STILL

STILL

by

Rebecca E. Bender & Kenneth M. Bender

North Dakota State University Press
Dept. 2360, P.O. Box 6050, Fargo, ND 58108-6050
www.ndsupress.org

North Dakota State University Press
Dept. 2360, P.O. Box 6050, Fargo, ND 58108-6050
www.ndsupress.org

Still
by Rebecca E. Bender and Kenneth M. Bender

First Edition

International Standard Book Number (ISBN): 978-1-946163-05-9
Library of Congress Control Number (LCCN): 2018967173

Cover design by Jamie Hohnadel Trosen
Interior design by Deb Tanner
Photo of Rebecca E. Bender by Lincoln Bernhard
Photo of Kenneth M. Bender by David Bender

The publication of *Still* is made possible by the generous support of donors to the NDSU Press Fund and the NDSU Press Endowment Fund.

Book team for *Still*: Shane Gomes, Rachel Grider, and Hannah Stevens

Printed in the USA

Publisher's Cataloging-In-Publication Data
(Prepared by The Donohue Group, Inc.)

Names: Bender, Rebecca E., 1958- author. | Bender, Kenneth M., 1916-2006, author.
Title: Still / by Rebecca E. Bender & Kenneth M. Bender.
Description: First edition. | Fargo, ND : North Dakota State University Press, [2019] | Includes bibliographical references and index.
Identifiers: ISBN 9781946163059
Subjects: LCSH: Bender family. | Bender, Rebecca E., 1958---Family. | Bender, Kenneth M., 1916-2006--Family. | Jewish families--Great Plains--History. | Jewish farmers--Great Plains--History. | Judaism--Great Plains--History. | BISAC: HISTORY / United States / State & Local / Midwest (IA, IL, IN, KS, MI, MN, MO, ND, NE, OH, SD, WI) | HISTORY / Jewish. | HISTORY / Women. | RELIGION / Judaism / History.
Classification: LCC F596.3.J5 B46 CS71.B4654 | DDC 978.004924--dc23

♾ This paper meets the requirements of ANSI/NISO Z39.48-1992 (Permanence of Paper).

Still

lyrics and music © by Rebecca E. Bender

In the quiet of the night
when no one is awake
when you think of your life
and how choice transcends fate
do you ever wonder
how you came to be you?
In the still of the night
what do you still hold true?

When it's close to the dawn
do you think of those before,
how they led you to here
how they breathe in your pores?
In their black and white pictures
when you see your own eyes
what else still continues
through your lows and your highs?

What we keep and we throw
who we hug and release,
does what's left in your heart
bring you heartache or peace?
Does your link still hold strong
in the chain they began?
In the still of your soul
do their ideals still stand?

If they met you today
and had two minutes to talk
would they say, "Job well done"
or continue to walk?
If you'd run after them then
then why not now,
to put still in your life
find your answers somehow.

Then at that divine moment
when the lake becomes clear
and you see your reflection
and beliefs you hold dear . . .
then your path will be even
your load will feel light
all because you're still you
and your still feels so right.

CONTENTS

Prologue ix

Chapter 1: St. Louis Park, MN, August 1965 1
Chapter 2: A Shtetl near Odessa, Russia, 1874 9
Chapter 3: Odessa, Russia, May 1903 19
Chapter 4: En Route to North Dakota, July 1906 43
Chapter 5: Ashley, ND, August 1906 49
Chapter 6: Ashley, ND, 1911 79
Chapter 7: Eureka, SD, 1927 101
Chapter 8: Rapid City, SD, November 1940 121
Chapter 9: Near Cardiff, Wales, June 1944 133
Chapter 10: Normandy, France, June 1944 143
Chapter 11: Eureka, SD, 1946 161
Chapter 12: St. Louis Park, MN, 1969 171
Chapter 13: St. Louis Park, MN, 1971 193
Chapter 14: Minneapolis, MN, 1976 223
Chapter 15: Eureka, Ashley, and Beyond, 2005 237
Chapter 16: New York, New York, May 2013 247

Epilogue 261

Acknowledgements
Appendix: "Still," lyrics and music © by Rebecca E. Bender
Bibliography
Index
About the Authors
About the Press

PROLOGUE

In 2014, a newspaper editor called to interview me as he was writing an article about immigrant Jewish farming homesteaders in the early 1900s. He had heard of my planned restoration work at the North Dakota Jewish cemetery where my homesteader great-grandfather is buried. In the course of our conversation, he inquired, "Are you *still* Jewish?" I said, "Yes," and we moved to other topics.

When I later reflected upon his question, I realized it was a valid one. My great-grandparents lived in a sod house on the prairie, far from any big city with a significant Jewish population. The editor justifiably thought that if my isolated ancestors had maintained their own Jewish identities, this would have been unusual. He might have assumed that to have passed this religion, which now makes up only about 1.5 percent of the American population, down five successive generations, was even more unlikely.

I thought about the choices that my family has made to "still" be Jewish and the Jewish compass that has guided our lives through the last century and a half. The challenges to faith, *emunah*, in *my* lifetime have been much more subtle than those faced by those before me.[1] Nevertheless, they still presented the same choice: to continue the traditions and religious belief systems or to break the chain.

The stories that follow provide a connection to our past and continue to give us strength. It is my hope that these tales of remembering our roots and living our beliefs will inspire you, and maybe even cause you to write down some of your family's history that has led you to be who you are.

---

[1]*Emunah* is the Hebrew word for faith.

Kiva (1858–1913) and Rebecka (1853–1932) Bender, Ashley, North Dakota, 1906. *Author files.*

***

Writing a book was not my original intention. Rather, this book is a welcome by-product of my attempts to preserve and retell my ancestors' history, for the reasons you will learn. This quest eventually led me on a path of discovery, through thousands of musty papers and numerous online searches, resulting in unexpected joyful outcomes.

Father William Sherman, a pastor, researcher, and former professor at North Dakota State University, made the following statement:

> The chronicle of North Dakota's Jews contains bits and pieces of genuine drama and tragedy, of success and failure . . . Heroic Jewish men and women were a veritable part of the State's pioneer past . . . Unfortunately, the whole matter of Jewish settlement in rural North Dakota has been completely overlooked by scholars. [These pioneers] await the hand of a poet, a playwright, or a movie producer.[2]

Though not a playwright or movie producer, in the course of my research I was spurred on with the adrenaline of an explorer, knowing I was uncovering information unknown to most. I admit to having some anxiety once I became aware of the breadth of previously unutilized resources regarding the Russian and Romanian immigrant Jewish homesteaders who made their homes in McIntosh County, North Dakota, in the early twentieth century. I felt a great responsibility to accurately document their lives and bring their stories to light. Some researchers, who had started on related projects fifty to seventy years ago, were not granted the gift of time to achieve their goals.

I obtained files and pictures from three primary collections as the foundation for my research with the help of the archivists listed: The Nathan and Theresa Berman Upper Midwest Jewish Historical Society Archives and Sharron and Oren Steinfeldt Photography Collection, housed at the University of Minnesota in Minneapolis (Kate Dietrick, Archivist); The Historical Society of North Dakota State Archives at the North Dakota Heritage Center and Museum in Bismarck (Greg Wysk, Archivist; Sarah Walker, Reference Specialist);

---

[2]William Sherman, "Jewish Homestead Communities in North Dakota, 1900–1920" (Bemidji: 17th Annual Northern Great Plains History Conference 1982); William C. Sherman, *Prairie Mosaic: An Ethnic Atlas of Rural North Dakota*, 2nd Ed. (Fargo: North Dakota State University Press, 2017).

and the North Dakota State University Institute for Regional Studies and University Archives, Fargo (John Hallberg, Archives Associate).

Decades before I came upon them, people whom I never had the opportunity to meet laid the groundwork for me by having donated their time and then their research files to these three locations. The late Alfred Thal, grandson of a German Jew who began farming in Lakota, North Dakota, in 1879, had wanted to write a book in the 1950s about North Dakota's Jews. Though he couldn't secure the necessary support for that project, he later took the time to travel around the United States with his little tape recorder to interview North Dakota Jewish homesteaders as part of the North Dakota American Revolution Bicentennial Oral History Project. He donated his materials to the North Dakota Historical Society Archives in Bismarck, as the "Al Thal Papers" and as part of the oral history files. My son and I had the privilege of listening to the homesteaders' voices (including my grandfather's) as they responded to Thal's questions.

Toba Geller, of Fargo, wanted to make Thal's vision a reality, intending to write a book on the Jews of North Dakota in the 1970s. She was driven and meticulous in locating North Dakota Jewish pioneers and their families and organizing family histories before her untimely death in 1978 at the age of sixty. She and her helpers, Ruth Landfield and Lorraine Kasden, left behind a wealth of first-hand accounts that in one more generation would have been lost. Two of these family histories in particular—that of the Miller family, written by Deborah Miller and Fanny Brudnoy, and that of the Schlasinger family, written by Ethel Schlasinger Overby—were especially detailed and helpful. The North Dakota Jewish Historical Project is housed in the University of Minnesota archives and, in part, at the North Dakota Historical Society Archives.

The late Frances Wold, the former Regan, North Dakota, Clerk of Court and writer for newspapers in Wilton, Regan, and Bismarck, had donated her files, some regarding the Jewish people in the area, to the State Historical Society of North Dakota, as well. In the North Dakota State Archives, I also located the family history compiled by

Susan Berman, the late daughter of a gangster, dealing with her father's formative years in Ashley, North Dakota.[3]

In Father William Sherman's "Jewish Settlement in North Dakota Collection" at North Dakota State University, I was able to review his scholarly research, analyses, speeches, and books describing North Dakota's various ethnic groups, including the Jewish homesteaders and business people. I utilized the online finding guide, requested relevant files to my research, and gained many insights from his impressive work.

Next I perused copies of Ashley and Wishek, North Dakota, and Eureka, South Dakota, newspapers, in hard copy and microfiche. Reading each of these cities' milestone celebration books and those of other North Dakota cities provided additional information about the lives and contributions of Jewish people living and working in these communities and the perceptions of their neighbors.

I was fortunate to have in my possession written sources specific to my ancestors and their experiences, including my late father Kenneth Bender's book.[4] His manuscript provided me with so many detailed recollections that he richly earned a co-author designation for this book. I also studied my grandpa Joe Bender's various handwritten versions of *This Is Your Life, Joseph Bender,* written for his children and grandchildren in the 1960s and 1970s. Letters written by Larry Schlasinger, my father's cousin, compiled and edited in a book by his niece, Regina Anavy, and letters written in the 1940s by my grandmother (Mary Bender), grandfather (Joseph Bender), father (Kenneth Bender), and uncle (David Bender), were also invaluable.[5]

I reviewed land deeds, plats, and land atlases, as well as marriage and immigration records at the McIntosh County Courthouse, where I was assisted by the knowledgeable County Recorder Carol

---

[3]Susan Berman, *Easy Street: The True Story of a Gangster's Daughter* (New York: Bantam Books, 1981).

[4]Kenneth Bender, *From the Prairies to the Beaches: An American Soldier's Story* (Minneapolis, 2005).

[5]Regina M. Anavy, ed., *Larry's Letters: The Personal Correspondence of Larry Schlasinger* (San Francisco: Hummingbird Imprints, 2nd Ed. 2005)

Fey and others. I visited the McIntosh County Heritage Center Museum, with docent Delores Schneider, where I was surprised to see a metal sign from the early 1900s in German and English, from my great, great uncle's general store in Ashley. I also toured the Eureka Pioneer Museum of McPherson County, in Eureka, South Dakota, finding additional information about my family and the Jewish community that lived near the border of North and South Dakota, with the enthusiastic assistance of curators Arlo and Bonnie Mehlhaff.

With the ease of online investigation not available to researchers forty years ago, I was able to view the annual American Jewish Yearbooks published in Philadelphia in the early 1900s (with entries submitted by my great-grandfather), contemporaneous reports concerning Jewish homesteaders found in the annual and other reports of the Jewish Agricultural Society published in New York, and the Bulletin of the National Conference of Jewish Charities. I also located books, chapters in books, periodicals, contemporaneous encyclopedia articles, and theses providing further background regarding the Jewish farming homesteaders, and their German-Russian neighbors. I learned more about North Dakota's Jewish cemeteries from information online, gathered as part of the International Jewish Cemetery Project. The United States laws and records — ranging from the text of The Homestead Act of 1862, to the Patent Records from the Bureau of Land Management, to the Manifests of Passengers for the United States Immigration Office found at the Ellis Island website, and certificates of naturalization for family members — further filled in the picture.

I spoke with family and non-family to flesh out additional stories regarding my father, my grandparents, and Ashley, North Dakota's Jewish residents. I enjoyed my time sharing tea in the home of Ashley historian Leona Neu, who maintains a collection of articles about Jewish people from the *Ashley Tribune*. Good friend Toni Schaeffer of Eureka, South Dakota, also shared stories about my grandparents I had never heard, and I found a recent response to a Facebook post from a stranger, over thirty-five years after my grandfather's death, referring to Joe Bender's kindness. I corresponded with Shirley Fischer Arends, who grew up in Ashley, wrote a book about the Central Dakota Germans, and, surprisingly, had a special connection with my family.[6]

At the Upper Midwest Jewish Historical Society in Minneapolis, Minnesota, I reviewed the articles, records, meeting agendas, and votes of the Ashley Jewish Cemetery Corporation, discovering the issues they had addressed since the 1950s. I also reviewed the North Dakota Secretary of State Annual Reports of the Ashley Jewish Cemetery Corporation.

Through all this work, I pieced together the causes for these immigrants deciding to leave Russia and Romania, as well as the confluence of historical events that allowed McIntosh County land to be available for farming once they arrived in North Dakota. At the conclusion of my research regarding my ancestors' past, I proceeded with the even more difficult task of writing about my own past — culling through memories to provide the reader with insights regarding more modern challenges to faith, traditions, and living a Jewish life. In the course of it all, I learned about everything from synagogues in Odessa, Russia, to North Dakota geology and climate, to Jewish burial practices, to the birth of the Jewish back-to-the-land movement, to the similarities that the Dakota Jews had to their German-Russian neighbors, to the historical role of Jews in America's military and women in synagogues, to anti-Semitism in the Midwest.

In addition to this targeted research over the last few years, I was simply at the right place at the right time through much of the rest of my life. As I was growing up, I was lucky to have lived in the same metropolitan area as my paternal grandparents, and right across the Mississippi River from my maternal grandparents. I also lived almost all of my life in the same city as my parents until their passing. I was an enthralled listener as they reminisced. From a young age, I liked helping to clean up in the kitchen after a multi-generation-

[6]Shirley Fischer Arends. *The Central Dakota Germans: Their History, Language, and Culture* (Washington DC: Georgetown University Press, 1989, updated version 2016 at Amazon.com).

al family meal, as that was a wonderful source of unknown family history. When I would attend a gathering that included elderly Jews I didn't know, I would make a beeline to talk with them, to see if they knew any of my family members. From the year 2004–2005, I was my dad's typist for his memoir, which provided us with time to further discuss our family history and for me to probe his recollections. I also spoke frequently over the years with my dad's siblings in Canada and California, and I am still fortunate to be able to speak with my dad's brother, David, and my mom's sister, Josephine. All of these interactions provided me with another layer of tales and fact checking, an oral history that made such an impression on me that I can recall the specific place I was when I heard certain stories.

As I look back at the desire that drove me through this process, I have come to realize that history and family are important to me because they were important to my ancestors. In 1911, my great-grandparents sent letters (in Yiddish) to my grandfather on his wedding day. These letters were sent by mail on horseback from Ashley to Minneapolis, Minnesota, traveled to Hudson, Wisconsin, via horse and buggy, were packed up and brought back to an Ashley sod house, were kept there for five years, then remained in a small town in South Dakota for thirty-three years, then in North Minneapolis for twenty years, then in St. Louis Park, Minnesota, for over thirty-five years. Though I could not understand what they said, I knew that my family considered these letters to be precious. I therefore protected the letters when they came into my possession and eventually found a translator for them in 2017, over one hundred years after they were written.

I am grateful to my family for being caretakers of this unique material and taking the time to tell their stories. I am also indebted to the researchers before me who preserved recollections and history of the North Dakota Jewish homesteaders. And I am appreciative that you have picked up a copy of *Still*. If a good story is ready to be told and no one is there to listen, there is no reason to tell the story.

CHAPTER 1

St Louis Park, MN, August 1965

MY SISTER, NANCY, NINE YEARS old, and I, seven years old, were so excited. We helped pack the white four-door Buick LeSabre before dawn, with all the necessities for the road trip: our matching pink culottes, travel bingo, one recently checked-out library book apiece with crinkly plastic protective cover, our favorite Danish troll dolls, "Dimples" and "Tina," and our spiral-bound notebooks and pencils to document the journey.

Our mom, who had just finished the dishes from an early homemade pancake breakfast, was in charge of food: peanut butter sandwiches, potato chips, and homemade sugar cookies in the shape of cars with orange sprinkles. We carried our apple juice and water over ice in red, black, and yellow plaid thermoses, and our parents brought out the hard ivory American Tourister suitcases with muted rose interiors. Gifts from my mom's parents to her eleven years earlier for a road trip from Minnesota to Banff, Lake Louise, they had transformed from honeymoon luggage into our family suitcases. Nancy and I climbed into the back seat for the trip to visit our dad's old stomping grounds in South Dakota.

I had lived my entire life in St. Louis Park, Minnesota, which was a first-ring suburb west of Minneapolis, with a population of around 45,000, about 25 percent of whom were Jewish in the mid-

1960s.[7] We lived about five minutes from Minneapolis, formerly known as Mill City due to its large flour production, home to a half million people, with a downtown complete with department stores, hotels, restaurants, and movie theaters. It was therefore hard to picture Eureka, South Dakota, this place of around twelve hundred people, where our dad Kenneth Bender, then known as Keva, grew up. His family was the only Jewish family in town for most of the time he lived there. The closest big town to Eureka was Aberdeen, an hour and a half away, and it had about 17,000 people in the 1930s.

Our dad was a good storyteller, and he told us fondly about his boyhood home Eureka, which means, "I found it!" in Greek. He would always brag, with a grin, about Eureka being the Wheat Capital of the World in 1892, with over two million dollars' worth of grain shipped out on the Milwaukee Road Railroad that year from its most profitable station. The town boasted forty-two crop elevators back then and thirty-two commission houses with agents ready to buy the grain. The farmers had to come to Eureka to sell their grain to the elevator owners at the end of the branch railroad line. The town, first noted on maps as "the end of the tracks" and later St. Petersburg, was "the funnel into which the wheat fields of the Dakotas emptied."[8] About twenty-five years later, the Benders settled in Eureka, when our dad's parents opened a general store in town and later a movie theater. Everyone knew everyone. He and his four siblings worked hard at school and were involved in everything from basketball to plays to band and glee club.

It would have been a nine-hour trip to Eureka, but our mom believed that every experience could be an educational one, so we stopped at each historical marker. In so doing, we learned about the Indian presence, Lewis and Clark's exploration route, Civil War history, and animal life on the prairie. We also saw fewer and fewer trees and more flat prairie land.

---

[7]Camille Andre, St. Louis Park City Manager, in *St. Louis Park Dispatch,* November 22, 1967.

[8]"Four Great U.S. Wheat Belts Yield a Rich Harvest," *Life Magazine*, August 1937: 20; Eureka Golden Jubilee Committee, *Eureka, South Dakota: 1887–1937 Golden Jubilee Book*, 1937, p. 227

"Eureka, South Dakota, Wheat Capital of the World," 1892.
Eureka Pioneer Museum Collection, Northern State University Archives & Special Collections, Williams Library, Aberdeen, SD, NSUdigital.org.

"We are getting close. When we cross the state line into South Dakota, I want you all to roll down your windows and inhale the sweet Dakota air," our dad said to us. He slowed down when it was about time. "Roll down your windows!" he said. We complied. Dust flew up in our eyes, and the unmistakable smell of skunk greeted us. "Roll up your windows, roll up your windows," our dad urged. "That wasn't quite the right place." Once we were on a better-paved road, he pulled over and said, "OK, *now* roll down your windows!" We did. "Isn't the air lighter and sweeter?" he asked. We sincerely agreed.

We arrived in Eureka and went to check into the Cal Cal Motor Hotel on H Avenue, two blocks down from where the former Bender house still stood. It was 95 actual degrees in the shade, in those days before weathermen announced heat indices. Our dad parked the car in the middle of the street, as was customary, and we all went into the motel. After waiting at the front desk in total silence, our dad called out, "Hellooo!" Still no response. We walked back outside, and saw one older man wearing a yellowish straw fedora, walking quickly down the street. “Hello sir!” yelled our dad, to get his attention. “We are trying to check into the motel. Do you know where the manager might be?”

“Everybody’s in Mobridge! It’s the big rivalry baseball game. No one will be back until it’s over.”

We thanked the man for the information, and he disappeared, leaving the street empty again. “There is a place not too far away that I want to show all of you. So this is the perfect time,” our dad said. We ate the last cookies, drank the rest of our hot, diluted apple juice, and returned to the car.

“Where are we going?” Nancy and I asked.

“It’s a very special place,” our dad said, “It’s in North Dakota, near Ashley.”

“Who is Ashley?” inquired Nancy.

Jewish Homesteaders Cemetery, on outskirts of Ashley, North Dakota. *Photo by Rebecca Bender, 2014, author files.*

"It's a town, not a person," explained our mom, as she looked for the correct page in our AAA TripTik.

After driving about a half hour, we arrived at our destination. Our dad pulled over as much as he could to park—not to be on the one lane country road, and not to be in the ditch. The prairie wind seemed to come from all directions when we exited our Buick. Our dad held my sister's and my hands as we walked down a little hill. Then he opened a chain link gate. "This is where my grandpa is buried. I was named after him."

We stepped carefully through the recently mowed grass, past the monuments. Our dad commented on different gravesites, as if he knew the people buried there, though he had never met any of them. "Mr. Bloom. He was a bachelor. He was a good man. And Uncle Auerbach. He married my grandma Becky's sister. He helped our family come over from Russia."

We then stopped in front of a tall, white marble monument that had an oval porcelain picture of a man with a flowing white beard. His nose was the same as Nancy's. I looked into the eyes of my great-grandfather for the first time and saw his English name on the stone, in addition to the writing in Hebrew. Kiva Bender was born in 1858, exactly one century before I was.

"He was a Jewish farmer with your grandpa Joe," continued my dad. "He came from Russia, where Jews were being killed just because they were Jews, and no Jewish person could own land. They were homesteaders who lived in houses made of prairie grass and dirt, and they farmed this land."

After a time examining every monument, we said the Mourner's Kaddish together, a prayer over one thousand years old, to honor the memories of the Jewish homesteaders.[9] The prayer ends with the phrase:

---

[9]The Mourner's prayer is traditionally said in Aramaic, a Semitic language closely related to Hebrew. Aramaic was the most widely spoken language among Jews around the time of the Second Temple's Destruction in Jerusalem in 70 C.E. Richard Gottheil and Wilhelm Bacher, " Aramaic Language Among the Jews," *1906 Jewish Encyclopedia*, available at www.jewishencyclopedia.com.

He who creates peace in His celestial heights,
may He create peace for us and for all Israel;
and let us say, Amen.[10]

On that trip, I learned about Eureka and about life in a small town in the 1920s, 1930s, and 1940s. The people were friendly. There

Kiva Bender, on Ashley Cemetery Monument.
Photo by Rebecca Bender, 2014, author files.

[10]The term "Israel" in this prayer refers to the Jewish people.

was lots of laughter and lots of "no kidding!" responses as my dad shared stories with his former neighbors. There were also genuine hugs with people I had never met before who immediately liked me just because of my family. But the face that stuck with me the most was my great-grandfather's.

I could not know then that decades later my path would bring me back here, to the people buried in this place and to their legacies.

Kenneth (Keva) Bender, showing his grandfather Kiva Bender's North Dakota grave to daughters Nancy and Rebecca.
Photo by Frima Bender, 1965, author files.

CHAPTER 2
A Shtetl Near Odessa, Russia, 1874

KIVA MYCHAL BENDERSKY WAS SIXTEEN years old and a Jew from a small *shtetl* (village) in Czarist Russia. His mother, Channah Nechie, died when he was young. His father, Schmeri, died eight days ago. With no parents or siblings, he was on his own.

It was the time of Czar Alexander II, known as Alexander the Liberator for his emancipation of the Russian serfs. There had been some level of optimism among Russian Jews regarding Alexander II's reign when it began in 1855, after the repressive rule of Czar Nicholas I, his father. Nicholas I had the homogenization of the culturally diverse Russian empire as one of his goals. He hoped to accomplish this by persecution of those who did not speak Russian and who did not practice Russian Orthodoxy, as well as by placing limits on the content of courses taught at universities. Czar Nicholas I also abolished the Jewish Qahal, the governing body of Jewish communities in Eastern Europe.

It was under Czar Nicholas I that the Cantonist Decree was passed, an order for twenty-five-year conscription in the Russian military for all Jewish boys, beginning at age eighteen. The leaders of each town had to produce the required numbers of twelve-year-old boys on a periodic basis to be put into training camps before their twenty-five-year service began. Kiva had heard the stories of children literally being ripped from their parents' arms to meet the quota, and of desperate parents cutting off their sons' index fingers so they would not be selected for Russia's military.[11]

Nicholas' son, Czar Alexander II, generally seemed more tolerant of Russia's diversity, including the Jewish population, and had even promoted local self-government councils. But optimism was short-lived when the Polish uprising in 1863 resulted in a crackdown against revolutionaries, the stripping of Poland's separate constitution, and the incorporation of Poland directly into Russia.[12] There was talk in Kiva's shtetl that Alexander II was beginning to lean more towards the repressive policies of his father. "*Es vet sai vi vider pasiren* [It is only a matter of time]," said Schmeri Bendersky with a sigh.

The Russian Empire had few Jews until the late eighteenth century. From 1791 to 1835, it acquired a number of countries — including portions of Poland, Lithuania, and Turkey — and the accompanying Jewish population residing in these areas. Jews were restricted to living in a designated area of southern Russia from the time of Catherine II in the late 1700s. This area, the Pale of Settlement, comprised much of Poland, Lithuania, Byelorussia, and the Ukraine. The Pale covered an area of about one million square kilometers (386,000 square miles) from the Baltic Sea to the Black Sea. Approximately

---

[11]The stories of the Benderskys' lives were told by Kiva and his wife, Rebecka, to their children. The author learned of them when Kiva and Rebecka's son Joseph told them orally to his children, who shared them with the author; when he wrote the stories down or recorded them in taped interviews; or when he shared them directly with the author.

[12]Pearl W. Bartelt, "American Jewish Agricultural Colonies," in *American Communal Utopias*, Ed. Donald E. Pitzer (Chapel Hill: University of North Carolina Press, 1997); *Jewish Agricultural Society Annual Report* (New York: Jewish Agricultural Society, 1909), summarizing the Society's first ten years; Lois Fields Schwartz, "Early Jewish Agricultural Colonies in North Dakota," *North Dakota History*, Vol. 32 (Bismarck: State Historical Society of North Dakota, 1965); Jyotsna Sreenivasan, "Jewish Agricultural Communities, 1881–1941," in *Utopias in American History* (Santa Barbara: ABC-CLIO 2008); Robert Sutton, "Nineteenth Century Jewish Farm Colonies," in *Communal Utopias and the American Experience: Religious Communities 1732–2000* (Westport: Praeger, 2003); Michael Stanislawski, "Kahal," *The YIVO Encyclopedia of Jews in Eastern Europe* (YIVO Institute for Jewish Research, 2010), www.yivoencyclopedia.org/article.aspx/Kahal.

Pale of Settlement, Russian Empire 1855. John Klier, *"Pale of Settlement,"* The Yivo Encyclopedia of Jews in Eastern Europe, *YIVO Institute for Jewish Research, 2010, http://www.yivoencyclopedia.org/article.aspx/Pale_of_Settlement.*

five million Jews, or 94 percent of the total Jewish population of Russia, lived in the Pale in the late 1800s. Yiddish — which has a Germanic base, with strong influences from Hebrew, Aramaic, Russian, Polish, Ukrainian, and even a bit of the Romance Languages — was the language spoken among the Jews, who made up about 12 percent of the general population in the Pale.[13]

Kiva Bendersky sat *shiva*, the traditional Jewish seven-day mourning period for close family, after his father's burial and recited

[13]See footnote 12

the Mourner's Kaddish with the men in town. Now, surrounded by the smells of rotting fruit from a basket given to him by a friend of his family, he had to make a choice. Kiva could stay there, in the brown, dusty world—a prisoner of the czarist class system placed upon him before birth—or he could start walking.

With no one to leave behind, the choice felt as liberating and easy as the last conscious breath before he fell asleep at night. He didn't know where he was going, but he started walking. He refused to believe that God would allow him, the only descendant of Channah and Schmeri, to be wiped out. Why would He create a family only to allow it to be extinguished entirely? Kiva believed that God would guide him.

This thought gave him comfort, *treyst*, as his late father used to say. As Kiva walked, the rhythm of his steps on the stones sounded like a march. But those who march have a destination. Kiva's destination was unknown. This could be a time of new beginnings. Kiva thought of how he could reinvent himself. Who would know? This could be a moment he would look back on as the day he raised his station. He could work, save some money, go to a larger city and appeal to a Russian Orthodox priest for compassion, offering to work for food and shelter. Eventually, he could become respected and known for his diligence and honesty. He could pass easily into Russian society. He smiled at the thought of wooing a Russian general's daughter, being the young man with no past who waltzes off with a brown-eyed beauty who smells of fresh fruits.

But in that moment, Kiva made a different decision—not to escape his heritage, but to walk toward it—to continue the learning he had begun with his father. His feet took the path toward a town, Zebricov, he had heard of with a larger Jewish population in the Kherson/Odessa region. German-Russians had formed the colony around 1818 when seeking religious freedom.[14] Kiva hoped to study with a rav, who might be willing to give of his time and knowledge to

[14]Ethel Overby, "Schlasinger Family History," The Jewish Historical Project of North Dakota records, Nathan and Theresa Berman Upper Midwest Jewish Archives, University of Minnesota Libraries, Minneapolis, https://archives.lib.umn.edu/repositories/15/resources/462; *This is Your Life, Joseph Bender* (Minneapolis: 1970); Dale Lee Wahl and Dayla Aspenleiter, *German-Russian Village List*, www.blackseagr.org/pdfs/village_list.pdf.

a young stranger eager to learn.[15] There were so many questions and so few answers in life. So other than a short ride on the back of an open wagon shared with thirty chickens, Kiva walked.

The familiar minor-key melodies of the prayers Kiva used to chant with his father and the men in town were the accompaniment for his journey. The words were the inspiration that made him feel stronger.

Adon Olam (Lord of the Universe)

V'hu Eli, v'chai go'ali.	And He is my God, my living God.
V'tzur chevli b'et tzarah,	To Him I flee in time of grief,
V'hu nisi umanos li	And He is my miracle and my refuge
M'nat kosi by'yom ekra.	Who answers the day I shall call.

Eyn Kelohaynu (There is none like our God)

Ata tooshiaynu.	You will save us.
Ata tokoom t'rakhaym tziyon,	You will arise and show mercy to Zion,[16]
Ki ayt l'khennawh,	for it will be the time to favor her,
Ki vaw mo'ayd.	for the proper time will have arrived.

Could Kiva really have entertained masquerading as someone else? God and these prayers were now his family. He could hear his father's words:

> *Ir heist Akiva noch der barimte Rabbi Akiva ben Yosef. In ein tog estu oych lernen andere, vi er hot geton. In ein tog vet dayn leben ayn a moshel tzu dayne kinder un einklech, un zayer kinder un einklech.*
>
> You, Kiva, are named after the great Rabbi Akiva ben Yosef. Someday, you too will teach as he did. Someday your life will be an example to your children and grandchildren and their children and grandchildren. Remember what God commanded in Deuteronomy, "And you shall teach it to your children."[17]

---

[15]"Rav" is Hebrew for a religious teacher.

[16]Zion is another name for the Jewish people.

[17]The conversation continued in Yiddish, though translated here.

Kiva's father had taught him of the determination of Rabbi Akiva ben Yosef. Born in 50 A.D. in Caesarea, Israel, Rabbi Akiva was a poor shepherd with no Jewish education. At age forty, he walked past a well and noticed a stone with a hole in it. He was told that the constant drip of water had made the hole. Rabbi Akiva decided that if water could wear down a stone, anything was possible, and went off with determination, studying the Torah for the next twenty-four years.

Kiva's father had also taught Kiva about the optimism of Rabbi Akiva. When Rabbi Akiva saw the condition of the destroyed Holy Temple in Jerusalem and his fellow rabbis were horrified, Rabbi Akiva laughed. He said, "From the bad I see the good. From the troubles, I see the redemption coming." His optimism, even in the darkest times, was legendary, as was the rabbi's unbreakable courage.

When teaching the Torah was outlawed by the Roman Emperor Hadrian, Rabbi Akiva stood in the public square and continued to teach the lessons from the Five Books of Moses. When Rabbi Akiva was captured, and as he was being executed, he continued to reaffirm his belief in God.

Over 1700 years after Rabbi Akiva's life, Kiva Mychal Bendersky carried the Rabbi's determination, optimism, and courage with him. It made his load lighter. Kiva arrived in the town of Zebricov as the sun began its ascent. People were scurrying around the marketplace at the center of town getting ready to sell their wares. Kiva felt invisible, and wondered if he blended in with his dusty clothes, or whether he, a tall, thin stranger, was intentionally ignored. He sat to rest behind an empty stall with a painted picture of grapes, and dozed off, with the smell of fresh bread and oniony, pickled herring filling his dreams.

He awoke to the sound of girls giggling and half opened his eyes to see three girls unloading a wagon with wine, making careful trips back and forth to the wooden stall with the painted grapes. One of the girls came right up and asked him, "*Ver bistu un farvos zitstu do* [Who are you, and why are you sitting here]?" The question was not asked in an accusatory fashion, but rather as one asks when purely seeking an answer.

"Ikh bin Kiva Bendersky, a id fun a dorf tsofn fun do [I am Kiva Bendersky, a Jew from a village north of here. I am seeking to work in exchange for food and education]."[18]

The girl replied, "I am Rivka [Rebecka], daughter of Aryeh Yehoshuah Michelovich, and these are my sisters Sarah and Esther. Our father is one of the most learned men in Zebrikov. He has lessons at our home a short way from here. Have some cool water from the town well, help us refill our stand during the day, and we will take you to meet him when we head home for Shabbos."

The parallel to the Rebekah-at-the-well Bible story was not lost on Kiva. He had studied the book of Genesis, with the tale of Abraham sending his trusted servant Eliezer to find a bride for his son Isaac. In biblical times, Rebekah appeared at the well, offering to give the stranger, Eliezer, and his camels some water. When Rebecka of Zebricov appeared and kindly offered traveler Kiva water from the well, he considered this a sign that he was on the right path.

Then Kiva's mind wandered back to his father, Schmeri, studying the well-worn Tanakh (Torah, Prophets, and Writings) in their home. Kiva could picture the two lines between his father's eyebrows as he leaned over the text, concentrating, and the careful way he would turn each page despite the thickness of his fingers. Kiva realized for the first time that he would never study with his beloved father again, and he felt loneliness wash over him.

Rebecka Michelovich persisted: "Shabbos . . . you do celebrate Shabbos don't you?" Rebecka, Sarah, and Esther chuckled.

"Oh yes," said Kiva. "I apologize. My father, Schmeri Bendersky, alav hashalom [may peace be upon him], died recently. In my mourning, the days and nights have not been as separate and as easy to count."

Kiva went back to the Michelovich house that afternoon after helping the girls sell their homemade wine in the marketplace. Faige

---

[18]The conversation continued in Yiddish, though translated here.

Toibe Michelovich, Rebecka's mother, was at first concerned there was something wrong with their new boarder, as he was so thin. But he soon proved his vigor and health with hard work, contributing his sweat and people skills to the Michelovich wine-making business. Kiva also proved his dedication to Jewish learning by staying up to study with Rav Michelovich: The Torah (the Five Books of Moses), Nevi'im (the Prophets), Ketuvim (including Psalms and Proverbs), and interpretations from the Talmud, including those of Rabbi Akiva of Caesaria. Kiva felt his father's presence as he studied, which made him even more anxious to delve into the ancient texts.

Within two years, Rebecka stood under the *chuppah* (Jewish wedding canopy) with Kiva Bendersky and became Rebecka Bendersky. Rebecka gave birth to nine children.[19] Five of them survived. Rebecka's parents passed away; the family closed their wine-making business and moved to the Black Sea port of Odessa for greater Jewish connections and occupational and educational opportunities. In Odessa, Kiva became a moderately successful grain broker.

Though Kiva was making deals to purchase and sell grain, it was all on paper. There was no preparing the soil, no planting seeds, no watering crops, and no harvesting. These farming activities were not a way for a Jew to make a living in the Pale in Russia post-1882, as Jews were prohibited from owning or renting land. Czar Alexander II was assassinated in 1881 when an anarchist threw a bomb at his carriage. His son, Czar Alexander III, blamed all the Jews for his father's assassination and reacted with anti-Semitic legislation called the May Laws. These laws were intended to restrict the freedom of Jews in the Pale and to reverse the greater integration of Jews into Russian society that had occurred during Alexander II's reign.[20]

In addition to Russian Jews not being allowed to own or rent land, they were banned from inhabiting rural areas and villages that had been established almost one hundred years earlier in the western portion of the Russian empire. Jews living in villages had to re-

[19]The children born to Kiva and Rebecka were David, Samuel, Chaim, Ephraim, Chaya, Bessie, Sarel, Lena, and Yosef.

[20]See footnote 12.

settle in towns. They could not obtain mortgages or manage land outside of the towns. Their education and occupations were restricted, with quotas on the number of Jews (10 percent maximum) who could study in high schools and universities, even if there were no non-Jews to take their places. Empty seats in schools were seen as preferable to having too many Jews in schools.[21]

There were also limits on the number of Jewish professionals and expulsion of Jews from any government jobs. Jews were not allowed to travel beyond the Pale into other areas of Russia without a passport. Jewish artisans could not work outside the Pale, and all Jews were excluded from participation in the Zemstvos (local administration bodies). Jewish people were straddled with harsh taxes, and Jewish boys were again conscripted into the Russian army for many years and pressured to convert to the Russian Orthodox religion. There was no security for personal property or homes belonging to Jews, which could be taken at any time for any reason. All of these restrictions would have been lifted if these descendants of Abraham adopted the official religion of the Russian Empire.[22] Most Russian Jews, like the Benderskys, refused to do this.

Also in the early 1880s, pogroms—large-scale, targeted massacres against Jews directly supported by Czar Alexander III and aided by the Czar's secret police, the Okhrana, and the Cossacks—broke out in southern Russia. Based on the rumor that the Jews were the ones responsible for the assassination of Czar Alexander II, the czarist regime had a reason, albeit a false one, to authorize attacks on the Jews and the destruction of their property. These so-called Storms in the Negev resulted in thousands of deaths, rapes, and injuries to Jews in the Pale, and successfully instilled fear within the Jewish population. Widespread famine crossed the land, and four hundred thousand Russian peasants died during Alexander III's reign. With poor living conditions and a corrupt, ineffective regime, the climate was ripe to look for a scapegoat. In 1884, when Kiva Bendersky was twenty-five years old, Konstantin Pobedonostsev, the government

[21] Ibid.

[22] Ibid.

official overseeing the Russian Orthodox Church, expressed the Czar's goals with respect to the Jews: to see "one-third of the Jews get baptized, one-third starve, and one-third leave the country."[23]

Kiva longed to have his family be allowed to live their lives in peace. He also longed to own land, to farm the land, and to raise food for his family and his community. But it was not to be. Every year at the Passover Seder, the Benderskys repeated the lines from the Hagadah, "*Avadim hayenu, Ata Bnai Chorin* [We were slaves and now we are children of freedom]."[24] The irony was felt by Kiva and Rebecka.

They were not free. Their children were not free. At any moment, their sons could be kidnapped and conscripted into the Russian army, with the likely outcome either being death or loss of their faith. At any moment any of them could be beaten or killed for no reason. Despite this looming danger, Kiva kept teaching his children the history of the Jewish people and its sacred books and tried to instill optimism in them for a better future. If not for him on this earth, he believed it would happen for his children.

Even for an optimistic man, this was the most Kiva could hope for.

---

[23]Edward Flannery, *The Anguish of the Jews: Twenty-Three Centuries of Anti-Semitism* (New York: Macmillan Company, 1965), pp. 189–90.

[24]The Hagadah is a Passover book retelling the story of the exodus of the Jewish people out of slavery in Egypt to freedom.

CHAPTER 3

Odessa, Russia, May 1903

THE SECOND MOSES WAS SUPPOSEDLY coming to Odessa. Like the original Moses, he was seeking to lead the Jewish people from persecution to freedom. Yosef Bendersky, the third oldest son of Kiva and Rebecka, was fourteen years old and attending the Trud School in Odessa when he heard the rumor.[25] But he had heard the rumor enough times that he figured there must be something to it.[26]

Yosef was born in 1888, when the sadness and anger from the early 1880s pogroms against Russian Jews were still fresh. Family members still mourned, breadwinners were absent, and buried mothers' soup strainers sat unused in cupboards, as dusk ushered in the Sabbath. The Jews in the Pale had learned again what Jews throughout history had learned: A spark, unrelated to the Jews,

[25]The Trud School, founded in 1864, was a professional school for Jews, with cutting-edge technical education, including mechanics, iron-foundry, and cabinet-making. The school attracted students from all over Russia due to its fine reputation. "Trud" means labor in Russian. Meir Dizengoff, the first mayor of Tel Aviv, learned the art of iron forging at Trud, and some of the forged balconies still visible in Odessa were made by him.

[26]The stories of Yosef (Joseph) Bendersky's life were told to Joseph's descendants, including the author, orally and in handwritten notes and an autobiography, *This Is Your Life, Joseph Bender*, and in taped interviews with Ellis Ellison in 1970 and Alfred Thal in 1974, collectively hereinafter referred to as "Joseph Bender Recollections."

could easily fan into flames of mistrust and violence against the Jewish people. Sometimes it seemed a spark was not even a requirement for killing the innocent. Mere dissatisfaction with the ruling class was enough to blame the Jews even though they were far removed from that ruling class.

A humorous folk tale has been passed down of a Jewish man in Russia in the late 1880s encountering Moishe, the poor Jewish peddler, eating some porridge for dinner while he reads the Russian government newspaper. "Moishe," the man says, "Why do you read such a newspaper, instead of the Yiddish paper?" Moishe the peddler responds, "When I read the Yiddish paper I read such sad news every day about how the Jews are treated in Russia. It's enough that I see that from dawn to dusk. When I read the Russian newspaper, I read that we Jews are so powerful, we are soon taking over the world! Even though it's fiction, it makes me feel better about myself."

There was nothing humorous in the Bendersky family's reality living in the Pale, surrounded by an ominous feeling that at any time, for whatever reason, they could lose everything, including each other. They didn't have to be taught to push these feelings down. Most everyone did, or it would have been hard to go on each day. Focusing on the precious gift of his family and his Jewish and secular education kept Yosef grounded. And he never stopped praying for a better life, a freer life, a safer life for his family and his fellow Russian Jews.

Odessa was a city of contradictions. Amid the tension, the port city could still be exciting and inviting. Young boys like Yosef would run to the docks before dawn to see what was coming off the ships from all over the world. It could be Greek sponges or Ceylon tea. Odessa was the fourth largest city in Russia and had the second largest Jewish population after Warsaw, the Capital of Poland, which had been absorbed within Russia's borders.

Odessa had eight impressive synagogues, with high ceilings and grand columns, and around fifty other houses of prayer. These smaller houses of worship were named after a particular trade or occupation; synagogues of tailors, carpenters, bakers, book binders, hat makers, woodchoppers, tin makers, butchers, and fruit sellers. Some synagogues were even named after charitable organizations such as Malbish Eronim (Clothe the Naked) Synagogue and Gmilut Hasadim (Benevolence) synagogue.[27]

The city was a center for Jewish charitable organizations. The community hospital had modern medical tools and provided health care even for those who could not pay. Kitchens served inexpensive meals for the needy, and charitable groups collected coal for winter heat and matzah meal for the poor for Passover. It was said that even beggars had a decent income in Odessa, which was a testament to the spirit of charity in the community.[28]

Odessa also had well-respected Jewish educational institutions for the child, the adolescent, and the adult. The vast majority of Jews in Odessa ate kosher meat, Sabbath services were well attended, and joyful Jewish holidays were greeted with relish. A few weeks before Sukkot, the Festival of Booths, big signs appeared in store windows for "Sitrus Frukht" (Citrus Fruit), so the Jewish families could purchase their *lulav* (fronds of the date palm tree, willow, and myrtal) and *etrog* (citron), symbols for the harvest holiday. During Chanukah, menorahs were customarily seen in windows of Jewish homes. In the spring, "white boats floated in a river washing over the many people in Odessa's streets," according to visiting poet Rabbi Shimon Yakov Gliksberg. The white boats were actually the white sheets wrapping matzoh-filled baskets on top of Jewish housewives' heads as they weaved their way home through the throngs of Odessa's population.[29]

---

[27]Herman Rosenthal and S. Penn, "Odessa," 1906 *Jewish Encyclopedia* (1906) www.jewishencyclopedia.com.

[28]Rabbi Shimon Yakov Gliksberg, *Jewish Odessa, Chapters From My Memoirs*, by grandson Alex Gliksberg (JewishGen.org), at www.kehilalinks.jewishgen.org/odessa/lif_gen_gliksberg.asp.

[29]Ibid.

Jewish writers, publishers, artists, and thinkers found a community in Odessa, in spite of the anti-Semitism.[30] It was not uncommon for Russian Jewish authors and philosophers to engage in lively conversations at the local bakery. On one ordinary day, Yosef met Russian author Maxim Gorky, picking up perogies and discussing politics with the men who frequented the place, more for the conversation than for the baked goods.[31]

But this vibrant city could change moods in a moment. Russian Cossacks on horses could suddenly make raids on the Jewish residents, beating them with clubs or slashing at them with swords. The Okhrana, the Czar's secret police, were equally brutal in their enforcement of the May Laws and their arresting of innocent "suspects" on unknown charges.[32]

"*Hostu gehert az er kummt tzu der Broder shul* [Did you hear he's coming to the Broder Shul]?" inquired Yosef's friend Shlomo one sunny May day.

"Who?" asked Yosef.

"Herzl, Theodor Herzl," responded Shlomo.

"I've heard it, and I want to believe it," said Yosef.

"Well believe it, because I heard it from Rav Smolsky, and he is not a man who deals in rumors."

* * *

It was hard for Yosef to sit still in mathematics class that day. He pictured Theodor Herzl leading the Jews across the Black Sea, like

[30]Ethel Overby, "Schlasinger Family History," "Deborah Miller and Fanny Brudnoy," and "Miller Family History," Jewish Historical Project of North Dakota records, Nathan and Theresa Berman Upper Midwest Jewish Archives, University of Minnesota Libraries.

[31]Maxim Gorky was the pseudonym for Aleksey Maksimovich Peshkov, a well-known Russian short story writer, novelist, playwright, and political activist who lived from 1868–1936 and was nominated for the Nobel Prize in Literature five times. Gorky is the Russian word for "bitter."

[32]See footnote 30.

Bendersky family and friends around a chessboard in Odessa, circa 1901. Sarel Bendersky (second row, left), Yosef Bendersky (second row, middle), Lena Bendersky (second row, right), Nuchen Schlasinger (front row, left), and one of Yosef's older brothers (front row, right). *Author files.*

Moses led the Israelites across the Red Sea in the Bible. If Herzl held out his staff, would the Black Sea split for the Russian Jews to walk on dry land to a life of freedom? Yosef's older brothers and father had spoken of Dr. Herzl in such reverent tones. Herzl was trying to find a way for the Jews living in the Pale to escape the harsh conditions, persecution and risk of death ever-present in their daily lives.

The coronation of the new czar Nicholas II, in 1894, had signaled more of the same poor treatment for Russia's Jews, but by April 1903, the situation had gotten worse. When a Russian boy was murdered, false rumors spread that the Jews were somehow responsible, as they allegedly needed a Christian boy's blood to make their Passover matzah. The truth was, instead, that the boy's uncle had killed him, that Jews have never used human blood for any purpose, and that matzah was made of flour and water. Nevertheless, Kishinev's Russian Orthodox Bishop refused to denounce the rumor. In addition, the semi-official Russian government newspaper, *Bessarabetz*, published by Pavel Krushevan, fanned the falsehood and printed it as a fact, openly preaching the extermination of Jews.[33] A proclamation signed by "The Party of the Workingmen Who Are True Christians" contained in Krushevan's newspaper stated that the killing of Jews was to be performed in support of the Czar "who watches over the wants of his people," and to show "good Christians' love of Christ." The last line of the proclamation was a direct threat: "Make your visitors [i.e., customers] read this, or else your establishment will be sacked. We shall be kept informed of this by those of us who go amongst you."

---

[33]James Harvey Robinson and Charles Beard, Eds., *Readings in Modern European History*, Vol. 2 (Boston: 1908), pp. 371–72; John Klier, "Pogroms," *The YIVO Encyclopedia of Jews in Eastern Europe* (Courtesy of YIVO Institute for Jewish Research 2010), www.yivoencyclopedia.org/article.aspx/Pogroms; Herman Rosenthal and Max Rosenthal, "Kishinef," *Jewish Encyclopedia of 1906* (New York 1906), www.jewishencyclopedia.com/articles/9350-kishinef-kishinev; Edward H. Judge, *Easter in Kishinev: Anatomy of a Pogrom* (New York: New York University Press. 1992); www.pages.uoregon.edu/kimball/kishinev.pogroms.htm.

Beginning after church services let out on Easter, 1903, rioters began attacking their fellow Jewish citizens. The governor refused to seek permission to use military force against the murders and ignored requests for help from the suffering Jewish population. Forty-nine Jewish men, women, and children were murdered; 1,200 were raped and/or otherwise wounded; and seven hundred families lost their homes and belongings, while police pointed out the Jewish homes to the mob and 12,000 Russian troops stood by.[34]

The first-person accounts were horrifying. *The New York Times* reprinted a report smuggled out of Russia that had appeared in *The Yiddish Daily News*. Though it could not print all that it knew, as the censors for the *Times* would not allow it, the article referred to Jews being dragged from their homes and savagely beaten into insensibility by a mob, the air being filled with feathers and torn bedding after Jewish households were broken into, the Jews in their terror endeavoring to hide in cellars and under roofs, and Kishenev's biggest synagogue being desecrated, with the Torah scrolls defiled. Disconcerting was the reported conduct of many "intelligent Christians," who made no attempt to check the rioting. "They simply walked around enjoying the frightful sport."[35]

Kishinev, the capital of the Bessarabi province, was only about one hundred miles northwest of Odessa. Nuchen Schlasinger, the boyfriend of Yosef's sister Sarel, had been born in Kishinev and received his pharmacy license there before moving to Odessa to manage an *apoteka* (pharmacy).[36] The violence felt to the Benderskys to be on their doorstep. The wounds of the Czar-endorsed anti-Semitic acts never seemed to have time to heal anymore, and they were becoming so gaping that no amount of time would heal them. Dr. Herzl's coming to Odessa at that time was more than just a speaking

[34]Ibid; www.simpletoremember.com/articles/a/the_czars_and_the_jews/; Paul Mendes-Flohr and Yehuda Reinharz, Eds., *The Jew in the Modern World* (Oxford University Press, 1995), p. 409.

[35]"Jewish Massacre Denounced," New York Times (April 28, 1903).

[36]Overby, "Schlasinger Family History," Jewish Historical Project of North Dakota records.

engagement. It was a showing of solidarity among Jews in Europe. It was a light in the darkness.

Yosef asked his father Kiva, when he came home from work: "*Tzu vet Dr. Hertzl takeh kummen do* [Is Dr. Herzl really coming here]?"

"Yes, Yosef, I've learned that he is planning to visit a number of towns in the Pale, and Odessa is one of them."

"Can we go to meet him?"

"Yes, Yosef, we will plan to go see him if we are able."

✲ ✲ ✲

The day finally arrived. Herzl, living in Vienna, was visiting Russia out of increasing concern regarding the treatment of Russia's Jews. He had come to observe first-hand the conditions the Jews were living under after the pogrom in Kishinev. As part of this quest, Herzl

Brodsky (Broder) Synagogue, Odessa, Russia.
Public domain, www.lubavitch.com.

was also trying to convince the Russian government to help the Zionist movement by allowing and facilitating the transfer of Jews from Russia to Palestine. Despite opposition from some Jewish factions, Herzl met directly with Viacheslav von Plehue, Minister of the

Postcard of Theodor Herzl with copied signature, from Bendersky home. *Printed by "Societe Libanon," Warsaw, circa 1900, public domain, author files.*

Interior under Nicholas II, who was known to have direct involvement in the Czar's anti-Jewish policies. Yosef and his father were among the first to arrive at the synagogue and sat in a pew closest to the *bima* (pulpit). There was excitement to hear Herzl speak, but caution was in order as well.

"Oib der Czar vil oishargenen asach yidden, ken er in gantzen farbrennen der shul [If the Czar wants to get rid of a lot of Jews, he could burn down this synagogue]," said one attendee.

"I wouldn't bring my children here," said another looking right at Kiva and Yosef. "It's too dangerous."

But Kiva Bender believed that any possible danger was worth it. He wanted his youngest son to hear Herzl's words. His son lived every day with the fear. This was an opportunity to hear of hope. The family had a framed postcard of Herzl that they kept in the back of a kitchen cupboard. To have hung it on the wall would have been inviting trouble. Kiva believed that it was important that his son not admire the image, but rather learn about the content of Herzl's thoughts and dreams to help the Jewish people. A common phrase among Jews in the Pale was, *"Di velt iz a rod un es dreyt zich eibig"* [The world is a wheel and it keeps turning]." Kiva felt it took a great man to make change and that Herzl was *"einer vos dreyt der rod* [one of the wheel-turners]" of their time.

Theodor Herzl spoke to a packed synagogue in Odessa on a hot August night in 1903, only months after the Kishinev pogrom. He spoke of the ties of faith that bind Jewish people all over the world, of the increasing danger to Jews in Europe, and of the Jews' biblical home. Herzl quoted the ideals from his 1896 book, *Der Judenstaat* (The Jewish State), and his 1902 novel, *Alteuland* (The Old New Land). In *Der Judenstaat* he stated:

> We are one people. We have tried to merge with the national communities in which we live, seeking only to preserve the faith of our fathers. It is not permitted us. In vain are we loyal patriots, sometimes superloyal; in vain do we make the same sacrifices of life and property as our

> fellow citizens; in vain do we strive to enhance the fame of our native lands in the arts and sciences, or her wealth by trade and commerce. In our native lands where we have lived for centuries we are still decried as aliens, often by men whose ancestors had not yet come at a time when Jewish sighs had long been heard in the country. Oppression and persecution cannot exterminate us. No nation on earth has endured such struggles and sufferings as we have. The Jews who wish for a State will have it. We shall live at last as free men on our own soil and die peacefully in our own homes. The world will be freed by our liberty. I believe that a wondrous generation of Jews will spring into existence. The Maccabeans will rise again.[37]

It was an inspiring evening. By the grace of God, it was also a peaceful one with no violence. When Dr. Herzl came down from the pulpit, he and his advisors were heading out to exit, right in front of the Benderskys. Yosef called out, "*Dr. Herzl! A dank* [Thank you!]!" and put out his hand. Theodor Herzl firmly shook the hand of fourteen-year-old Yosef Bendersky and said, "*A shaynum dank* [Thank you very much]." Maybe Yosef was seeing things, but Yosef believed he saw a halo around Dr. Herzl's face, like a light shining from some unearthly source.

On their way walking home, Kiva had a mixture of emotions as he watched his beaming, optimistic young son with a bounce to his step. He was a little embarrassed at the brazen way in which Yosef had called out to this important Jewish leader. On the other hand, he was proud that his youngest son had the *chutzpah* (boldness, audacity) to shake the man's hand. More importantly, Kiva saw that his son refused to accept that any man should be treated as the Jews were treated in the Pale. The Maccabees had fought for religious freedom in the Syrian-Greek Empire 2000 years before. The Russian Jews in attendance at Herzl's speech, despite personal risk, were affirming that they would accept nothing less.

---

[37]Der Judenstaat translation from German by Sylvie D'Avigdor (1896, public domain), Joseph Bender Recollections.

Kiva put his arm around his teenage "Maccabee" as they headed home. That was when Yosef began whistling *Maoz Tsur* (Rock of Strength), a hymn that dates back to the fourteenth century in Germany, traditionally sung in the winter on Chanukah.[38] *Maoz Tsur* celebrates the Jews' deliverance from slavery under the Pharaoh in Egypt, from the captivity in Babylonia under Nebuchadnezzar, from Haman's plot to kill the Jews in Persia, and from the Syrian/Greeks' attempts to extinguish the Jewish faith. Yosef whistled the tune on the street. As they closed the gate of their apartment building behind them, Yosef and Kiva softly sang the words of the first stanza:

Ma oz tsur, y'shuati	Rock of Ages let our song,
l'chanaeh l'shabeach	Praise thy saving power;
tikon beyt t'fillati	Thou amidst the raging foes,
v'sham toda n'zabeach.	Were our sheltering tower.
L'et tachin matbeach	Furiously they assailed us,
mi tsar hamnabeach	But Your arm availed us
az egmore b'shir mizmor	And Your word broke their sword,
chanukat hamizbeach	When our own strength failed us.
az egmore b'shir mizmor	And Your word broke their sword,
chanukat hamizbeach.	When our own strength failed us[39]

Even though it was summertime, and the song is traditionally sung in winter, not even the strictest Rabbi could say it was the wrong time of year to sing God's praises and pray for redemption on that night. It felt like the perfect time for faith. Rebecka had stayed up late, making two big pans of *kasha varnishkes* (buckwheat groats, onions, and bowtie pasta) for the next day's meal, as she

---

[38]The Chanukah holiday commemorates the miracle of the Maccabean-led Jewish victory of the few over the many in 165 BCE., defeating the much larger Syrian-Greek army, so the Jewish people would be allowed to rededicate their temple and practice their religion.

[39]This is the popular non-literal English translation of the first stanza of the hymn by Talmudic linguists Marcus Jastrow and Gustav Gottheil, based upon the German version of the ancient hymn, *Schirm Und Schutz* (Mo-os zur), literally, Shield and Protector, written by Leopold Stein in 1838. Both versions use the same German melody. Dianne Ashton. *Hanukkah in America.* (New York: NYU Press, 2013), *Leopold Stein's Maoz Tzur,* leopoldstein.net/html/stein_leopold_maoz.html.

couldn't sleep. When she heard Kiva and Yosef approaching, she thanked God.

Herzl left Odessa, but the problems for Russian Jews remained. The Bendersky family continued turning for hope to a movement called *Am Olam* (Eternal People). Formed by two Jewish teachers in Odessa, the organization was named after Perez Smolenskin's famous essay of the same name. The movement's emblem was an image of a plow with the Ten Commandments, signifying the right to own and farm land while still being allowed to follow Jewish laws and traditions. The motto of the group was, "Arise from the dust, throw off the contempt of the nations, for the time has come!"[40]

Another movement that formed around the same time in Russia was known as BILU, an acronym in Hebrew for the quote from the book of Isaiah 2:5, "Let the House of Jacob go!" The BILU movement's goal was to form communal agricultural colonies in Palestine, and several thousand "Bilu'im" emigrated from Russia to participate in this movement in 1882. Unfortunately for Jews seeking to immigrate to Palestine, the Turkish government, then in control, had an inconsistent policy regarding allowing Russian Jewish immigrants into the country; sometimes they were allowed in, and other times, they were forbidden from entering or owning land.[41]

---

[40]Joseph Brandes. *Immigrants to Freedom: Jews as Yankee Farmers!, 1880s to 1960s* (University of Pennsylvania Press, 1971), p. 15–16. Prior to the Am Olam movement, there had been some Jewish agricultural colonies in the United States. The first one was formed in 1820, on Grand Island in the Niagara River in New York. It was called Ararat, after the mountain where Noah's ark settled after the flood. Seventeen years later, Sholom (Peace) was formed in Wawarsing, Ulster County, New York. The colonies did not last long, primarily due to lack of funds and lack of farming expertise. Pearl W. Bartelt, "American Jewish Agricultural Colonies," in Donald Pitzer, *American Communal Utopias* (Chapel Hill: University of North Carolina Press, 1997); Max Rosenthal, "Agricultural Colonies in the United States," *Jewish Encyclopedia of 1906*, www.jewishencyclopedia.com/articles/909-agricultural-colonies-in-the-united-states.

[41]Walter Laqueur. *History of Zionism: From the French Revolution to the Establishment of the State of Israel* (Knopf Doubleday Publishing Group, 2009). Though the BILU model for the cooperative farm was not successful due to lack of experience and supplies and Turkish government policies on immigration, it was seen as the precursor to Israel's later kibbutz movement.

Rather than facing east toward Palestine, Am Olam "looked westward to the New World."[42] Its goal was to help Jews escape the conditions in Russia by moving to the United States and becoming farmers. Though Jews generally worked as peddlers and merchants in Russia due to the laws prohibiting them from owning land, Am Olam suggested that the negative stereotype sometimes associated with Jews in Russia was due to this very situation. With 90 percent of non-Jews in Russia being farmers, the Jews were—in obeying the May Laws—outsiders. This was exactly what Czar Alexander III and his son, Czar Nicholas II, wanted. Am Olam's goal was quasi-religious: to assist Jews to not only earn a livelihood on the land, but also to empower them to attain full citizenship, returning to agriculture as in biblical times, to provide food for humanity, to regain their independence, to be strong again. Men and women were invited on this bold adventure.[43]

By 1903, it had already been twenty years since a number of Am Olam communal colonies had been started in the United States, and shortly thereafter, failed for various reasons ranging from flooding of the Mississippi, to internal disagreements, to poor land, to poor economic management. The first one had been in Sicily Island, Louisiana, in 1881; the next two in South Dakota (at Cremieux, twenty-five miles southwest of Mitchell, South Dakota, and Bethlehem Yehuda, three miles away) in 1882; and then at New Odessa, Oregon, and Cotopaxi, Colorado, the same year.[44] These and other lesser-known

---

[42]Violet and Orlando Goering, *Am Olam* (South Dakota Historical Society, 1983); Abraham Menes, "The Am Oylom Movement," *YIVO Annual of Jewish Social Science* 4 (1949): 9.

[43]Peter Adams, *Politics, Faith, and the Making of American Judaism* (University of Michigan Press, 2014).

[44]The Russian Jews' arrival at the train station in Mitchell, South Dakota, in 1882, prior to setting up their colony at Crimeaux, was unusual in the history of Jewish immigrants to largely non-Jewish rural areas in the Dakotas. Usually, the Jewish arrivals would only distinguish themselves from their neighbors with their Yiddish language and religious practices, and otherwise strived to adapt to their new environment. The Jewish immigrants to Mitchell, conversely, attracted attention by ordering a large can of boiling water and then celebrating their arrival by drinking Russian tea on Mitchell's main street. Goering, *Am Olam*, p. 238.

colonies, with varying levels of joint and private ownership, did not meet their goals of setting up lasting agricultural utopias.[45] However, the seeds of the Am Olam movement had continued to grow in the imaginations of disenfranchised Russian Jews. So much so, that over ten years after the last Am Olam commune in the United States had disbanded, songs were still being published in Eastern Europe regarding the impetus for the movement.

The powerful lyrics of the 1882 poem "Am Olam" were written in the midst of the horrific pogroms in Russia, and put to music in 1898.[46]

> What was often heard was as exhausted voice
> Do our people mourn withered?
> Our strength, no more,
> Our spirit melted,
> No more life in our hearts?
>
> We can't fear every murder
> We will not wither forever,
> A nation that brings forth many men of spirit—
> the priests, the Levites,
> poets and prophets, engraving God's words on a tablet,
> generals like tigers and lions were in our midst
>
> Also, David is with us
> Above everyone
> Hero and poet combined
> He has a harp to joyfully play
> And arrows like lightening
> He was not fearful, or ever afraid

---

[45]Ibid; Jeanne Abrams, *Jews in the Wild West* (May 26, 2011), www.jewishaction.com/jewish-world/history/jews_in_the_wild_west_cotopaxis_orthodox_pioneers.

[46]This poem, translated in 2017 by Minneapolis teacher, religious lay leader and linguist Uri Koppel, was written by Mordekhai Tzvi Mane when he was twenty-three years old. Mane died four years later of tuberculosis. "Am Olam" (Eternal People), Lyrics by Mordekhai Tzvi Mane, music by Cantor/Composer Avrom-Moyshe Bernshteyn (Abraham Moses Bernstein), 1898, Vilna, African and Middle Eastern Division, Hebraic Section, Yiddish Sheet Music, Box 6, Library of Congress, public domain.

Even after we fell
And the destruction of our land
When all that we loved was desolate
Other heroes arose
Our enemy was stunned

Yes our hearts
Are forever heavy
But we are mighty
Great Babylon disappeared
Persia and Media are gone
And yet despite all we are here

And in the waves of life under heaven
Many more will be erased
But us, a grieving nation
will live forever
And God's light will shine for eternity.

In the late 1800s and early 1900s, Am Olam, along with other Jewish organizations in Russia, actively assisted in the formation of Jewish young men's self-defense clubs and watch groups to defend against the physical threat of pogroms.[47] Without *koeach* (strength), the Jewish people would not survive to observe God's commandments. Yosef, like his brothers before him, became a member of such a self-defense gang. Not being a large boy, he was taught how to take away the height advantage of an aggressor with a head butt to the midsection. Once they were on the ground wrestling and punching, everyone was equal . . . except if the combatant had a weapon.

To say it was a tense and intense time for Jews in Russia would have been a significant understatement. The Russian police force would recruit hooligans to enter Jewish homes and apartments for unprovoked searches. When asked what they were looking for, the recruits claimed they were looking for evidence of anti-government revolutionary activity.[48] It was unclear what "anti-government revo-

[47]Brandes, *Immigrants to Freedom*.

[48]Lena Bendersky Miller recollections in Miller/Brudnoy, "Miller Family History," Jewish Historical Project of North Dakota records, Nathan and Theresa Berman Upper Midwest Jewish Archives, University of Minnesota Libraries

lutionary activity" entailed, and whether they were enlisted more to instill fear and destroy Jewish homes than really to search for anything. These sudden searches were more frequent in homes where young adult male students were living. Educated young Jewish men were seen as the greatest threat to the Czar. The Bendersky home was subject to sudden searches, with the apartment building where they resided in Odessa housing ten young men, including three young Benderskys — Yosef, Chaim, and Ephraim — aged fourteen through twenty-one, and Yosef's sister Sarel's fiancé, Nuchen Schlasinger.[49]

The Benderskys' property and lives felt increasingly threatened. The probability of a sudden search caused them to be careful with even the articles and novels they brought into their home. Would an article by a member of the Am Olam movement, advocating that Jews leave their Russian homes for the pursuit of farming in America, be considered revolutionary? Could their own family Bible in Hebrew be considered lack of allegiance to the Czar? It was like living under a secret set of laws and not knowing if any act they were taking violated the secret code, until they were arrested, beaten, or worse.

The young men in the Benderskys' apartment building in the Jewish Quarter on Bazarnaya Street took turns watching. In 1905, Jewish settlements throughout Odessa received warnings through the grapevine that a pogrom was coming. The Benderskys, Nuchen, and others lived in a two-story apartment house with a big heavy iron gate in front, which they kept locked. Non-Jewish neighbors had also heard the warnings, and many of them wanted to help the Jews. Even some men from the Black Sea docks, mutineers from the Imperial Russian Navy's Black Sea Fleet battleship Potemkin, came to help with the watch. On many nights, there was a damp fog that rolled in from the Black Sea, making the watch more difficult. Those seeking to do harm to anyone could easily hide among the low clouds.[50]

---

[49]Overby, "Schlasinger Family History."

[50]Noah Schlasinger recollections in Overby, "Schlasinger Family History."

* * *

After a series of workers uprisings, strikes, and naval mutinies — later referred to as the Russian Revolution of 1905 — on one foggy night in the summer, the word spread that a pogrom had indeed started, away from the Benderskys' section of town, closer to the seashore. The government-endorsed Cossacks started burning the grain warehouses by the port. Even in the fog, those on watch could see the flames. They knew that the Cossacks were on their way. The Jews in Yosef's neighborhood had nothing to defend themselves with other than some knives they had collected and rocks. They moved all the women and children to the second floor of the apartment building. Yosef heard his mother quietly crying as he left the house to join his watch group. Rebecka and the other Jewish women in the building were boiling water on the stoves to pour down in case of attack. Nuchen, a pharmacist, had brought home a small amount of sulfuric acid from the drugstore to use if they had to.[51] He reported that as they were on watch,

> a droshky [horse-drawn cab] driver stopped and came over to us and asked, "Do you have anything to defend yourselves?" When we told him no he gave us three weapons — a Finnish hunting knife, a whip made of a door spring and a lead weight, and a revolver with some ammunition. None of us had a gun — it wasn't permitted for Jews in Russia — and if you had one you could get killed by the police. Well, I put that gun in my pocket. The cab driver told us the students at the University of Odessa had been hiding away weapons for a long time, and now they were distributing them to Jewish settlements all over the city. I decided to go into the house to try to calm down Sarah and her family — they were inside, terribly scared. Well, I did that, and as it turned out, we had a very close call. I was in the house just a few minutes, and when I came back to the gate, the other men told me the police had come past the house, checking to see what's going on. Our men had got a warning from a stranger who called from across the street, and they managed to slip back quietly into the

[51]Ibid.

> yard, so the police didn't see them. If they had been seen, the police would have questioned them and there would have been trouble. And if I had been out there with a gun in my pocket, they would have taken me away, and the others too. And we would never have come out alive.[52]

Such were the days in the summer and early fall of 1905 in Odessa for its Jewish citizens. As the revolutionary movement had been gaining strength, the press—supported by the czarist regime—had intensified the anti-Jewish propaganda. Then in October of 1905, Czar Nicholas II published a manifesto in response to the revolution that promised liberties to all of Russia's citizens and the establishment of a Duma [parliament] in which the people would be represented.[53] Joyful celebrations of Jews and non-Jews erupted in impromptu processions down Odessa's streets. But the joy for the Jews was short-lived.

These processions soon developed into pogroms against the Jews. In late October of 1905, around four hundred Jews (men, women, and children) were killed in Odessa alone, and thousands more were wounded. The police stood and watched or actively participated in the worst pogroms in Odessa's history. Two of those killed were Yosef's only brothers, Chaim and Ephraim. Ephraim had completed his service in the Russian army, maintained his Jewish faith, and was critically beaten by Cossacks for defending an old Jewish fruit peddler being harassed in the market, his back "smashed in by rifle butts." Chaim was targeted and killed by the Czar's secret police solely because he was a Jewish young man living in Odessa.[54]

The glass windows of Jewish businesses on Deribasovskaya Street were smashed, riff-raff ran into the night wearing boots and fur coats that were not theirs, and the Bendersky family ached with

---

[52]Ibid.

[53]"October Manifesto," *Encyclopedia Britannica*, www.britannica.com/event/October-Manifesto.

[54]Regina M. Anavy, Editor. *Larry's Letters: The Personal Correspondence of Larry Schlasinger.* (San Francisco: Hummingbird Imprints, 2nd ed. 2005, p. 228); Joseph Bender Recollections; Sarah Schlasinger recollections in Overby, "Schlasinger Family History" and Lena Miller recollections in Miller/Brudnoy, "Miller Family History", both in Jewish Historical Project of North Dakota records, Nathan and Theresa Berman Upper Midwest Jewish Archives, University of Minnesota Libraries.

Photograph of Ephraim Bendersky, one of Yosef Bender's brothers, killed in the October 1905 Odessa pogroms. Note the fold mark from Yosef carrying it with him. *Author files.*

sorrow. The killing spree continued in over sixty other towns and over 620 small villages. Within only a few days, more than eight hundred Jews had been killed in the Pale, and Yosef was the only boy left in the Bendersky family.[55]

The Daily Tribune in Bismarck, North Dakota, referring to the continuing actions against Russian Jews, had as its headline on November 7, 1905: "No Cessation is Noticed in Butchery of Jews . . . Troops and Officials Do Nothing to Stop the Slaughter and Awful Crimes are Openly Permitted." The report went on to say the "anti-Semitic actions are in full swing again in [Odessa] and surrounding districts," and,

> the agitators of the movement have distributed circulars assuring the villagers that the authorities have received the Czar's ukase [a czarist proclamation having the effect of law] and state that it commands the extermination of all

[55]John D. Klier and Shlomo Lambroza, Editors. *Pogroms: Anti-Jewish Violence in Modern Russian History* (Cambridge: Cambridge University Press, 1992), *Modern Jewish History: Pogroms,* Jewish Virtual Library, www.jewishvirtuallibrary.org, citing to The Gale Group, *Encyclopaedia Judaica* (2008).

> the Jews. As a result the wholesale slaughter and pillage continues. The local authorities refuse to interfere either standing idly by refusing to check the riots or participating in the same. A dispatch from Akkerman near the city reports that the town is in flames and a great many of the Jewish people killed or wounded. The hospitals are crowded with the [5000] injured. Many of the wounded are being placed in temporary infirmaries established in private houses. The news continues to reach the city of terrible massacres at various points along the railway, especially between here [Odessa] and Kieff [Kiev].

After sitting Shiva to honor their sons' memories, Kiva and Rebecka reached a decision.[56] *No more.* They began to make plans to get themselves and their three remaining children to safety in America.

Israel Auerbach, living in Ashley, North Dakota, and married to Rebecka Bendersky's sister Sarah, offered to lend the Benderskys and Nuchen Schlasinger passage money for the long journey to this North Dakota agricultural community. Rebecka's sister and her husband had written of free land for farming in North Dakota, where everyone was treated the same. Jews could worship and farm land. Most importantly, there were no pogroms.

The Benderskys also had cousins named Margolin who had already resettled in New York and opened a restaurant. They indicated their willingness to help the Benderskys in any way possible. But the draw of the land was too great for Kiva and his family. The Benderskys agreed instead to accept the Auerbachs' kind offer.

***

Yosef's sister Sarel and her fiancé Nuchen left first. They didn't tell their family when they were leaving—for their protection and that of their family. One morning in March 1906, when Yosef awoke, they were gone. The Bendersky family prayed that God would watch over them until they were safe with family in North Dakota.

---

[56]Shiva is the seven-day Jewish period of mourning after a close Jewish family member's funeral.

Although the Russian government showed its contempt for the Jews in their midst in numerous ways, it still wanted to make their attempts to leave Russia as difficult as possible. Therefore, the Russian government would not grant exit visas for Russian Jews.[57] Yosef knew that at a moment's notice, whenever his father Kiva told him, he should be ready. He also knew that he could not say good-bye to his classmates or neighbors or give them any indication that his family was planning to leave.

With emigration close at hand, Yosef found himself noticing more carefully the everyday sights, sounds, and smells around him — the glow of the rows of black-iron double streetlamps at night; the mixed smell of businessmen's cigars and cinnamon from sweet noodle *kugel* at Fanconi Café on Yekaterin Street; the humid, biting salt air on his face when he stood on the docks facing the Black Sea; the bright yellow acacia flowers on trees along the avenues. But with his brothers gone, every soon-to-be memory was now laced with heartache and anger.

✲✲✲

On the way home from picking up the items requested by his mother at the market, Yosef took two detours. First, he bounded up the two hundred Richelieu steps as fast as he could, with the monument of Frenchman, Duke de Richelieu, the first Odessa mayor, looking down upon him. Yosef used to race his brothers up the steps in the early morning as part of their ritual after visiting the pier to see the ships. Now only Yosef's feet echoed on the sandstone steps. Yosef also made one last visit to the cemetery where his brothers Ephraim and Chaim were buried. He told them, "*Du vest zany frai mit mir in Amerika* [You will be free with me in America]."

"*Vi bistu geven* [Where have you been]?" asked Rebecka when Yosef returned with the tomatoes, garlic cloves, and bay leaves for

---

[57]Paul Spickard, *Almost All Aliens: Immigration, Race and Colonialism in American History and Identity* (New York: Routledge, 2007), cited in Ethan Forbes, Suzanne Lauer, Kathleen Koonz, and Pam Sweeney, *Russian Jewish Immigration*, 1880–1920, www.fitchburgstate.edu.

the brisket. Without waiting for an answer, she dried her hands on her apron and gave him a hug. That night, he and Lena each packed a bag and hid them under the feather quilts above the ceiling in their attic.

Two months after his sister had left, in mid-June 1906, Yosef went to bed as usual on the pillowcase bordered with garlands of roses, lovingly needle-pointed by his mother. He woke up when he heard his parents talking. Then Kiva came into the room Yosef shared with his sister Lena, and said softly but urgently, *"Es iz tsayt kinder* [It is time, children]."

With God's help — providing a cloudy night and contacts Kiva had made as a grain merchant, who were his go-between for payments to Russian border guards — the Benderskys were off to Antwerpen (Antwerp) to catch a ship to America. Even if the payment to the border guards got to the right place, they had another risk: the danger of highway gangs as they crossed the Russian border. They climbed into a wagon heading into Eastern Galicia, where they were to catch their first train. Four people with suitcases and sacks being transported at night were the perfect target for thieves looking for a quick profit. God watched out for them again.

The tickets purchased by Uncle Auerbach were combination railway-steamship tickets, for the two-thousand-mile railway from Eastern Galicia to Warsaw to Berlin to Antwerp. The route included crossing the Carpathian Mountains through tunnels. Their tickets were to cover their food, lodging between connections, and ultimately the steamship transport to New York.

There were a number of charitable organizations along the way that had been set up to assist the emigrating Jews and non-Jews. In 1906, the emigration business was a thriving one in Poland and Germany. The migration market fares paid to the railroads and steamship companies and the money paid to the boarding houses and food vendors increased these businesses' usual profits substantially. For this industry to continue, it was in everyone's interest to keep the emigrants flowing smoothly through, and then to get them on ships to their new homes.

Kiva, Rebecka, Yosef, and Lena arrived in Antwerp and anxiously headed to the port with their tickets. With their ship, the *S.S. Zeeland*, at the port, they were given bad news. The amount that had been paid by Uncle Auerbach for their tickets was suddenly only enough for two of the four of them to get to America. They were told that they needed to pay more money that they did not have.

It was decided that Kiva and Rebecka would go first, to begin the process of staking claims for homesteading in North Dakota. Yosef would have had to wait to claim land, as he was not yet twenty-one years old, as was required under the Homestead Act. Kiva and Rebecka also felt their children were safe in Antwerp staying at a boarding house supported by a Jewish charity until the Margolin family in New York would send the additional necessary funds. A little Jewish shtetl had formed in Antwerp by this time, with many Jews trying to leave czarist Russia for the United States on the Red Star Line of ships out of Belgium. Of the 2.5 million people who left czarist Russia for the United States out of Antwerp between 1899 and 1914, 40 percent were Jewish.[58]

"*Mir vellen zich zeyn in Amerika* [We'll see you in America]," said Yosef, as he hugged his mother and father goodbye, trying to seem older than his seventeen years. "*Baruch Ha Shem* [God willing]," said his father.

Yosef strained to keep watching his parents, carrying their only belongings, walk by themselves onto the pier. His mother looked back once. Then Kiva and Rebecka blended with hundreds of others, as colors in a dark watercolor painting. Kiva Bendersky only looked forward.

---

[58]30-40 perent of Jewish Americans have ancestors who sailed from Antwerp on the Red Star Line. Golda Mabovitz was in steerage on the Red Star Line with her family the same year as the Benderskys (1906), and Israel Baline had left with his family in 1893 . Ms. Mabovitz was later known as Golda Meir (Israel's first female prime minister) and Israel Baline was the composer of "White Christmas" and "God Bless America," Irving Berlin. National Archives at Philadelphia, www.archives.gov/philadelphia/public/red-star-line; redstarline.edu; Philip Heylen, Vice Mayor for Culture and Tourism of Antwerp, "The Red Star Line," Speech, Congregation for Humanistic Judaism, Unity Church, Sarasota, Florida, August 6, 2011. www.erraticimpact.com/~feminism/html/pdf/fuentes_en_sarasota_speech.pdf.

CHAPTER 4

En Route to North Dakota, July 1906

THE TRAIN RIDE WEST WAS bumpy, but Yosef was relieved that he and his sister Lena were soon to be reunited with their parents and sister. He had said Shehecheyanu more times on this journey than he had his entire life.[59] The train was hot, and Lena had fallen asleep with her head resting on his chest, her traveling coat for a pillow. Each time the train jolted on the track, it sounded to Yosef like his mother, back in Odessa, pressing down on a wooden board to knead the dough for Shavuoth cheese blintzes, making sure that the flour, eggs, and milk were uniformly mixed.[60] As Yosef sat, watching America's vistas go past his train window, he had time to recall all that had happened from the time he and Lena had left Belgium. He thought back to seeing the wealthy Russian men on board the Red Star Line ship from Antwerp to New York, with their pocket watches and shiny shoes. Yosef and Lena were in steerage (third class) on the four-masted ocean liner. July 7, 1906, was the maiden voyage for the *S.S. Samland*, formerly the *S.S. Mississippi*. The name change was to honor America and Uncle Sam as the schooner had been built at

---

59Shehecheyanu is a Jewish prayer of thankfulness to God for a new experience or joyous occasion.

60Shavuoth is a Jewish holiday celebrating the Israelites receipt of the Ten Commandments, when dishes made with milk are commonly prepared.

a Camden, New Jersey, shipyard.[61] The festivities involved with the name change never filtered their way down to Yosef, Lena, and the 750 others crammed into the steerage area, originally designed for transporting cattle. Pots and pans were used for human elimination, the brown bread served was rock hard, and the stew ladled out to hungry passengers contained an unknown tough meat. So Yosef and Lena were thankful for the pickled herring offered, even though it was over-salted, so as not to violate their kosher eating restrictions.[62]

Yosef had snuck up from the lower level to look for water for himself and his sister, as the amount of water provided would not have been enough for a cool journey, let alone one in July, or after eating salty pickled herring. To Yosef's surprise, he was invited to play cards with several of the wealthy men who were looking for a fourth for Konchinka. To his even greater surprise, he was successful in earning a little money playing cards with the first class passengers. The men were amused at his good luck, in continuing to turn over the ten of diamonds and the two of clubs, giving him more points.

One of the card players slapped Yosef on the back and said in Russian, "*Amerika ne pokhodit ni na kakoye drugoye mestopolozheniye v mire, moy mal'chik* . . . [America is unlike anywhere in the world, my boy! Did you know that before and after the fighters fight in America, they shake hands with each other? No one shakes hands with us before they fight us in Russia! Have you ever heard of another place where they do that]?" Raising his glass, the Russian man made a toast, "Here's to America, where you shake hands with your enemy!"

***

[61] Jonathan Kinghorn, *The Atlantic Transport Line, 1881–1931* (Jefferson: McFarland, 2012); www.whitestarhistory.com/belgic3.

[62] The Bible, in Leviticus, Chapters 3,11, and 17, provides for the types of animals that are permitted to be eaten by Jews. Following these and other rules, e.g., relating to not eating meat and milk products together, is referred to, generally, as "keeping kosher," or following the laws of kashrut.

Yosef and his sister waited in the long lines at New York's Ellis Island immigration center. The biggest fear among all the immigrants was being sent back to their homelands. Lena whispered to Yosef, "*Dos iz vi Yom Kuppur, ven Gott beshlist unzer goierel. Nor do, blois a mentch bashlist unzer tzukunft* [This is like the Day of Atonement, when God decides our fate. Only here, a mortal man decides our future]."

Yosef whispered back, "*Zorg zich nisht, Gott is mit untz vi mir zenen, tayere shvester* [Don't worry. God is with us wherever we are, dear sister]."

The single lady waiting in front of them in line had fainted, possibly due to lack of food or water. She had been taken away, and they hadn't seen her again. Yosef recalled the faces of other fellow immigrants in the bottom of the ship . . . the faces of Moische and Rachel Davidowitsch of Bialystok and their nine children. Had smiley four-year-old Fanny Davidowitsch been allowed entry?

No one had told Yosef or Lena that there was a fifty dollar (three thousand ruble) minimum to enter America. Though Yosef and Lena passed the health testing, they then stood in another long line. This was where Yosef first heard a man he had met in steerage repeating over and over with a raspy voice to everyone in the line who would listen, "*Oib du host nisht genug getl, vet men dich tzurik shiken! Oib du host nisht genug getl, vet men dich tzurik shiken* [If you don't have enough money, they will send you back . . .]!"

Yosef relived their encounter with the immigration officer, a man with a high neck collar and shiny gold buttons, who smelled like peppermint sticks. The officer assigned to them spoke Yiddish, had the ship's Manifest of Alien Passengers, and was cross-examining them with the information gathered in Antwerp. First, he asked them their names. "*Yosef aun Lena Bendersky*," said Yosef.

The immigration officer and the Benderskys continued in Yiddish:

"The Manifest says your last name is 'Benchersky'" How do I know that you are the same persons who boarded the ship in Antwerp?"

Yosef answered, "Sir, we are those people. We have always been Benderskys. The ship made a mistake."

Next, they were asked their nationality. Yosef and Lena, without hesitation, each said, *"Rusishe yid* [Russian Jew]." The manifest had listed their "Nationality" as Russian and their "Race or People" as Hebrew.[63] Their answer was a match for the officer. Then the immigration clerk asked how much money they each had.

With his face flushing, Yosef said he had the money for both he and his sister. He took out a few rubles from one pocket and a few rubles from another. Then, knowing that he didn't have the required amount, he began an act of checking real and imaginary pockets—in his pants, his shirt, his coat, his sack—for the non-existent rubles. The immigration officer watched him go through the charade and then said:

"Halt oif [Stop]!"

"Yo, mayn har [Yes, sir]?" Yosef said, and put his hands at his sides. First Yosef noticed that the man was smiling. Then the man started laughing.

"Ales vet zayn fayn far dir, Yosef. Nor di neimen zenen tzu lang and tzu Rusish. Du vest zayn Lena Bender, un du vest zayn Joseph Bender. Boruch haba tzu Amerika [You'll make it just fine, Yosef. But your names are too long and sound too Russian. You will be Lena Bender and you will be Joseph Bender. Welcome to America]."

No sooner had Joseph, Lena, and a group of other Jewish immigrants starting walking out of the immigration processing center, then a bystander threw a rotten tomato towards them. Joseph had only been admitted into the United States moments earlier, but his blood started to boil, he dropped his packages on the ground, and started to fight with the man. The crowd of Jewish immigrants cheered him on. Joseph got the best of the tomato-thrower, and he ran away.

---

[63]Jews do not consider Judaism or being Hebrew as a "race," but rather consider Judaism to be a religion, and the Jews a people or nation who practice this religion. Among the reasons given for this understanding is that a race is not something that can be joined, and people are allowed to convert to Judaism, though Jews traditionally do not proselytize.

✲✲✲

Joseph and Lena's sponsors in the United States, the Margolin cousins, lived in New York City, had a son about Joseph's age, and ran a restaurant. Joseph and Lena had stayed with them after arriving in New York while the cousins assisted them in making contact with the Hebrew Immigrant Aid Society. The HIAS was formed in 1881 to address the needs of many Russian Jews immigrating to the United States. The charity provided some of the funds to Joseph and Lena to travel by train from New York City to North Dakota.

✲✲✲

"*Ende der gleis!* End of the line—Eureka, South Dakota! Ende der gleis! End of the line—Eureka, South Dakota!" The engineer's announcement in German and English woke Joseph and Lena with a start.

"*Mir darfen do aropgeyn, shvester* [We've got to get off here, sister]," said Joseph. "*Noch dem vet men unz ariberforen tzu* Ashley [Then we are to get a ride to Ashley]."

"*Ich ken nisht gloiben az mir zenen shoin bald in unzer naye heym* [I can't believe we're almost at our new home]," said Lena.

"*Baruch Hashem* [Thank God]," said Joseph.

Eureka, South Dakota, was known as Odessa of the North, as so many people arrived there by train from Odessa—Jews and non-Jews—either to make Eureka their home or to settle in neighboring areas. It looked like such a young town to Joseph compared to Odessa, Russia. The buildings were lower and newer, except for the tall grain elevators. But that was fine with him. He was ready for a new start, and said to Lena in Yiddish, "This is good. We are getting in on the ground floor!" Joseph and Lena climbed onto a horse-drawn wagon bound for Ashley, North Dakota, to begin their American lives. They were already pioneers, as over 70 percent of Russian Jews who immigrated to the United States through Ellis Island settled in New York.[64]

To an outsider, Joseph and Lena probably looked small, riding in the big, empty wagon. But with the hopes and dreams accompanying them, the wagon was near capacity.

[64]Janet E. Schulte, "Proving Up and Moving Up—Jewish Homesteading Activity in North Dakota 1900–1920," *Great Plains Quarterly* Vol. 10 no. 4 (2010): 228–44.

CHAPTER 5

Ashley, ND, August 1906

AFTER REUNITING WITH HIS FAMILY in Ashley, Joseph learned that his sister Sarel, now Sarah, had already filed for a homestead and then had married Nuchen Schlasinger, now Noah. But unbeknownst to Joseph, Sarah and Noah had married in Odessa in a secret Jewish ceremony prior to leaving for America. Sarah's parents, Kiva and Rebecka, would not allow their eldest daughter to travel alone to America with a man who was not her husband.[65]

The Homestead Act allowed a woman of any religion, who had not taken up arms against the United States and no matter whether single, divorced, or widowed, to file her intent at the closest land office to homestead 160 acres that were not already claimed.[66] Sarah would not have been allowed to file for her own claim had her marriage been known to the state, but as it was not, she and her sister Lena were each able to take ownership of their parcels. In this way, in America, there was equality of women (except married ones) and men in regard to taking on the backbreaking work of making the virgin prairie soil productive on their own claims and then to own the land.

---

[65]Stories of Sarah Schlasinger told to her grandchildren, including Ronnie Sigal Hartman.

[66]The Homestead Act of 1862, 37th Congress, Session II, Chapter 75, May 20, 1862: "An Act to Secure Homesteads to Actual Settlers on the Public Domain."

Unbeknownst to Joseph upon his arrival to America was that much of the available "public lands" for homesteading in the Dakotas were originally occupied during some seasons by the Great Plains Indian tribes. McIntosh County, North Dakota, where Joseph's family settled, had originally been called Buffalo County.[67] The United States government broke a series of treaties with the tribes, and in the 1870s the United States Army and hunters engaged in the purposeful slaughter of the bison. These actions, together, ended the tribes' nomadic way of life and ability to live off the land. They also set the stage for forcing the Native Americans onto reservations to make way for settlers the railroads were bringing west. Thirty years later, once the buffalo were gone and the tons of sun-bleached buffalo bones littering the prairie had long ago been sold for fertilizer and bone china, Jewish settlers escaping Russian persecution began to farm the land where the Native people had once freely lived and hunted.[68]

Joseph was anxious to begin living the independent life of a farmer. However, even with adding a couple years to his real age at Ellis Island, Joseph was still too young to file for a homestead claim. But there was no time to waste to beat the learning curve necessary to survive on the prairie and to help Lena and his parents with advancing their claims.

Joseph had never ridden a horse before and knew nothing about farming. He hired himself out as a farm hand at the home of an Ashley German farmer so he could learn. He learned how to rotate crops, how to handle a single-blade plow with a team of horses, and how to break in wild bronco horses. Joseph was a hard worker and a fast learner. He used the skills he acquired to help his family on

---

[67]In 1873, Logan County was created from Buffalo County. In 1884, McIntosh County was created from Logan County. *Dakota Territory, South Dakota and North Dakota: Individual County Chronologies*, Dakota Territory Atlas of Historical County Boundaries (The Newberry Library 2006); Nina Wishek, *Along the Trails of Yesterday: A Story of McIntosh County* (*Ashley Tribune* 1941).

[68]State Historical Society of North Dakota, Great Plains Indians, www.ndstudies.gov, Tessa Sandstrom, "Buffalo Bones" in *Dakota Datebook* (November 2, 2006), www.prairiepublic.org.

their land. Soon Joseph was even a consultant for other farmers new to the area.

Then, on July 5, 1907, the day Joseph turned nineteen (and pretended to turn twenty-one), a little less than one year after arriving in America, he took his horse and headed for Bismarck, North Dakota. This was the closest Land Office for him to file his homestead application papers.

Two red-tailed hawks soared and swooped with Joseph along the 120-mile route, keeping him company. Joseph smiled to himself thinking how free he was—just like the hawks—and remembering his promise to his two brothers before leaving Odessa: "*Du vest zayn frai mit mir in Amerika* [You'll be free with me in America]."

Joseph was seeking to farm a 160-acre parcel, located between his parents' and his sister Lena's, in Township 131N, Range 69W, in McIntosh County. McIntosh County is situated in south central North Dakota, the second county east of the Missouri River, and its southern boundary forms part of the border between North and South Dakota. The Ashley Jewish homesteaders arrived a little late to the party—over twenty years after McIntosh County was opened for homesteading—and about five years after the Soo Line railroad came to Ashley.

By this time, the best land had already been claimed. Most of the Jewish homesteaders ended up with land in the hilly sections of the county, and this is where Joseph's proposed plot was located. The German residents in the county referred to the Jewish homestead lands as "Judenberg," or "the Jewish Hills."[69] On his journey to the Land Office, Joseph carried with him the $10 filing fee, the $2 commission to the land agent, and the hope that no one had claimed the plot already. The land agent excused himself to check for previous ownership claims for the requested plot, using the survey coordinates. Joseph could feel his heart. Then a door closed and the agent reappeared.

[69]William C. Sherman, notes from interview with Ashley residents Max Wishek and Dr. Leo Cohen, circa 1980, NDSU Institute for Regional Studies and University Archives (Fargo, ND); Susan Berman, *Easy Street: The True Story of a Mob Family* (New York: Dial Press, 1981).

"Good news, Mr. Bender," said the agent. "The land is clear for your filing. Good luck!"

"Thank you, sir!" said Joseph.

The way back home seemed longer, as Joseph was anxious to tell his family the good news. He would be farming right next to them. He had looked over the slopes and valleys of his land and knew just where he wanted to start building his home. Building a home on one's land within six months of filing for a claim was one of the requirements under the Homestead Act.

Early the next morning, standing on *his* land for the first time, Joseph spun around in a full circle. The sky touched the ground, endless, with nothing in the way. The wind moved the prairie grasses like waves in a green sea. Joseph inhaled the sweet, Dakota air, perfumed with the natural scent of coumarin. *This is God's country*, thought Joseph. He said the prayer Shehecheyanu, typically said to thank God for living to see a particular day or occasion, but he took the liberty to change the words slightly: "Blessed art Thou, O Lord our God, King of the Universe, who has sanctified us with His commandments, and has allowed us to reach this *place*." Even though Jews think of each day of life as a gift from God, Joseph was even more thankful for the safe place where his family was, and the limitless opportunities the place presented. He was far away from the sorrow of Odessa, where doing nothing wrong could lead to death. Joseph then began the process of building his house.

With few trees on the prairie, there were only two real options for homes: a dugout, like a cave with no windows, protected from the moisture and frost by horse manure, or a sod house, with a respectable wooden door and real windows. Joseph opted for the latter, as he had learned that sod houses provided excellent insulation against the Dakota cold and wind.

The native western wheatgrass, with densely packed intertwining roots to hold the soil together, was ideal. Joseph borrowed a special plow with a curved steel blade and hooked it up to a horse to cut through the tough roots, which made a loud, tearing sound. Joseph next used a spade, to cut the strips into three-foot lengths. Each freshly-cut sod brick was placed root-sod up, so it would continue to grow into the brick above it and strengthen the walls. Joseph was like the sod he struggled to remove — ripped from its original home, and hoping to continue to grow even stronger in another place. For a sixteen-by-twenty-foot house, about three thousand bricks were used. After over a month, and with help from neighbors, Joseph's sod house was completed, with a wooden door and two windows. He hung a muslin sheet from the ceiling to keep dirt and snakes from unexpectedly dropping inside his new home or on top of his food.[70]

Joseph closed the door, and sat by himself in his home. He tried to think of an appropriate prayer for the occasion. He recalled the biblical story of a prophet, Balaam, who would have been paid by the King of Moab, Balak, had he agreed to curse the Israelites. But the prophet refused and instead, looking out over the wilderness where the Israelites were encamped tribe by tribe, said: "*Mah Tovu. Ohalecha Ya'akov, meeschkino'techa, Yisrael* [How beautiful are your tents, o Jacob, your dwellings, o Israel]." Joseph repeated these words. His dwelling place in the Dakota wilderness was beautiful to him. However, when Joseph began preparing the soil to plant, he realized what many of his homestead neighbors had realized. There were thousands and thousands of rocks, stones, and boulders peppering his mixed-grass prairie claim. When the last glaciers advanced from the north 12,000 years earlier, they pushed Canadian Shield core bedrock over the land at varying depths. The rocks remained on Joseph's land until he arrived.[71] The process of clearing the land foot-by-foot, and eventually acre-by-acre, was the highest priority. Crops would not grow in and around the stones and rocks. This tedious, time-consuming work was, of course, done without the benefit of any modern machinery.

Removing rocks too big to be dug out of the soil required creative methods. If the pickaxe and crowbar didn't work, Joseph would

---

[70]"Searching for Shelter: Building a Sodhouse," *Homestead Act: The Challenges of Living on the Plains*, www.nebraskastudies.org; Joseph Bender Recollections.

[71]Lauren Donovan, "Between Rock and a Hard Place," *Bismarck Tribune* (May 6, 2017), quoting Ed Murphy, State Geologist for North Dakota Geological Survey.

Homesteader pyramids of cleared rocks dot the Dakota prairie, McIntosh County, ND. *Photo by Rebecca Bender, 2014; author files.*

build a fire on one rock, then pour water over the hot rock to crack it. Following this procedure, he could more easily dig out the pieces. The smaller rocks were removed with persistence and backbreaking labor. The women homesteaders worked alongside the men in this process. Joseph's sister Sarah would load rocks that her husband Noah dug up by throwing them into the stone boat that the horses would then haul to the ravine.[72]

[72]Overby, "Schlasinger Family History"; Joseph Bender Recollections

Joseph and the other homesteaders worked on their land with sore and bruised arms, backs, and legs until they "found gold."[73] Like his neighbors, after digging by hand for what seemed like forever and pulling up dirt in a bucket on a rope, Joseph eventually located his land's water supply. This was a significant occurrence, and worthy of another prayer to thank God. However, one set of challenges was replaced the next day with a new set.

The Benders, like their Jewish and non-Jewish neighbors, were required to deal with the harsh climatic conditions in the area. Temperatures exceeded 110 degrees on multiple summer days, and dropped to forty below zero with heavy snow in the winter. Joseph learned from the older German-Russian farmers that it was dangerous to leave horses or cattle outside for more than a short time during the extreme cold. Their breath could freeze over the ends of their noses, resulting in suffocation. Joseph was also taught to use the rope technique to stay alive and keep his animals alive in the extreme winter conditions. When he went to feed his animals, Joseph tied a thick strong rope around his waist and attached it to the door of his barn. Otherwise, if a blizzard suddenly came up, he could easily lose direction. Joseph knew that if he couldn't find his way back to shelter during a blizzard, he would die.

Noah discussed the intense climatic conditions with his brother-in-law, Joseph, saying, "I have never felt such heat or such cold."

Joseph responded, "But it's our land, so it's not as hot or as cold as the thermometer at Uncle Auerbach's store shows."

"That's the *emes* [truth]," laughed Noah.

✲ ✲ ✲

In its 1903 report, prior to the Benders' arrival in North Dakota, the Jewish Agricultural Society (JAS), part of Baron de Hirsch's charity set up to aid Jewish immigrant farmers escaping persecution in Russia, referred to the "intense climatic risks of Dakota," stating:

---

[73]Noah Schlasinger quote, from Overby, "Schlasinger Family History"; Joseph Bender Recollections.

> There is no advantage in seeking such remote places for our people. We shall in no case assist any farmers . . . sen[t] out to the Northwest at any date after May 1903, unless conditions alter materially.
>
> While the land is practically free, everything connected with its tilling is expensive, and the chances of crop failure are very great—since the season is a very short one and droughts and frosts are both very likely to occur. The cost of all supplies being great, the new farmer must run deeply into debt to the local storekeepers before he can harvest his crop and a debt so incurred runs at the legal interest of twelve percent . . . so without a large supply of ready money during the first year of his residence, the farmer is certain to become hopelessly involved in permanent indebtedness. We are fully in accord with the opinion of our manager that much might be gained if we could [provide support to farmers on] farms whose fertility had already been tested, together with [providing] information as to the best crops to be raised and methods of the same, that he [the farmer] would be spared the many disappointments which are encountered at the present time.

The Benders, along with the other wave of Jewish immigrant farmers in the second immigration boom to North Dakota, knew nothing of the JAS's pessimistic report issued prior to their arrival. The railroad companies for years had referred to the same area as the Garden of Eden and The Land of Golden Grain in order to encourage settlement.

The Jewish homesteaders kept working at the never-ending job of clearing rocks to increase the amount of tillable soil. They planted wheat first, before diversifying their crop with flax, barley, oats, and spelts. They harvested what they could, depending upon the weather situation each year. When Joseph saw his first field of golden wheat catching the sun's light, next to the intense blue of a natural pool on his land, he was awestruck. "Have you noticed that colors are brighter in America?" he commented to his sister Lena.

The Bender clan and the other homesteaders also found jobs off their land to make ends meet. Some found part-time work in stores in or near Ashley. Others painted the McIntosh County Courthouse.

Joseph worked as a member of a threshing crew, pitching bundles of hay from stacks to wagons. The other spike pitchers received two dollars and fifty cents for a day's work. Joseph was proud to receive fifty cents more. His boss said he worked faster and took no breaks. Joseph told his parents, "I love it, and want to prove we can do it . . . that Jews can be farmers."[74]

Meyer Mackoff, a Jewish homesteader who spoke English well, recruited Jewish immigrants for a crew to build a road crossing on the Milwaukee Railroad near Monango, North Dakota. The pay was good, $1.50 per day, and Noah and Joseph took advantage of the opportunity. Sarah Schlasinger and her cousin took their cook stove, a cow, dishes, and pots and set up a kitchen in an empty house near the road job. There they made money for their families, feeding the crew of men, baking fresh bread every day, and serving milk direct from the cow.[75]

The Benders and the rest of the Jewish homesteaders near Ashley in McIntosh County changed the minds of the New York-based Jewish Agricultural Society, which had determined that it would no longer support North Dakota Jewish farmers "in the Northwest" with loans. The JAS Report in 1907, provided:

> Though hit hard by this year's extremely unseasonable weather, [the Jewish farmer] has not suffered from its effects any more than his gentile neighbor.
>
> During the last two years there has been a large influx of Jewish settlers in [North Dakota], the fourth largest number in the United States. Many of them were obliged to file on poor land, owing to the fact that most of the desirable homesteads had already been preempted. The settlers, however, are promising young men, filled with a pioneering spirit and not afraid of hard work. This is especially true of those settlers in McIntosh County. The largest and youngest settlement is around Ashley. Most of these homesteaders have started with little or no money, but by working out for other farmers, on the section roads, or with threshing crews, have managed to make ends meet.

---

[74]Joseph Bender Recollections; Overby, "Schlasinger Family History."

[75]Ibid.

> To enable them, however, to work their homesteads, they require horses and farm machinery. These they generally buy on credit at exorbitant prices, giving in payment notes bearing twelve percent interest [rather than the 4 to 6 percent interest typically charged by the JAS] and becoming deeply involved in debt, they apply to us for assistance. This accounts for the 59 loans we were obliged to make this year in North Dakota.
>
> Owing to the difficulty of supervision so far from New York, we had almost concluded not to assist any more settlers on homestead claims. [These] men, however, have convinced us of the wisdom of in some measure changing our decision.

Local newspapers also began to notice that the Jewish farmers in the area were exceeding expectations. An article in the *Grand Forks Herald* in 1907, "Jews Take to the Farm—Colony in Ashley, ND, prospering at beginning of Third Year," stated:

> The Jewish colony which was started near Ashley, ND, in September 1905 is prospering wonderfully. At that time, twelve families moved to the colony and since then it has grown rapidly. There are now thirty-two families there who have taken homesteads. They are proving daily that the Jews make as good farmers as students, vindicating that they are willing workers, and many of them would have long been "tillers of the soil" had they but had the opportunity.[76]

Even those Jewish homesteaders who were farming in North Dakota sensed something unique about the Jews who "came out" to the Dakotas to homestead: "They were a different kind of people there . . . they came to the Dakotas not only to make a living, but to be independent, self-made people. That was really their aim.[77]

* * *

[76]The Grand Forks article begins by referring to "the Jewish problem" that "may be taking care of itself," recognizing that the Jews have been persecuted in other lands and the possibility of a Jewish homeland is far off.

[77]Joseph Bender, in interview with Alfred Thal, May 1974.

With the never-ending job of trying to succeed as a farmer, amid drought, early frost, tornadoes, hailstorms, swarms of grasshoppers that could destroy fields of crops, and the howling wind, it would have been understandable had the Jewish immigrants in McIntosh County put their religion on hold temporarily. But to do so would have been akin to asking them to stop breathing or eating. Even when the homesteaders had been persecuted for their beliefs in Russia and Eastern Europe, they continued their religious traditions, oftentimes at great personal risk. Once coming to the United States, where practicing their religion and being allowed to live were not mutually exclusive concepts, these same Jews were not prepared to ignore their religious history. They felt they could be good citizens of their adopted country, while observing their Jewish customs and rituals.

There was no lag time from the time of the Jewish homesteaders' arrival until they picked right up with their religious observances. Part of their Jewish observance required a quorum of ten men (a *minyan*) for certain religious services and prayers, with the belief that God would then be present. Once a family member died, the children honored the memory of the deceased by reciting a prayer (the Mourner's Kaddish) for eleven months and then again on the annual anniversary of the person's death, according to the Jewish calendar.

The Benders were among Jews who believed that when the Mourner's Kaddish was said, the soul of the deceased rises higher in heaven and closer to God. When a child of the deceased praises God, this action becomes a source of merit for the deceased, as a child inspired to continue serving God is one of the greatest legacies left on earth when a Jewish person dies.[78] The requirement of ten to say the Kaddish makes those saying the prayer thankful to the others who make this mitzvah (good deed) possible. On the North Dakota

[78]Many Jews also strive to perform good deeds specifically in memory of deceased family members, so the departed is found by God to be worthy of *lictig Gan Eden*, a "luminous Paradise." Yeruchem Eilfort, "Why Do Mourners Recite Kaddish?" www.chabad.org.

prairie, this feeling of appreciation was amplified due to the distances fellow Jews had to travel to make the minyan.

By Joseph Bender's sixth day in North Dakota, he was just beginning to get comfortable riding a horse. Lipman Bloom, a fellow bachelor homesteader, rode his horse and brought along another horse to the Bender home for newly arrived Joseph. Kiva Bender, his son-in-law Noah, Lipman, and Joseph set out for Yankel Greenberg's house, to recite the Mourner's Kaddish for Yankel's mother on the anniversary of her death. "This is America!" said Joseph to his father Kiva, as they mounted their horses. As he grabbed the reins and began his gallop, dust from too many hot days without rain flew up from the horses' hooves. Joseph smiled, being part of the minyan brigade on the prairie. He had never enjoyed participating in a minyan as much as he did on that day.

The Ashley Jewish homesteaders also gathered at different neighbors' farms for the Sabbath and to recite the important prayers that were thousands of years old. Homesteader Sol Jamplolsky joked with Joseph one day when they had all gathered for services. "I wish we would always try to get eleven men instead of ten. Then," he said, "we wouldn't have to stop praying when one person has to go outside to relieve himself."[79]

As there was no ordained Rabbi in the early years, Kiva Bender would oftentimes lead the prayer services and chant the *parsha* (weekly Bible portion) from the Torah scroll in the Bender barn. Kiva rolled the parchment scroll to get to the correct place with the help of another of those assembled. The old Torah they used had been loaned to them from a congregation in Minneapolis. It was a simple Torah, unlike the one at their former synagogue in Odessa with its ornately embroidered mantles (covering) and silver finials on top of the staves on which the scroll was wound. But it was a kosher Torah, and that was all that mattered.

---

[79]Sol Jampolsky, "Jampolsky Family History," Jewish Historical Project of North Dakota records, Nathan and Theresa Berman Upper Midwest Jewish Archives, University of Minnesota Libraries.

The words of the Torah were handwritten by a *sofer* (pious scribe) using a turkey quill dipped in ink made from gallnuts. The *gevil* (parchment sheets) were made from kosher animal hides sewn together with dried stretched animal veins and tendons. And in keeping with tradition, no iron or steel was used to create any part of the Torah, even to hold the wood spindles together, as these materials are used to manufacture instruments of war. As Kiva stood in front of the congregation, in the special place he had set up in the Bender barn, he remembered the words of his late father, Schmeri, that someday he would be a teacher and a leader like Rabbi Akiva. Kiva knew his father could never have imagined that he would be a teacher on the American prairie, from a barn with hay on the ground. But he knew his father would be proud.

In addition to reciting the mourners' prayers and observing the Sabbath, the residents of the Ashley Jewish Homesteaders settlement celebrated the major Jewish holidays with each other—Rosh Hashanah (The Jewish New Year), Yom Kippur (The Day of Atonement), Sukkot (Feast of Booths or Feast of Ingathering), Shavuot (Feast of Weeks, celebrating the giving of the laws to Moses and the Jewish people at Mount Sinai), Simchat Torah (celebrating completion of reading the Five Books of Moses, and the beginning of the same again), and Pesach (Passover, celebrating the Jews' exodus to freedom, from slavery in Egypt). For these major Jewish holidays, the families would initially travel to one home in or near Ashley, or later, to Bismarck or Aberdeen, South Dakota, for services. The Jewish young adults and children especially enjoyed having a full house of visitors for the major holidays. There were sometimes eight children in one bed, with all the men sleeping with the horses in the hayloft in the barn, and all the women sleeping in the house. But no one minded.[80] Bender cousin Rose Rapaport Schwartz opined that "Simchas Torah was the most fun — they'd hire a hall in Ashley, get

[80]Pauline Auerbach Greenberg, "Auerbach Family History," Jewish Historical Project of North Dakota records, Nathan and Theresa Berman Upper Midwest Jewish Archives, University of Minnesota Libraries.

a small band, get goodies from Brochins in Minneapolis, and everyone would have a good time."[81]

Besides the challenge of getting together a minyan and gathering together for the holidays over significant distances, there was another significant religious obstacle faced by the early McIntosh County Jews. The Bender family in Russia, like most of their Jewish neighbors, ate only kosher meat, i.e., meat from animals approved in the Bible, and only from animals killed in a humane way, by a trained *shochet* (Jewish butcher trained in humane slaughter of animals). Prior to having a person trained in the proper way to slaughter animals being available in the Ashley settlement, the Bender family made a number of attempts to get kosher meat shipped on the trains from Minneapolis or Grand Forks. As the meat was not properly refrigerated and trains were frequently delayed, when Joseph went to the train station to pick up the anticipated package, it was always the same conversation with the railroad employees: "Are you Bender?"

"Yes."

"Your delivery really stinks. Will you get it out of here?"

"Yes, sir." Though hope sprang eternal for many challenges on the prairie, it soon became obvious that transporting butchered chickens and beef from bigger cities was not a realistic option. This led to some members in the Ashley Jewish community learning on their own the kosher way to slaughter meat. Homesteader Isadore "Izzy" Jampolsky even took the initiative to travel to Brooklyn from North Dakota, to get a degree in *hechsher* to slaughter chickens in the kosher way. He would then travel by train at his own expense and spend entire days butchering chickens for the Jews in neighboring towns.[82]

For many of the homesteaders during these times, including the Benders, the food eaten was a result of the family's financial condition. If rabbit and pheasant were readily available on the prairie, and

[81] Rose Schwartz, "Rapaport Family History," Jewish Historical Project of North Dakota records, Nathan and Theresa Berman Upper Midwest Jewish Archives, University of Minnesota Libraries.

[82] Sol Jampolsky, "Jampolsky Family History." History," Jewish Historical Project of North Dakota.

the previous year's crop had not been as successful as they hoped, by necessity they would hunt for their own food, whether or not it was kosher or slaughtered in the traditional way. Though the Benders were sometimes forced to adapt the rules they were used to living by in order to survive, they felt no less Jewish than when they had lived in Odessa. To the contrary, Joseph felt that his religious commitment was even stronger in America, as, though he was safer, he had to work harder for his Jewish observance than he had in Odessa.

In 1908, less than two years after Kiva Bender arrived from Russia with no knowledge of English, with no rabbi, and with no synagogue building, he registered the new Ashley Jewish Congregation in the prestigious annual American Jewish Year Book. The Book was published by the Jewish Publication Society of America based in Philadelphia. When Joseph saw his father writing out information to submit to the Jewish Year Book, after a full day of seeding in the hot sun, he inquired as to why it was so important to let people in the East know about them. Kiva replied, "I am not only sending this information so they know we are here, and so more will come to join us. I am sending it so the Ashley Jewish farmers know that we are a congregation that is recognized nationally. This is even more important. I want them to know that we are not alone out here, but are part of something much bigger."[83]

Less than one year later, Kiva Bender also organized and registered one of the first two Jewish farmers associations in the United States, which he named The Sulzberger Colony, after Cyrus Sulzberger, a friend of the Ashley Jews on the board of the Jewish Agricultural Society. Kiva realized that there was strength in working together to purchase seed and supplies and to obtain credit. He was one of the

---

[83]"My Dad used to write in the Jewish paper and ask for volunteers to come to our colony. We had a few from New York but they didn't stay very long." Joseph Bender, in Alfred Thal Inteview, 1974. After a "brief bout with the North Dakota climate," one of these New York couples returned to the city. Joseph Miller, Joe's sister's husband, offered them $20 for the contents of their home, and then owned a round, solid mahogany dining table, a buffet and six mahogany chairs covered in genuine black leather. Miller/Brudnoy, "Miller Family History," Jewish Historical Project of North Dakota records.

original founders of the Federation of Jewish Farmers of America, which in 1909 boasted twenty-five farmer associations throughout the United States. By identifying mutual needs and goals with Jewish farmers in other communities within and outside of North Dakota, the group of Ashley Jewish farmers made connections with those beyond their county's boundaries.[84]

The Federation of Jewish Farmers of America held its first meeting in New York in October 1909, in conjunction with the Jewish harvest holiday of Sukkot. The fair offered Jewish farmers an opportunity to exhibit their produce, as well as to familiarize themselves with the benefits of being a member of the Federation.

Sukkot is one of the three pilgrimage festivals for Jews. In ancient times, these were the three times each year when Jews would travel from their homes to the Holy Temple in Jerusalem. The holiday has a dual significance: historical (commemorating the forty-year period when the children of Israel wandered in the desert while living in *sukkot* [temporary shelters]) and agricultural (also called the Festival of Ingathering, a thanksgiving to God for the harvest). As New York City was a long way from Ashley, the only known "attendee" from Ashley at the First Annual Convention was a woven wreath of three-inch head millet sent by Joseph's sister, Sarah Schlasinger. The Ashley farmers had been contacted by the JAS, asking for specimens of their grain for the exhibition in New York City. By the time the Ashley Jewish farmers learned of this request, all their good quality wheat had been sold. Sarah crafted a wreath from their chicken feed millet and won a silver medal and certificate of merit.[85]

In 1908, the same year that Kiva Bender was connecting with the broader Jewish community and providing the local Jewish farmers a sense of belonging, the JAS began its publication of *Der Iddusher Farmer (The Jewish Farmer)*, at a cost of three cents per copy or twenty-five cents per year. *The Jewish Farmer* was an agricultural monthly newspaper published in Yiddish and English to help edu-

[84]Jewish Publication Society, Jewish Agricultural Society Annual Report, 1910; Schulte, "Proving Up and Moving Up"; Miller and Brudnoy, "Miller Family History."
[85]Overby, "Schlasinger Family History."

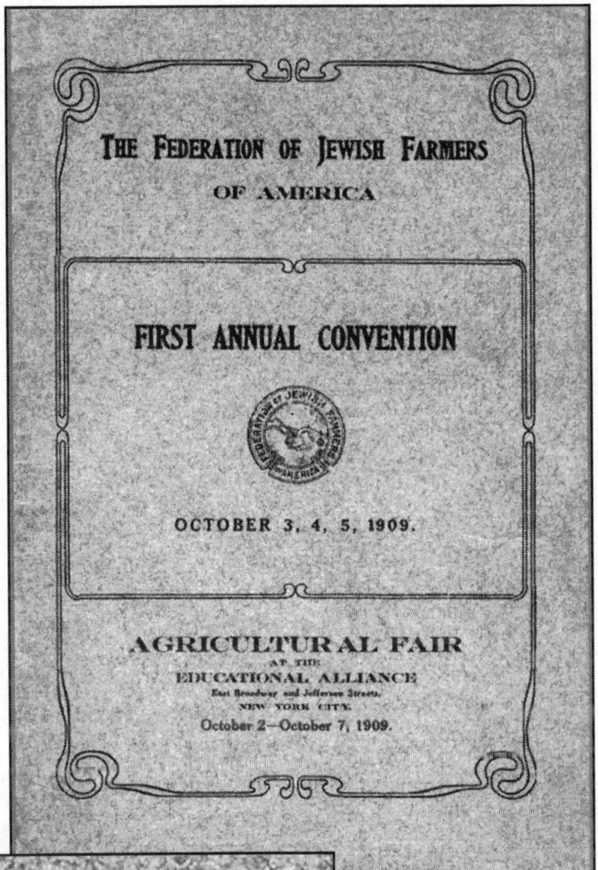

Program from First Convention of The Federation of Jewish Farmers of America. *Courtesy of The Jacob Rader Marcus Center of the American Jewish Archives, Cincinnati, Ohio, americanjewisharchives.org, 1909.*

cate farmers regarding techniques of farming and to offer solutions to the problems of farm life. Kiva's brother-in-law Israel Auerbach subscribed to this periodical and his family and friends shared his copy.[86]

One summer day in 1909, Joseph was pitching hay to his sister, Lena. She was arranging it in careful stacks, shaped to drain off water in case of rain, the way she had seen the German farmers do. The team was working with such momentum, they didn't realize that the stack on which Lena was standing had become so high, there was no way for her to come down. Joseph ran from farmer to farmer until he found a ladder long enough to rescue her from her perch.

The story spread throughout the area, of the young Jewish lady stuck on top of the high hay pile. A short time later, Joseph and Lena were in the field when a well-dressed gentleman approached them. "He's not from around here, Lena," said Joseph.

"Hello. I'm Mr. Blaustein from the Jewish Agricultural Society in New York. I'm looking for Joseph and Lena Bender," the man said.

"I'm Joseph Bender and this is my sister Lena."

"We have been so impressed with the work of the Ashley Jewish homesteaders. We would like to feature your settlement in a story in our *Jewish Farmer* magazine. Would you continue your work, as on a typical day, and I'll take pictures?" Joseph and Lena were pictured in a future edition of *The Jewish Farmer*.

In 1910, another gentleman who Joseph could tell was also not a farmer, was pacing in front of Joseph's home when Joseph came in from the field. The man had a big leather satchel. "Are you Joseph Bender?" asked the man.

"Yes, I am," said Joseph, a bit apprehensively.

"Your parents said that I could find you here. May we go inside?" Joseph got each of them some water from the well and invited him in.

"I am conducting the 13th census of the United States of America and need to ask you some questions, to make sure that you are counted. Do you know what a census is?" asked the census taker.

---

[86]Miller and Brudnoy, "Miller Family History."

דער אידישער פארמער

THE JEWISH FARMER

The Jewish Agricultural and Industrial Aid Society

Der Iddisher Farmer (The Jewish Farmer) *Magazine*, published by the Jewish Agricultural Society.

Joseph Bender with single blade plow and horse on his homestead land near Ashley, North Dakota, circa 1909. *Photo taken by JAS representative; author files.*

"Yes," said Joseph. "In the Bible, about 5,000 years ago, God told Moses and his brother Aaron's son to count all the men 20 years and up who were able to serve. They counted 60,000."[87]

"Well I'm glad I don't have to count that many people," laughed the census taker, "and I'm counting men, women and children." After the initial questions, the census taker inquired, "What is your occupation?"

"Farm laborer," responded Joseph proudly. Joseph slept well that night, feeling like the Jewish farmers were making a name for themselves and being counted.

The JAS was also counting the Ashley homesteaders, and counting on them to continue the back-to-the-land movement. Its report on North Dakota farmers in 1908 referred to 216 Jewish farmers in the area, with the "most important Jewish settlements" being in the Ashley section in McIntosh County and the Wilton section in Burleigh County. Leonard Robinson, the general manager of the JAS wrote in his report that he was

> much impressed" with the "spirit with which the homesteaders set about to work out their destinies in a new country . . . When we remember that these settlements are still in their infancy, the strides made by our farmers are certainly inspiring . . . There was a pervading spirit of hopefulness which was contagious.

But there was no escaping the fact that conditions for crop production in the area were less than ideal, even on the best homestead land in the area. The JAS report for 1909 stated that in North Dakota, the state "experienced an almost general crop failure" that year. Regarding "the McIntosh County settlers," the JAS states:

> This year's crop was almost a total failure . . . few if any farmers will have grain to sell. All that they will realize is enough for seed and feed. However, in spite of the crop conditions, our settlers have held their own in the past year, contracting few new debts.

[87]Numbers 26:51

The 1910 farming report was not much better for the farmers in the area:

> In the Dakotas, where the average farmer depends largely upon his wheat crop, this year's failure, following immediately upon the heels of that of last year, was most disastrous in its effects. To the new settler who has not yet had time to gain a foothold and whose cultivable area is as yet small, the two successive crop failures proved a severe setback. In some sections the drought was so severe that the farmer did not even harvest enough to pay him for his seed. Many of them were obliged to abandon their homesteads, at least temporarily, in order to find work for the winter. This is true of both Jewish and non-Jewish settlers.

Though the farming conditions were poor, Joseph and his family had diversified by raising cattle and buying and selling cream. In this way, they were not so dependent upon the varying weather conditions. On October 17, 1910, Joseph was successful enough to purchase his land outright with cash, after only about three years and prior to the five-year waiting period prescribed in the Homestead Act. Kiva, Lena, and Sarah had also obtained their land patents early.[88]

Joseph rode his horse to the Bismarck Land Office and presented full payment for his 160 acres at $1.25 per acre—two hundred dollars in cash. Now, the "south half of the southwest quarter and the south half of the southeast quarters of section twenty in township 131 north of range sixty-nine west of the fifth principal meridian in North Dakota containing 160 acres," was his. He was told that his patent papers would next be forwarded to the General Land Office in Washington, DC, for its stamp of approval. Joseph explained this exciting process to his newer immigrant friends: "Then, I will be sent my patent, with the approval of President William H. Taft, no less!"[89]

[88]The Patent records show that Sarah, who arrived to Ashley first, owned her land in 1908; Kiva owned his homestead land in 1909; and Lena and Joseph owned theirs in 1910.

[89]As long as they had begun the process to become a United States citizen, homesteaders were able to own their land prior to completing the process.

***

The Ashley Jewish community gathered whenever they had the opportunity to talk, sing songs, play chess, and drink hot tea sweetened with lump sugar or *varenya* (jam). The Rapaports, one of the homesteading families, had purchased a phonograph, and homesteaders visited their home to listen to operas, great violinists, and Jewish cantorial and other music.[90] Joseph sometimes brought his dance music record entitled *Odessa Mama*, by the Jewish Russian Orchestra, complete with trumpets, flutes, clarinets, cymbals, tuba, and snare drum.

"Odessa Mama" was a common phrase among residents of Odessa, referring to the love they had for their city. Several years later, when the Ukrainian song "Odessa Mama" came out on a 78, Joseph enjoyed listening to the lyrics, translated, in part, from Yiddish below:

> Whoever has not been
> In the beautiful city of Odessa
> Has not seen the world
> And knows nothing of progress
> Who cares for Vienna or Paris,
> They're puddles, jokes, no comparison
> Only in Odessa is a paradise, I say

---

[90]"Schlasinger Family History" and "Rappaport Family History," Jewish Historical Project of North Dakota records. The recording of oral history Yiddish music on "78s" (shellac discs which spin around at 78 revolutions per minute) began in the late 1800s. Approximately six thousand Yiddish/Hebrew recordings were released between 1898 and 1942 in the United States, and another ten thousand or so recorded in Europe during this same time period. Sherry Mayrent, "Why Listen to Scratchy Old 78s," 2016, klezmeracademy.com/blog/2016/9/23/why-listen-to-scratchy-old-78s, citing Richard K. Spottswood, *Ethnic Music on Records: A Discography of Ethnic Recordings Produced in the United States, 1893–1942* (University of Illinois Press, 1991), and Michael Aylward, www.yidisher-gramofon.org. Sherry Mayrent is a clarinetist, composer, and music producer who collected over nine-thousand 78-rpm recordings of Yiddish and Hebrew music, the largest collection in the world, which she donated to the University of Wisconsin—Madison at the Mayrent Institute for Yiddish Culture.

There in a restaurant
They serve you beer
And with it a bite
Of fresh skombri [mackerel from the Black Sea]
Bashmala [loquat fruit] and balik [finest Russian smoked salmon]
And with them a shashlik [lamb skewer]
With a good glass of wine—
What could be better?

Your avenues, promenades
Are light, beautiful.
The cafes, the boulevards,
One can never forget.
The carriages, the gypsies,
The tumult, ta-ra-ram,
The hotels, the young ladies
Still are on my mind

Oh, Mother Odessa,
You're forever dear to me.[91]

The sound of the klezmer arrangement in the song brought Joseph back to happier times, when he was the youngest male in his family, instead of the only son. However, despite the lyrics of the song, whenever Joseph was asked if he missed his homeland of Russia, he always responded the same: "How can a person love a country that treats its people so badly? I love America."[92]

Far from the lights and cafés of Odessa, when the weather allowed, the homesteading women in North Dakota walked across the prairie to visit each other with their small children holding onto their long skirts. In early summer, they gathered rose petals together from the wild rose bushes and made rose-amber jelly. Later in the summer, they picked chokecherries, poking the almost black fruit with their hairpins to remove the pits before boiling, and making jam. When they canned jam and jelly together, it was a social activity

[91] Translation found at yiddishlyrics.blogspot.com/2007/05/Odessa-mama-3272.html.

[92] Bender, *From the Prairies to the Beaches.*

as well as a way to provide a little variety for their families during the long, cold winter months.[93]

The settlers made their own fun and developed their own distractions from otherwise challenging lives. Lena Bender had become a proficient horsewoman, who would ride to Ashley for mail and other errands. She soon started racing on horseback with the German girls in the area.[94] On Saturday nights, after the Sabbath was over, Joseph Bender started his own tradition. He would take a big wagon — a hayrack — filled with hay. He would pull it from one Jewish homestead to the next, and the single men and women would climb in. Heated rocks wrapped in gunnysacks under quilts kept everyone warm. They would sing and sometimes hold dances in barns. The single ladies would prepare cakes and sandwiches for the trip.[95]

In addition to socializing within the Jewish farming community, there was also communication and friendship between the Jewish farmers and their German farming neighbors and those living in town. There was a sense that they were all in this together. When the harsh climate resulted in crop failures, they all suffered. When the rains and temperatures were favorable, they all triumphed. The Jewish women learned to make cheeses, winterize vegetables, and store eggs — skills they did not previously have — from their welcoming non-Jewish neighbors.[96]

In the spring of 1912, Joseph was riding his horse from his land, nine miles northwest of Ashley, into town. Mattias Kapp, a German-Russian farmer, owned 160 acres near Ashley. Joseph noticed that Mr. Kapp had not seeded his land yet and it was getting late to plant wheat. He stopped at the Kapps' house and asked Mr. Kapp if anything was wrong. Mr. Kapp, with tears in his eyes, said his horses were sick and this would be the first year that he wasn't able to plant. Joseph rode to see his dad and said, "We've got to help him." Kiva

[93]Overby, "Schlasinger Family History."

[94]Miller and Brudnoy, "Miller Family History."

[95]"We didn't have any money to spend, but the social life among the people was wonderful." Thal, Interview with Joseph Bender (1974).

[96]Rose Schwartz, "Rapaport Family History."

told Joseph, "you know all the homesteaders. See if you can get them to all help the Kapps together."

Joseph went from farm to farm that evening on horseback, explaining the situation to the neighbors. He told them of his plan — that they would all meet at the Kapp farm the next morning. When Joseph arrived at the Kapp farm before dawn with his team of horses, plow, and seed, he was the only one there. His heart fell. Joseph closed his eyes to concentrate, thinking of the Bible quote from Leviticus, *"V'ahavta L'rayachah K'mohcha* [Love your neighbor as yourself]." Suddenly, he heard the rumble of horses' hooves and then more horses' hooves, just as the sun started to rise. Thirty Jewish homesteaders with thirty teams of horses and thirty plows had come to help their neighbor, Mr. Kapp.

In one day they plowed and seeded the Kapps' 160 acres. Mr. Kapp came out and looked with disbelief. "Why did you do this for

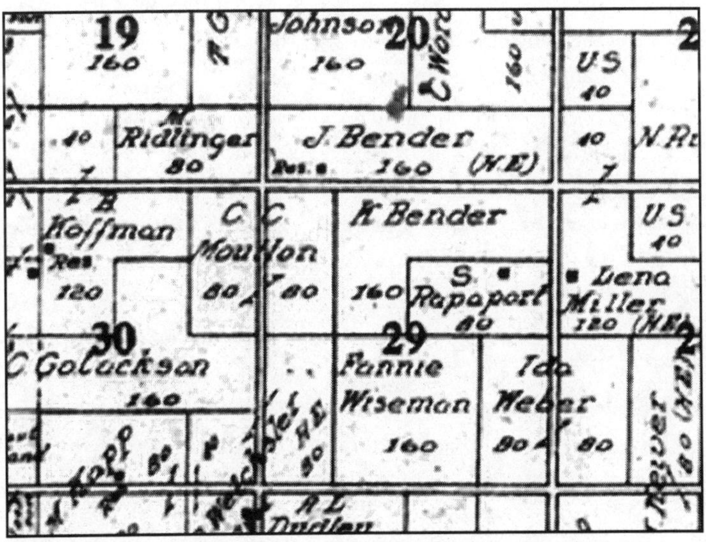

Portion of 1911 McIntosh County Standard Land Atlas for Township 131, Range 69W, showing K. Bender, J. Bender, Lena Miller, S. Rapaport, and M. Kapp farms. *Geo. A. Ogle and Company, State Historical Society of North Dakota.*

me?" he asked. Joseph responded, "What we did for you, you would have done for any of us."[97]

***

McIntosh County was considered part of the base of the German-Russian Triangle in North Dakota. The German-Russians had moved from Germany to Russia to farm beginning in the 1760s, based upon promises of Catherine the Great that they could own land and would be allowed to maintain their culture and language as well as be exempt from Russian military service. In 1804, Duke Richelieu, appointed by Czar Alexander I, issued a decree with similar promises to the Germans who were willing to relocate. These promises that induced them to move were later broken. By 1874, the conscription exception was removed by Czar Alexander II, and by 1892, the Russian language was required to be taught in German village schools in Russia, rather than German, per Czar Alexander III's decree. This increase in anti-German sentiment resulted in a great hegira of the German-Russians to the Dakotas.[98]

As many of the immigrants in Ashley, North Dakota, only spoke German, Yiddish, and/or Russian, and could not speak English, Rebecka Bender's sister (Israel Auerbach's wife) Sarah served as a go-between for the American doctor when the non-Jewish and Jewish women were ready to give birth. Farmers would come to the door of the Auerbachs' house and knock at all hours. Sarah would go with the farmers to get the doctor and would stay to translate directions from the doctor and comments of the women until the baby was born. Sarah's generosity exemplified just one of many types of good deeds that flowed both ways, between the Jews and the German-Russians, cementing the growing friendships between them in and near Ashley.[99]

---

[97]Thal, Interview with Joseph Bender, 1974.

[98]Gordon L. Iseminger, "The McIntosh County German-Russians: The First Fifty Years," *North Dakota: Journal of the Northern Plains*, Vol. 51, no.3 (1984); Arends, *The Central Dakota Germans*.

[99]Greenberg, "Auerbach Family History."

Many of the homesteaders had become friendly with members of what was then called "the Sioux Tribe," who lived near their homesteads. Joseph had noticed that the tribe's horses were faster than the ones typically ridden by the homesteaders. He approached one of the owners to purchase a horse, and a deal was struck for a pinto. The horse was so fast that Joseph won the Ashley Fourth of July races three years straight. Some people in town used to say, "Oh no, here comes Bender with that horse, again!"[100]

* * *

The hard work on the farm did not diminish the creative spirit nor the community building among the Jewish homesteaders. Sarah Schlasinger was determined to make her sod house a home. She "painstakingly painted the wooden floor by hand, to look like the parquet floors of Odessa."[101] Mrs. Walder, another Jewish homesteader, played the piano for the town movies in Ashley.[102] Louis Reuben, a homesteader with a large family who grew wheat, a standard crop for the area, also had a large, productive garden, with a wide variety of fruits and vegetables, which were far from standard. Homesteader Rachel Minenberg Baker recalls "with what joy this large man with a full reddish beard cracked open a muskmelon on a rock and ate it dripping in the garden."[103]

During the second winter in North Dakota, a group of homesteaders including the Schlasingers and Nathan Minenberg decided that if they could not attend plays, they would put on their own. Among the books that Sarah and Noah Schlasinger had brought from Russia was a volume of plays by Chekhov and other Russian writers, including two one-act comedies that they produced: *The Bashful Bridegroom* and *The Devil and the Belle*. The Jewish theater group rented the Ashley Town Hall, and it was a full house. Noah

---

[100]Kenneth Bender, *From the Prairies to the Beaches*.

[101]Overby, "Schlasinger Family History."

[102]Minenberg Baker, "Minenberg Family History."

[103]"Schlasinger Family History" and "Minenberg Family History."

wrote a synopsis of the plays in Russian, and a local banker translated the synopsis into German and English for the playbill.[104] A February 7, 1908, article in the *Ashley Tribune* provided: "The Jews who gave the Russian entertainment in Ashley a few weeks ago are advertising the same plays to be given in Lehr . . . in Kulm and Eureka in the near future."

Though many of the Jewish settlers who arrived were married in Russia or shortly after they arrived, there were also single members of the community who were looking forward to getting married and to starting a family. Homesteader Pearl Rapaport, urged to come to Ashley with her husband by her Uncle Kiva Bender, convinced her brother Joseph Miller to move to Ashley. Miller was living in Pittsburgh, where he was a cigar maker. Once arriving in Ashley, he offered to teach English to single homesteader Lena Bender. Soon Mr. Miller proposed marriage.[105] An August 6, 1909, article in the *Ashley Tribune* stated: "A Jewish wedding in which Joseph Miller and Miss Lena Bender were the consenting parties was solemnized at the Bender home, a few miles north of Ashley, Sunday."

This brief notice did not begin to describe the event, which Lena Miller later did:

> The wedding took place in the Bender barn. Fresh green grass was strewn inside and boards were propped up for tables and covered with fresh tablecloths. Cookies and cakes were baked in great quantity by relatives and friends. Kiva [Bender] had bought grapes and made several huge barrels of wine, far more than he expected to need. Nathan Minenberg made a Star of David. All Jewish families in the colony were invited. Everyone came to join in the festivities.
>
> The day was calm and beautiful. No wind was stirring. The chupa was set up outside. Their German neighbors, who had never seen a Jewish wedding before, came to watch. Kiva invited them to have a drink, and in less than an hour all wine and pastries were gone. The guests danced on the prairie, reveling in the joy of the

---

[104]"Schlasinger Family History," Jewish Historical Project of North Dakota.

[105]"Miller Family History," Jewish Historical Project of North Dakota.

> occasion. The men vied for a dance with the bride, so Jake Raich stepped in to organize the dancing. He asked the musicians to shorten their numbers, charged 25 cents for a dance with the bride, and cleared twelve dollars to present to the new couple.
>
> The musicians had been engaged to play until midnight. When midnight arrived and the guests clamored for more dancing, the musicians were offered more money and urged to continue, but they refused, so the groom [Joseph Miller] accommodated the guests by taking his fiddle, and to the accompaniment of a washtub drum, played waltzes and polkas far into the night.[106]

In addition to following Jewish traditions for the happy milestones, the Jewish community did the same during sad times. When people in North Dakota were getting sick and dying from the Spanish Flu pandemic, homesteader Sol Jampolsky's brother Leo in Mercicourt, North Dakota, caught pneumonia. Sol, whose family had sold their farm near Ashley and was then living in Braddock, North Dakota, had just given away much of the merchandise in his general store, closed his store, and sent his parents to live with Leo, so he could report to Bismarck, North Dakota, for World War I service. Sol had previously been sent home from Bismarck and told to wait until called to report. Sol hired a man to bring his sick brother to the nearest doctor, fearing the worst, and headed to Bismarck again to report for duty. Sol's father, Izzy, was watching from inside as his son Leo was being laid on the sled. The sight was too much for him, and he fell to the floor and died.

In Bismarck, Sol was told once again that his call to service was temporarily cancelled, and he was advised that his father had passed away. He arranged for a car to take him and his deceased father to the Ashley Jewish Cemetery for the burial. However, a snowstorm came up and the car stalled. They walked the rest of the way to Ashley and placed the body in a barn, as it was by then the eve of Sabbath, and no funeral could be held on the Sabbath. After the funeral

---

[106]Ibid

on Sunday, Sol took the Soo Line train back to Merricourt. Deep in his thoughts and sorrow, he stepped down off the train. Then he heard bells ringing and saw people laughing and dancing, with tears of joy. When Sol asked what was going on, he was told that World War I had just ended. Within a matter of several days, he had given away his business to serve in the war, his brother had gotten severely ill, his father had died, he had walked through a snowstorm, buried his father, and the war had ended. As he made his way through the boisterous crowd back to his now widowed mother, he must not have been sure of the source of his own tears.[107]

[107]Sol Jampolsky, "Jampolsky Family History."

CHAPTER 6

Ashley, ND, 1911

IN 1911, DR. MORRIS LOEB — scientist, chemistry professor at Columbia University, philanthropist, and member of the Board of Directors of the Jewish Agricultural Society — stated in an editorial in *The Survey*:

> The Jewish farmer is not only a fact, but is gradually becoming a factor. Failures, it is true have been numerous, but it is no longer popular to dismiss them with the off-hand statement that the Jew cannot be a farmer. Every failure, it was shown, can be traced to specific causes that are inexorable and that operate without regard to creed, race, color or previous condition of servitude.[108]

As the Jewish farmers near Ashley continued working on the land, big changes were in store for Joseph and the community in 1911. While picking up supplies at a store in Wishek, North Dakota in 1910, Joseph, twenty-three years old, met a sixteen-year-old raven-haired girl born in Baltimore, with enchanting dark eyes. Mary Rievman had big city department store experience. Because she was strong and mature, she had been able to secure a job at a Baltimore department store at age fourteen. She had left school at that time to

[108]Dr. Loeb's December 23, 1911, quote included language from the Fifteenth Amendment to the Constitution (1870) giving former slaves the right to vote. His speech was cited in the Jewish Agricultural Society Annual Report, 1913.

work, as her parents needed help supporting the family. Her family eventually moved to Minneapolis, and she had begun working in Wishek for her uncle when Joseph happened in.

Though Joseph and Mary had never met until that day, Joseph's mother, Rebecka, and Mary's mother, Esther, were sisters. Mary's

Postcard of Joseph, sent to Mary while courting, August 15, 1910. *Author files.*

parents, Max and Esther Rievman, left Russia and settled in Baltimore almost twenty years before Joseph and his parents immigrated.

Joseph and Mary's respective experiences growing up in different countries not only made them strangers, it made them interesting to each other. Mary was fascinated to hear what life in Russia was like, and Joseph listened intently to Mary's descriptions of growing up in a big American port city. They hit it off immediately. Joseph soon made the decision to sell some of his flax crop, to buy a suit,

Joseph and Mary Bender, wedding picture, 1911. *Author files.*

and to go to Minneapolis to ask Mary's parents for permission to marry. They had a small religious ceremony in Mary's parents' home on a sunny, crisp day in October 1911.[109]

Kiva and Rebecka could not attend the wedding ceremony of their only living son, Joseph, as they didn't have the funds to do so. Their pain while accepting God's will and affirming their faith in God, is expressed in the handwritten letters they sent from Ashley:

> Hoshana Raba [final day of Sukkot], 5672[110]
>
> My pen is too weak for me to be able to express my thoughts that I feel now, at this moment, when I am writing. Nothing turns out the way a person thinks and imagines in his mortal thoughts. I certainly did not think this would be so . . . Thank God your mother and father were merited to marry off their oldest and youngest daughters and they were not sad that they were not present at the great simcha [joyous occasion], where the entire family was present—at a place where it would have been the most wonderful hours of a person's life. This was very likely God's wish, and we take this on with love and we say with a full mouth and full heart the blessing "Shehechyanu lazman hazeh." We send you our warmest wishes for long years and many good things. We also wish the in-laws now from our hearts good health, mazal tov, good things, they should always have plentitude, pride in their family, good fortune and joy.[111]
>
> Akiva [Kiva] and Rivka [Rebecka] Bender
> [in Kiva's handwriting]

---

[109]Joseph Bender Recollections; Frances Rievman and Lenore Haasl recollections told to author, circa 1990.

[110]The Jewish calendar year of 5672, the same as the Gregorian calendar year of 1911, is based upon the number of years elapsed since creation. Though the book of Genesis states that the world was created by God in six days, common interpretations to allow the literal text of the Bible to coexist with present scientific knowledge include that what are referred to as "days" in the Bible could have actually been millions of years, or that God created and destroyed worlds prior to the present world He created.

[111]This prayer, "Shehechyanu lazman hazeh," is said at special occasions, thanking God for sustaining a person to reach that time. Letter translated from Yiddish by Pamela Russ, 2017.

My dear and beloved,

I am sending you a Mazal Tov. May God grant that it be a time of good fortune with much joy and long years. May God help that we should all have pride in all our children and in you, our dear ones. We would certainly want to be present when our one son is led to his chuppah but probably God wanted it this way. So I say, thank God for this. May God grant that we have much nachas [Nachas is the Hebrew word for pride, especially at a child's achievements] in even this little bit. And may you live to see, from

"Post" sent to Joseph and Mary Bender on their Jewish wedding day. Sent from relatives in New York. The telegram begins with *"Mazel Tov"* written three times and the wish, "May your bond be eternal." Design includes idyllic pictures of couples farming, holding abundant harvests of wheat and grapes, and stamp showing Theodor Herzl, founder of the movement for a Jewish homeland. *Author files.*

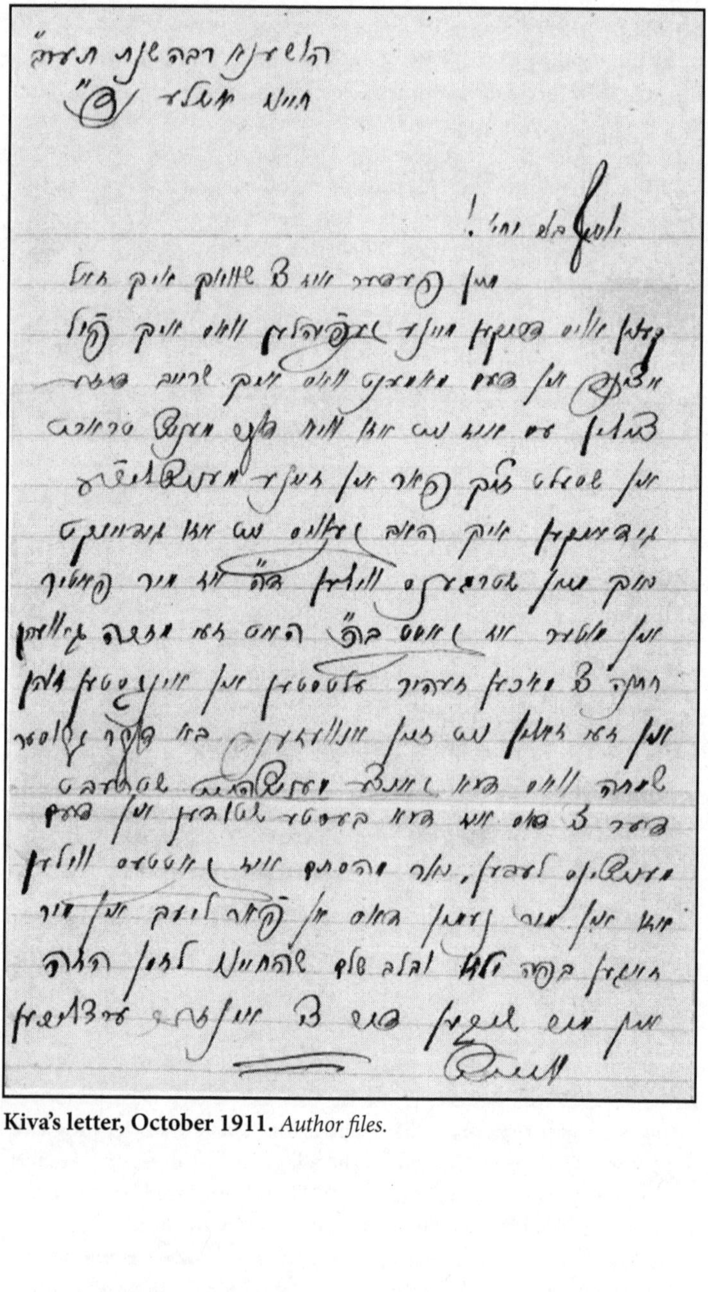

Kiva's letter, October 1911. *Author files.*

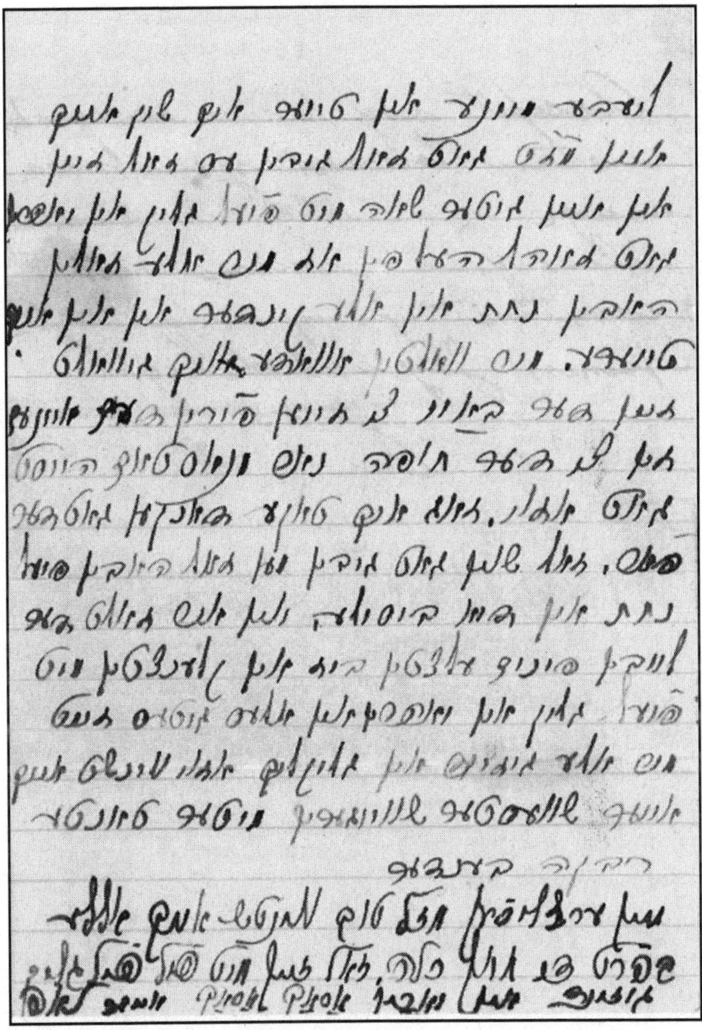

Rebecka's letter, October 1911. *Author files.*

your oldest to the youngest, much joy, and long years, and all good things. Be well and happy, all of you. This is what I wish for you.

Your sister, sister-in-law, mother, aunt,
Rivka Bender[112]

As Joseph and Mary were cousins, they then were required to travel to Wisconsin to obtain their civil marriage license, to make their union comply with state laws. On October 12, 1911, Joseph Moses Bender from Odessa again married Mary Rievman from Baltimore—this time in a civil ceremony at the courthouse in Hudson, Wisconsin. Their wedding reception consisted of their sharing a chocolate bar while walking around the block together.

After the wedding, Joseph took Mary by horse and buggy to their new home on the acres he was homesteading near Ashley. Mary unpacked her belongings. She picked up a broom to begin tidying up. As she swept, the dirt would not come up off the floor. She fell to the ground in the sod house lit only by candlelight and began to cry. Seventeen-year-old Mary had realized that she couldn't get the dirt off the floor because the floor was dirt.[113]

Considering the major change in lifestyle from waiting on customers in a Baltimore department store, to cooking whatever food her husband could hunt and kill on the prairie and living in a house made of dirt and grass, Mary adapted very quickly. She and Joseph took turns filling the little stove in their house with coal every hour or two.[114] Mary made friends quickly with the Jewish and non-Jewish neighbors. She put feminine touches on their home—making curtains for the windows, throwing flower seeds on the windowsills and up on the roof, to brighten the place a bit when the flowers would

[112]Trans. from Yiddish by Pamela Russ, 2017.

[113]Mary Bender told these stories to her daughter-in-law (the author's mother, Frima) years later.

[114]Joseph Bender later said about their lives at the time, "We were happy and satisfied." Joseph Bender Recollections.

bloom, and suggesting the addition of a raised wooden floor to Joseph's bachelor home. She also became a "real farmer's wife"—successfully selling one of their calves to a neighbor so Joe could make the first payment on a life insurance policy.[115]

The other big change in 1911, was that a rabbi moved to town. Prior to his arriving, Kiva Bender had officiated at Ashley and Wishek Jewish weddings, in addition to conducting services for High Holidays and other religious services.[116] In 1911, with the help of the Jewish Chautauqua Society from Philadelphia, Rabbi Julius Hess came to live in Ashley, North Dakota.[117] Several of the members of the Ashley Jewish community had advertised for a rabbi and paid a small part of his salary. Rabbi Hess was also a cantor, a person trained to sing the liturgical notes that accompanied the sacred texts and prayers. The Chautauqua Society felt that no child of a Jewish farmer, no matter how remotely located, should be without at least some religious instruction.

Rabbi Hess, born in Lithuania, part of the Pale of Settlement in the Russian Empire, married Francesca Feist while living in Germany. As a Jew born in Russia, he was told he could never become a German citizen and that he had to apply for a permit each year to continue living in the country, despite having been educated at the University in Marburg, Germany. In 1901, after their first child was born, when Rabbi Hess attempted to apply for his permit, he was told, with no explanation, that his permit was denied and that he had to leave Germany within twenty-four hours. He immigrated to the United States, and his wife and child followed soon after. After living in Chicago for several years, and then starting the first Conservative Jewish congregation in Tampa, Florida, the rabbi and his wife moved to McIntosh County, North Dakota, where they lived

---

[115]Ibid.

[116]Ibid.

[117]American Jewish Yearbook, Volume 9 (Philadelphia: Jewish Publication Society, 1907).

from 1911–1922 with their eight children, including a son named Abraham Lincoln Hess.[118]

Even with a rabbi close by, Kiva Bender always said, *"Di eltern zol lernen* [It is up to the parents to teach]." Rabbi Hess agreed, and he obtained copies of the *Jewish School and Family Bible* for McIntosh County Jewish families who requested them, including the Benders.

While living in McIntosh County, Rabbi Hess also traveled to Wilton, Regan, Minot, and Williston, North Dakota, to assist with the education of Jewish children and to officiate at weddings, funerals, baby namings, and *brises* (circumcisions). The 1912 Bulletin of the National Conference of Jewish Charities reported that in the Ashley, North Dakota, settlement, services were led by Rabbi Hess on Rosh Hashanah, with seventy-eight adults and thirty-one children attending. It also reported that Rabbi Hess spent the first part of Sukkot in McIntosh County and killed 350 fowl for the month of September and two beeves a week.[119] Rabbi Hess also visited Fort Lincoln, a military post on the Missouri River. He obtained a three-day furlough for the Jewish soldiers in the fort for them to observe the Jewish High Holidays. In January, 1913, Rabbi Hess appeared at the meeting of the Chicago Rabbinical Association, representing the Jewish Chautauqua Society in the Jewish Colonies of North Dakota, seeking funds to enable him to continue his work.[120]

Rabbi Hess was seen in Bismarck in 1915 and asked what he was doing there. He said he was there to see a performance by his brother's son at the Chautauqua. "Who is your nephew?" he was asked.

[118]Al Thal taped interview with Joe Miller, 1974, and Al Thal taped interview with Joseph Bender, 1974, The Historical Society of North Dakota State Archives, Bismarck Heritage Center and Museum; Ron Vossler, "The Lost Jews of McIntosh," *North Dakota REC/RTC* (July 1986): 24. Rabbi Hess also served as the rabbi at the Bnai Isaac Synagogue in Aberdeen, South Dakota, beginning in 1917 and at the Sons of Israel Congregation in Sioux Falls, beginning in 1922. Goodye Becker article about her father: Al Thal Papers, The Historical Society of North Dakota State Archives; Steven Weinreich, "Virtual Cemetery," findagrave.com/cgibin/fg.cgi?page+gr&Grid+106150029.

[119]National Conference of Jewish Charities, *Jewish Charities: Bulletin of the National Conference of Jewish Charities* (Baltimore: 1912, 4th ed. Vol. III).

[120]*The Reform Advocate: America's Jewish Journal*, Volume 44 (Chicago 1913).

"His name is Al Hesselson," said the rabbi.

"Never heard of him," said the other gentleman.

"He goes by another name, Al Jolson," said the rabbi. Al Jolson would go on to star in the first talking movie, *The Jazz Singer*, in 1927 and became the first star to entertain troops in World War II (where he contracted malaria and subsequently lost a lung), and in the Korean War, where he performed forty-two shows in sixteen days. He died at age sixty-four in 1950, shortly after returning from Korea, and he was awarded the Medal of Merit by United States Defense Secretary George Marshall. Despite his use of blackface in his career, Al Jolson crusaded for equal rights for black Americans in 1911, insisted on fair hiring and treatment of fellow black performers, and he "helped to introduce African-American musical innovations like jazz, ragtime, and the blues to white audiences."[121]

Once Rabbi Hess took up residence in Ashley, it made sense for the Congregation to have one place where its members would meet, rather than going to different homesteaders' homes or barns. The Ashley Jewish Synagogue building was purchased in 1917 from the Ashley Baptist Church. The building had been built by and owned by the Baptist congregation for fifteen years prior to the Ashley Jewish Congregation of Beth Itzchock (House of Isaac) purchasing the structure. The synagogue building was located outside the city limits of Ashley between 1917 and 1924, but then moved into town in 1924. The Jewish Congregation bought the lots for the synagogue's Ashley site from John Wishek for $125 with the understanding that the property would revert back to Mr. Wishek if and when the property was no longer used as a synagogue.[122]

Another rabbi, Rabbi Ostrowsky, arrived around 1918 and served the Ashley Jewish community for several years, as well. During the period from 1918 through 1922, McIntosh County boasted the presence of two rabbis. By this time, there were also two synagogues in

---

[121] *St. James Encyclopedia of Popular Culture* (St. James Press, 2000); "Al Jolson Remembered," Paramount News, December 6, 1950.

[122] Ashley Golden Jubilee Historical Book Committee, *Ashley Golden Jubilee Book* (1938); Al Thal taped interviews with Joe Bender and Joe Miller, 1974.

the same North Dakota County. In 1916, one year prior to the Ashley Jewish community's purchasing the Baptist church building for their synagogue, the neighboring Wishek Jewish community, also in McIntosh County, built its synagogue. The program for the Wishek

"Jewish Church," from Ashley's Golden Jubilee Book. *Courtesy of Ashley, North Dakota Golden Jubilee Committee, 1938.*

Wishek Synagogue and congregants, circa 1917.
Courtesy of Nathan and Theresa Berman Upper Midwest Jewish Archives, University of Minnesota Libraries.

synagogue dedication service listed one rabbi (Julius Hess) and three Protestant Ministers.[123] Having these two synagogues in one North Dakota County made praying more convenient for the homesteaders, rather than evidencing any rift between them.

Israel Auerbach ("Uncle Auerbach" to the Benders), who had assisted with providing funds for the Benders to leave Russia, purchased a general store in Ashley shortly before the Benders arrived in North Dakota. He would post signs in the window, "Closed for Jewish Holiday," in English and German on the days when a holiday was taking place and he was praying. The *Ashley Tribune* also carried notices of the days that Auerbach's — or The Israel Store, as it was also called — and other Jewish-owned stores were closed for Jewish holidays. The *Ashley Tribune* reported: "No business of any kind was

[123]*Wishek News*, August 18, 1916. The warm feelings between the Christian and Jewish clergy echoed the feelings between the Christian and Jewish neighbors in McIntosh County.

done by the merchants as the Hebrewish New Year was honored that day. Services were held at the local synagogue and a crowd of people assembled in the city Sunday evening and early Monday morning so as to be present when the services commenced."

Israel Auerbach's son Nate, as well as Ashley storeowners Max Kelber and Louis Straus, continued the tradition of notifying customers in the *Ashley Tribune*, regarding the dates of Jewish holidays when they would be closed. The ads were always in English and German.

The *Ashley Tribune*, during and after World War I, also ran advertisements periodically for the Jewish Relief Campaign to help the "thousands of Jewish families in Europe whose only home is a rude cart open to the snows and rains," who have "suffered the hardships and brutalities of war" in the "devastated countries of Poland, Galicia, Rumania, Lithuania, and Palestine." The ads sought contributions from "Americans—red-blooded, charitable, humanitarian Americans of every religion and creed."[124] Though Jews made up the majority of contributors, many non-Jewish residents of McIntosh County also responded, as they did in many other counties in North Dakota at the time. Father William Sherman's research found that over eighty different North Dakota towns had representatives working to assist the American Jewish War Relief Committee. Exhaustive reports showed the wide distribution of the funds to towns, villages, and cities in the war zones. President Wilson even named January 27, 1917, as a special day for contributions to the Jewish Relief Fund to help spur donations throughout the United States.[125]

An article in the *Ashley Tribune* on April 4, 1913, expressed the common view of the citizens of the town toward their Jewish neighbors:

---

[124]*Ashley Tribune*, various.

[125]Albert Lucas, "American Jewish Relief in the World War," Albert Lucas, *The Annals of the American Academy of Political and Social Science*, Vol. 79, War Relief Work (September 1918), pp. 221–28.

> Since history began, the Jew has been the middleman and the lender of money — reason for this is found in the law of other countries forbidding him ownership of real estate. In the US today, this is changing and the Jew is going to the land in ever increasing numbers. Statistics on file with the North Dakota Development League at Grand Forks show that there are now 7500 Jewish families on farms in the US, with 37,000 Jews engaged in agriculture. On the land the Jew is proving competent and making for himself a place of importance in the agricultural life of the country.

There was a mutual respect between Jewish and non-Jewish neighbors. When Gertrude and Getzel Ourach and their three children left their farm near Ashley, it was their non-Jewish neighbors who held a going-away party for them.[126] At the Auerbach Store, Israel Auerbach and later his son Nate used to sell many staples at cost, such as sugar and flour. He would also extend credit to farmers who were down on their luck. Israel's customers paid him back when he was forced into bankruptcy by an Ashley moneylender. Israel's non-Jewish customers cosigned notes for him at the bank so he was able to start in business again.[127]

Despite the community's praise for their efforts, 1913 was a difficult year for the Benders and the Ashley Jewish community. First, Mr. Bloom, a good friend of Joseph's, a caring uncle to the son of his widowed sister, Rebecca Cohen, and a good man to all who met him, took ill and passed away at thirty-nine years. He was the first adult to be buried in the Ashley Jewish Cemetery, an area designated by Jewish community leaders for Jewish burial, a few miles north of

[126]Alfred Thal interview with Mrs. Jake Marcovitz and Mrs. Julie Lewis Ourach, 1974, The Historical Society of North Dakota State Archives, North Dakota Heritage Center and State Museum, Bismarck; Jewish Historical Project of North Dakota records, Nathan and Theresa Berman Upper Midwest Jewish Archives, University of Minnesota Libraries.

[127]Greenberg, "Auerbach Family History." Though articles in the social pages of the *Ashley Tribune* identified that certain residents were "members of the Jewish colony" or "Jews," it was never in a pejorative way.

town, on land then owned by Jewish homesteaders Wolf and Alta Fenick.[128]

Then Kiva Bender became ill, passed away, and was buried in the same cemetery. The *Ashley Tribune* ran an article on its front page referring to Kiva's passing, calling him a "well known Jew." The article stated, in part, "The remains were interred, with rites and according to customs of those who hold the Jewish faith, in the Jewish cemetery three miles north of Ashley."[129] The Jewish community in Ashley mourned, as they had lost one of their primary leaders and visionaries. Kiva's death was a demoralizing blow to the Benders, who looked to Kiva for guidance and support. "He has so much more he wanted to accomplish for the Jewish farmers. He just became a United States citizen last year," said his son Joseph.

Then, the joy of Mary's first pregnancy ended with sorrow, as their baby, Rose Bender, passed away shortly after she was born.[130] On top of all of this, 1913 was a year of drought conditions, affecting the quantity of marketable crops.[131] With this backdrop, Joseph looked for more work off his farm.

After working in the roundhouse at the Wishek Railroad Station for several months, Joseph passed the examination for fireman. Heizer, stoker, fireman, coal heaver—this job was called by lots of names and was known to be the toughest work on the locomotive train. This was before dieselization of trains, and there was a high fatality rate. There were no shift maximums or safety rules to protect the railroad workers.

---

[128]Based upon the Silverlieb Family History, Jewish Historical Project of North Dakota records, Nathan and Theresa Berman Upper Midwest Jewish Archives, University of Minnesota Libraries, conversations with Sarah and Noah Schlasinger granddaughters Ann Kay and Ronnie Hartman, Susan Berman's book and Recollections of Joseph Bender, it is believed that infants Mary Schlasinger, a Silverlieb baby, and infant Nathan Berman had been buried in the infant section of the cemetery by this time.

[129]*Ashley Tribune*, June 27,1913.

[130]Conversation between Mary Bender and children.

[131]Farmers Bulletin, No. 563, "Estimated average of yields of all crops combined by states (1913) - North Dakota was at 70% of the previous year."

The Wishek station manager said to Joseph, "It's hot, backbreaking, and dangerous. I want you to know what you're getting into. Do you have children?"

Joe responded, "No."

The station manager replied, "Good. If anything happens . . ." His voice trailed off as he reached for something behind him. "Here's the kind of scoop you'll use. You have to fire light and often. The men will show you how to direct a light load of coal to the right spot on the bed of burning coals on the firebox grate. If you can space out your shots with no holes and no thick spaces, we'll keep you on. If you can't do it, you're done. What do you think?" It was the only open spot on the Soo Line from Wishek to Minneapolis and back.

So Joseph said, "Sure I can!"

"Then be here at 6 a.m. tomorrow to get started. The train from Venturia will be coming through at 7 a.m. tomorrow. It'll stop here, then head east to Minneapolis."

Joseph needed to make some more money and there was nothing the railroad man could have told him that would have dissuaded him. He went home to tell Mary the good news, leaving out the part about the danger.

Joseph showed up two hours early, and working hard over the next several winter months, earned the respect of his fellow workers. The temperature in the firebox was over two thousand degrees Fahrenheit. Each time he shoveled the coal in, Joseph felt a burning blast on his face. Joseph learned to keep his eyes open enough to see where he was placing the coal, but closed enough to keep them from burning. He also learned to exhale right before shoveling the coal, so he didn't breathe in the coal dust. Joseph didn't mind that it was a tough job. It was a job.

After several months, the train engineer approached Joseph. "What kind of a name is Bender?" he asked him. Time stood still as the question bounced off the walls of the engine car, like a raindrop off of tin. When Yosef had arrived from Belgium to Ellis Island, he had been questioned and questioned again. *Where are you from?*

What language do you speak? Do you have family in America? How much money do you have with you?

He thought he was done with the questions once he had been allowed into America seven years earlier. This was supposed to be the land of the free. He wanted to be free from questions. And the engineer's question, "What kind of a name is Bender?" was another way of saying, *Where are you from, who are your people?* The engineer persisted, "Is it German?"

"No, I'm a Russian Jew," said Joseph, matter-of-factly.

"You can't be a Jew. I've heard that Jews don't work hard. I've never seen a Jew shovel coal," said the engineer, trying to egg Joseph on.

"Well, now you have," said Joseph. The train started going, and Joseph began scooping coal, again.

But the engineer wouldn't give it a rest. He kept returning, making negative and stereotypical comments about Jews. Joseph told him to stop. The engineer refused. Joseph told him that if he didn't stop, they would fight at the next station, and see "who's who." Joseph's training in the street gang in Odessa came back to him. He would run at his opponent with a head butt to his stomach to take him down to the ground. The railroad workers in North Dakota were not used to the Russian way of fighting. As soon as they stopped in Cayuga, Joseph flew off the train and rammed into the engineer's midsection. After knocking the man down and punching him, Joseph said, "Have you had enough?" The engineer said he had. Joseph helped him up and went into town with him to get a piece of meat to put on the engineer's eye. As they were walking, the engineer said, with a degree of admiration, "I've never seen a Jew fight."

"Well now you have," said Joseph.

Joseph won the fight, but not the war. He was called in to his supervisor when the train stopped in Minneapolis, who insisted that he sign a resignation letter. Joseph told the supervisor that he had not started the fight and that he came to the United States because he heard that all people were accepted here, no matter who they were, as long as they were good people and good Americans. Joseph said that he knew he was being asked to resign because he had admitted to being a Jew, and the engineer didn't like Jews. Joseph refused to sign the resignation letter. The supervisor said, "Someday you should run for office, Joseph Bender. You're fired."[132]

Joseph got a ride back to Ashley with a traveling Shores salesman, selling patent medicines. Bouncing along in the buggy, he had time to think. He had lost his only brothers in pogroms in Russia because they were Jews. Now he lost his job in the United States because he answered the engineer honestly, telling the engineer that he was a Russian Jew. Should he have answered differently? That thought was immediately dismissed from his mind.

He closed his eyes and said to himself, "I am Joseph Bender, son of Kiva and Rebecka. I am a Jew, and I am an American. No one will ever have the power to make me lie about who I am." Joseph felt proud, as he knew that he did the right thing. He thanked the salesman for the ride, jumped down from the buggy, and began his walk across the fields to give Mary the news.

Months passed. But without the railroad job, the Benders' financial condition became more precarious, especially after baby Frances was born. One night, Joseph and Mary were sitting by the fire.

"I love this land, Mary."

"I know you do, Joseph."

"It's a symbol of everything we couldn't do and have in Russia. But now we're starting a family. Sweet baby Frances is here with us now, and God willing, there will be more children to grow up in this great country."

"What are you thinking?" inquired Mary.

"We own the land. We bought it outright even before the five-year homestead period. I think we should sell it and use the money to rent a building for a general store and buy supplies to sell to farmers. I saw a nice storefront on the main street in Eureka. Lots of traffic. You have experience helping customers in a store. I speak German, Yiddish, Russian, and English. I understand the farmer and

---

132 "This is your life, Joseph Bender," Al Thal interview with Joseph Bender; Bender, *From the Prairies to the Beaches.*

what he needs because I am one. You speak German, English, and Yiddish. I think we could do it."

"I think so, too, Joe," said Mary.

Joseph and Mary sold their land and Kiva and Rebecka's land just as their planted flax crop was starting to bloom with violet flowers. With funds from their life savings, $750, they made the first month's rent payment for a general store on the north side of Main Street in Eureka, South Dakota, thirty-five miles away, on land originally purchased by the Milwaukee Railroad Land Company, and began to build their inventory, purchasing everything from pickles to heavy-duty cloth. They soon moved to their new home in town with baby Frances and mother Rebecka. In about a year, Mary sensed it was almost time to give birth to their second child. As there was no hospital in Eureka and only one doctor, who traveled around the area as needed, she boarded the train alone to Minneapolis, to be with family and closer to medical attention if needed. There, at her parents' home, where she had married Joe, she gave birth to a healthy baby boy. He was named Keva, after the grandfather he never met, who had inspired and led the Ashley Jewish homesteading community. Mary traveled home on the train with baby Keva.

While living in Eureka, the Benders traveled to Ashley for major Jewish holidays with their children in tow. Joseph always stopped by his former homestead parcel on the way to services, to show his children the beauty of the land and to tell them that their father used to be a farmer. He also told them that in America, Jews could be farmers or anything else they set their minds to and said, "Thank God, who gave me the strength, patience, ambition, and lots of nerve, to earn money from this land . . . I could never have done it alone."[133]

✲✲✲

Over the years, Benders' General Store became a place for a good deal, good quality, good service, and a good story. Joe had taught himself to read and write English once he arrived at Ellis Island. He

[133]Joseph Bender Recollections; Al Thal interview of Joseph Bender; Bender, *From the Prairies to the Beaches.*

had a melodious way of speaking English, with strategic pauses for drama and emphasis. Mary's retail training was invaluable in knowing how to order merchandise, ring up sales, and make signs. Joe and Mary, elegant with her slight Baltimore accent, were well liked.[134]

Thanks to Joe and Mary, Benders' General also became a place where compassion was the norm. When a farmer's car broke down and his son needed to register for classes at the University of South Dakota in Vermillion over three hundred miles away, Joe took off his apron, grabbed his keys, and said, "Let's go."[135] When a local family was down on its luck, brown bags of clothes and food appeared on their doorstep, courtesy of Benders' Store.[136] When a widower with seven children was short on cash and was looking for work, his "grocer friend" Joe drove him to Ashley with a lawn mower and rake. Together, they cleaned up the Jewish cemetery where Kiva Bender and other Jewish homesteaders were buried, and Joe was "especially kind" to the gentleman in paying him for his work.[137] And if you were a child in Eureka who had been saving your pennies, the display on the west wall upon entering Benders' General Store was the place in town to get the most candy for your money.[138]

Joe and Mary never hid from anyone the fact that they were Jewish, though for most of their years in Eureka, the Benders were the only Jewish family in town. To the contrary, Mary made signs to hang in the window, "Closed for Jewish High Holidays," just as the Jewish storeowners had done in Ashley. And when Joseph and Mary returned after the Jewish Holidays to the store with the awning that proudly proclaimed, "Benders Farmers Cash Store," all of their customers came back, too.

[134]Bender, *From the Prairies to the Beaches.*

[135]Conversation between author and USD graduate at Eureka Centennial Celebration, Eureka, 1987.

[136]Bernice Bender Ellison recollections in Grenz, Anderson, and Straub, "If These Walls Could Talk: Eureka Family Dental Clinic," *Northwest Blade,* Germans from Russia Heritage Collection, NDSU Institute for Regional Studies and University Archives.

[137]2017 public Facebook post of Kenneth K. Grenz, about Grandfather John Junker, February 2016.

[138]Stan Stabler, conversation with author, Eureka, 2015.

Joe and Grandma Becky Bender at Benders' General Store, Eureka, SD, circa 1925. *Author files.*

CHAPTER 7

Eureka, SD, 1927

WHEN KEVA BENDER, THE SECOND oldest child of Joe and Mary, was eleven years old and with a full head of black hair, his dad told him "for the last time" to stop at the barbershop to get a haircut after school. Keva was leaving school with his good friend Otto Eckman to go home for lunch. Otto suggested that they take the longer way home, past the lake. As they approached Lake Eureka, they spotted an abandoned fishing pole on the ice. Keva ran out to bring it to shore.

Without warning he heard the ice crack under his feet and suddenly sank into the icy, cold water. He heard Otto yell for help. Everything went black. Keva was going down and then bobbing back up, but when he tried to grab the ice, it cracked off in his hands. Otto kept yelling and waving his arms, getting the attention of five men from town who were heading home for lunch. One of the men was Doctor O. H. Gerdes, "Doc" Gerdes, the town doctor who was from Hanover, Germany.[139] His grandfather had fought Napoleon with the Prussian army at Waterloo. The doctor was walking home at the

---

[139]"Doc" Gerdes served the people of Eureka for forty-three years, from 1893–1936, as the town doctor and at Koch and Gerdes Drug Store from 1896–1912. "Western Druggist," *Eureka 1887-1937 Golden Jubilee Book*, Vol. 18 (University of Michigan, 1896).

time, carrying his little black bag. The men and Doc ran to the lake. By then, Keva was nowhere to be found. Otto showed them the area where Keva had gone under.

The men formed a human chain from the shore, with those on the ice lying flat on their stomachs. The one on the end, closest to the hole in the ice, had his arm in the icy water up to his shoulder and

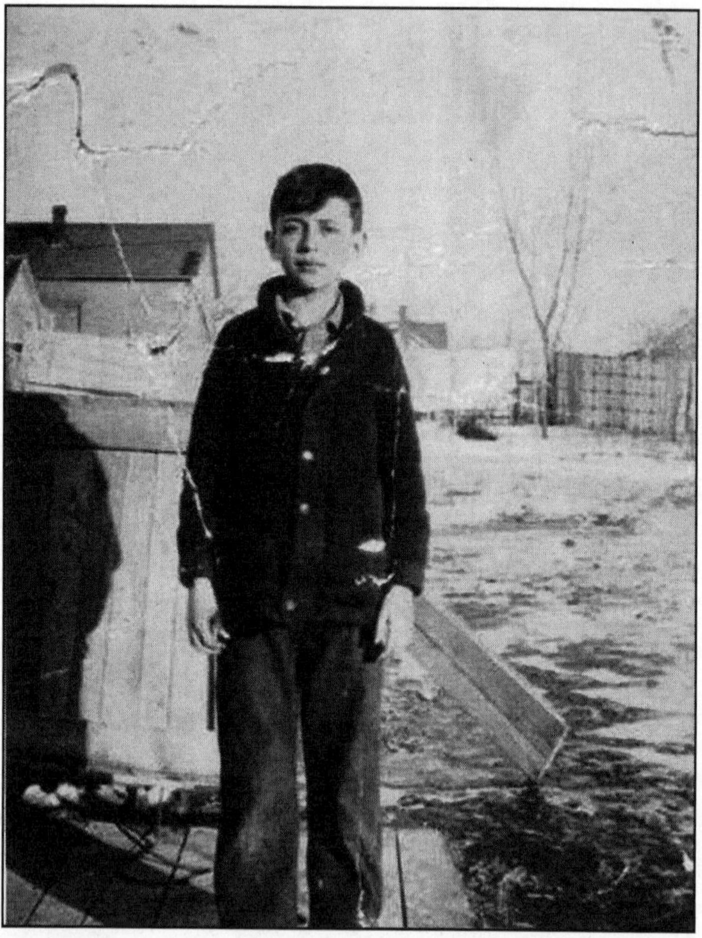

Keva Bender, eleven years old, Eureka, SD, 1927. *Author files.*

kept reaching around in the water. Then he felt something. He pulled up: it was Keva's hair. He pulled Keva out, but he was unconscious and not breathing. The men covered Keva with their jackets and Doc Gerdes felt for a pulse. He sadly told the onlookers the bad news: "There is no pulse." Two of the men carried Keva up the steep hill to Doc Gerdes's house nearby, while the third man ran to tell Joe.

Out of breath when he entered Benders' Store, the man shouted, "Joe, bad news, your son is dead! He drowned in Lake Eureka. We pulled him out by his hair, but it was too late."

"Where is he now?" Joe cried.

"At Doc's house," said the man. Joe ran the six blocks to Doc Gerdes's. The men had taken Keva into the bedroom. Doc Gerdes had given Keva a shot of adrenaline and was at his side listening for a heartbeat. Joe knelt beside his son and silently prayed.

Suddenly, Doc Gerdes said, "I hear it! I hear Keva's heartbeat!"

Soon Keva opened his eyes. He was confused and surprised to see his father kneeling beside him, saying, "I will never tell you when to cut your hair again, my wonderful son! Thank God! Thank God!" The Benders felt forever indebted to the people of Eureka, who together saved Keva's life.[140]

Keva was the second oldest of four Bender children at the time, with three sisters: Frances, Sara Lee, and Bernice. Joe's mother, Rebecka — Grandma Becky — tiny in stature with a bun high atop her head, primarily took care of the children while Joe and Mary worked at the store. After her husband passed away in 1913, Grandma Becky could have focused on herself and her loss. Instead, she became a pillar of strength while showing love and instilling Jewish principles in her grandchildren's lives.

The house might have seemed crowded with seven people and only one outhouse about twenty-five feet from their home, but no one noticed. The Bender children never wanted much they couldn't

[140]The stories of Keva (Kenneth) Bender's life are contained in his book, *From the Prairies to the Beaches: An American Soldier's Story* (Minneapolis, 2005), supplemented by written notes and memories of parents, siblings, and children, including the author.

have, and the family was very close; the children learned respect for elders through Grandma Becky's presence. Keva also respected how hard his parents worked and the good example set by his older sister, Frances—typing champion for the entire state of South Dakota, valedictorian of her class, and lead actor in the senior play when she was a freshman.

Keva lived a typical small town life. He played the clarinet with his sister Frances in the school marching band (because his father got a good deal on two clarinets while on a buying trip to Minneapolis). He learned the meaning of his dad's admonition, "Don't take any wooden nickels," when the traveling carnival came to Eureka, and—despite swinging the mallet and ringing the bell at the "strongman" test of skill—he still could not win a large Kewpie doll for his sisters with his dimes and pennies.

***

In 1928, when Keva was twelve years old, he was sent to Minneapolis to live with Joe's sister Lena and her husband, Joe Miller, for the purpose of studying for his upcoming bar mitzvah. Keva enrolled at Lincoln Junior High, and Uncle Miller would study prayers and Torah portions with him after dinner. One of his cousins in the house was about Keva's age (and also named "Keva," after their mutual late grandfather). Keva Bender was happy when, after Sabbath services at the synagogue, he found a ball in the back of the Millers' closet. Keva walked outside with the ball, and a boy wearing short pants and suspenders in the yard next door called to him, "Hi, what's your name?"

"Keva," he answered.

"What's your name?" Keva asked.

"Harry," said the neighbor.

"Why are you holding that ball, Keva?" continued the boy.

"I was going to throw it and catch it; do you want to play catch?" asked Keva.

"Don't throw the ball!" yelled the boy with alarm.

"Why not?" asked Keva.

"It's Shabbas," loudly whispered the neighbor, "and we can't play ball on Shabbas."

"I don't see how playing ball is work," said Keva.

"Just don't do it, or you'll get yourself and me in trouble," said Harry. "I know your uncle, and he will not like it at all." Harry ran back into his house.[141]

Just then Keva's cousin walked outside from the house, "What are you doing with that ball, Keva!" he yelled.

"I know, I know," said Keva softly. "We can't play ball because it's Shabbas." Keva went back into the house, missing his family and friends and Eureka. Keva was used to hearing his sisters and mother and father and Grandma Becky all chime in at the dinner table, talking, giving opinions, and laughing. But in Minneapolis, his uncle was very strict and the children were not allowed to speak at the table. The silence caused Keva to lose his appetite, even though his Aunt Lena was a good cook. Keva wrote a letter to his father, saying that he knew it was important for him to study for his bar mitzvah but begging him to be allowed to come home.

Joe and the rest of the family had missed having good-natured Keva around, and it hurt Joe to read the letter from his son. "I'm going to leave at 6 a.m. tomorrow, Mary," said Joe, once the rest of the family was asleep. Mary didn't have to ask where he was going. Joe drove to Minneapolis, paid his brother-in-law for supporting his son for a month, and drove Keva home.

In the car, Keva asked his father if he would still be a good Jew, even if he didn't have a bar mitzvah. Joe paused a moment and then answered, "Having a bar mitzvah is a wonderful thing. It's a chance to learn more of our prayers and traditions and to begin to be counted as a man in the congregation. But being a good Jew is a lot more than having a bar mitzvah or going to services. It's the way we act towards each other, the way we treat each other — Jews and Gentiles. It's not enough to pray in the synagogue and fast on Yom Kippur. Your actions should show that you are Jewish. In everything that

---

141 Recollections of Harry Friedman and Kenneth Bender told to the author, circa 1974.

you do, you have to be an example. That's what God commanded. That's what Moses and Joshua taught the Israelites. You have always lived a Jewish life, Keva. You show respect to your teachers at school, you mow the lawn for our elderly neighbor, you help out around the house, you tell the truth, you stand up for the underdog, you like to learn about our heritage . . . Keva, even if I don't live to see it, I know, sitting here with you today, that you always will live a Jewish life."

They pulled up to the Bender house in the wee hours of the morning. "See the light?" Joe asked Keva. "I think Mother has been waiting for you to come home," and Joe put his arm around Keva's shoulders and Keva put his arm around his dad, and they walked up the steps to the front door.

Keva happily returned to his usual Eureka life and his family's talkative dinner table. He enjoyed doing odd jobs around town, including trapping gophers. McPherson County paid one cent per gopher tail to try to lessen this destructive digging population. He also helped unload watermelons being brought from the farms to his parents' store. But he felt he had really made it when his dad gave him the most prestigious job for a pre-teen in Eureka: stomping on sheep fleece. The farmers would bring bundles of fleece, tied together with a rope, and Joe Bender would toss the bad-smelling fleece onto the dirt floor in the basement of the store until there was enough to compress and sell. Keva would then climb up a fifteen-foot ladder, jump into a big bag, and wait for the sheep fleece to be thrown down on top of him. He would jump with his hands to his sides and stamp on top of it in the bag, to pack it down. Keva ended up covered with the lanolin fleece grease and debris, but it was well worth it for fifteen cents per day.

These were tough economic times throughout the United States. After the stock market crash in October 1929, there was less spending by consumers and less investing in bank instruments; bank runs occurred when depositors feared for the safety of their funds, withdrawing their cash and liquidating their investments. Eureka was not immune to this crisis. In December 1930, all the banks closed in Eureka. What made Eureka somewhat unusual, was that in less than three months, in March 1931, the Eureka State Bank opened for business. Doc Gerdes, the same man who had been instrumental in saving Keva's life when he fell through Lake Eureka's ice, saved the life of the town by borrowing against his own life insurance policies to provide funds to open a bank.[142]

When the school year ended in 1930, Keva was fourteen, helping out in his parents' store, and playing ball with friends. He was about 5'6" and everyone thought he was probably ending his growth spurt. Then something unexpected happened. That summer, he shot up a full six inches more. Word spread quickly, and there was a knock at the Benders' door. Frank Manders, the high school basketball coach (whose brother Jack played football for the Chicago Bears) paid a visit to Joe and Mary. He told them that Keva's height would be an asset to the team. He encouraged Keva to start coming to practices. He also told Joe and Mary that players who don't have enough stamina are not able to play the game. Coach Manders was concerned that the sudden growth spurt had left Keva too gangly and thin.

Grandma Becky sprang into action. Whenever she would make beef for dinner for the family, she would drain the fat — which she called the *koeach* (strength) — from the beef. She would store the liquid fat in the icebox. Each day when Keva came home for lunch, she would heat up a full glass of the concoction and stand watching him drink it before he started the rest of his lunch. Grandma Becky only attended one of Keva's basketball games, as she said she saw little point in watching people running back and forth and back and forth. But Keva felt that he played his best, including his high game of eighteen points, because his family was supporting him, and because he was drinking beef fat made with love by his grandma.

Keva and his grandma had a very close relationship over the years. She taught him to play chess, a common pastime from Russia. She first patiently taught him the way that each piece moved, from knight to king, and eventually they played against each other. This

---

[142]Grenz, Anderson, & Straub, "If These Walls Could Talk: Currently Great Plains Bank, Part 1," *Northwest Blade*, September 1, 2011, citing Ted Straub biography of Dr. O. H. Gerdes, www.library.ndsu.edu; www.history.com/topics/bank-run.

went on for a number of years, until one day Keva won a chess match against his grandma. As Keva put the chess pieces away in the box, Grandma Becky stated quietly and calmly, "*Ikh vet nit shpiln mit ir enimor. Ikh hobn gelernt ir ale ikh kenen* [I will not play with you anymore. I have taught you all I can]." Keva respected his grandma too much to ever question her decision.

If Grandma Becky said it once to her grandchildren, she said it a hundred times, "*Ir zent geboyrn a id. Ir vet shtarbn a id. Keynmol fargesn vas ir zent* [You are born a Jew. You die a Jew. Never forget who you are]." Being the only Jewish family in Eureka didn't bother Keva. Sara Lee, one of his sisters, when she was six years old used to sing quietly in school, "Onward Jewish Soldiers," instead of "Onward Christian Soldiers." This was her way of preserving her religious identity.

Grandma Becky made sure that the only Bender boy preserved his identity, too. Joe taught Keva how to put on *tefillin*.[143] However, it was Grandma Becky who watched him put them on his arm and head and say the accompanying prayers every morning before school from the time he turned thirteen. Tefillin are sometimes called phylacteries, from the ancient Greek *phylassein*—to protect. As Keva put his Grandpa Kiva's tefillin away each morning, he would always hear his Grandma Becky give a barely audible sigh. Having completed his prayers in the morning gave her a feeling that God was now watching out for Keva as he headed out into the world.

Keva and his siblings looked forward to the Jewish High Holidays. On the way to Ashley, or Bismarck, or Aberdeen for services to pray with fellow Jews from around the area, Joseph would tell the children how fortunate they were to be able to pray in Hebrew in a public place, without fear of being injured or worse. "America is the most beautiful place on earth," Joe would say. Mary would respond, "Amen."

[143]Tefillin are small black leather boxes with parchment inside inscribed with Torah verses.

When it was the eight days of Passover, the Benders would eat matzah and products made from matzah meal instead of flour. This is the Jewish tradition to recall when the Israelites were forced to prepare and eat food quickly in the desert after fleeing from slavery in Egypt. There was no time to wait for bread to rise. Grandma Becky rationed out her precious matzoh cake flour to make certain she had Passover sponge cakes available for the family throughout the eight days. She would keep her sponge cake, light as a feather, in one of her high dresser drawers and would make sure that all family members received equal portions. The framed postcard of Dr. Herzl, which used to be hidden in the Benders' kitchen cupboard in Odessa, now hung out in the open in Joseph and Mary's bedroom in Eureka.

Any anti-Semitic incidents experienced in Eureka were fewer than could be counted on one hand over decades, and they were a small footnote to the Benders' warm experiences in the community. Joseph's sister Lena and her husband Joseph Miller had sold their homestead lands near Ashley. They had used the proceeds from the sale to open a general store in Hillsview, South Dakota, about eleven miles from Eureka.[144] One of their daughters, Fanny Miller, who was six years older than Keva, lived with the Benders for a time so she could attend school, as Hillsview did not have a high school.

One day, Fanny came home from school in tears. Her Uncle Joseph Bender asked her what was wrong. She said that the superintendent at the school was saying bad things about Jews and Catholics. Joe went to the school, closed the door of the superintendent's office, and locked it. The superintendent said, "Why are you locking the door?"

Joseph said to him, "Don't worry about what I'm doing. I hear that you have a problem with Jews and Catholics. Whatever are your views are your own. But you are a leader in this school, and you will not tell lies about any group of people to your students. If I ever hear again that you are doing this, you will have me to deal with. Do you

[144]The Millers later moved to Minneapolis.

understand?" The suddenly pale superintendent swallowed and said he understood. Joseph unlocked the door and left. There were no more similar comments made at Eureka High School.[145]

This incident was the impetus for Joseph to run for and obtain a seat on the school board. He informed the school board what had been said, and they did not renew the superintendent's contract. Joseph then ran for and was elected alderman from Ward 2 and then became mayor. The words of the Minneapolis railroad supervisor to recent immigrant Joe Bender as he fired him fifteen years earlier had been prophetic. The fact that Joe Bender was selected to represent his ward and city after speaking out against this type of behavior, evidenced that the community of Eureka had no place for prejudice.

* * *

Some of the traditional Jewish foods eaten in the Benders' home distinguished them from their neighbors—*mamaliga* (cornmeal porridge); *perogies* (mashed potato and onions wrapped in dough); *tzimmes* (sweet carrot dish with prunes, flour, and brown sugar); chopped liver spread; *hamentaschen* (three-sided, fruit-filled pastries eaten during the Purim holiday)—but what separated Keva from the other children much more than being Jewish, was the fact that his parents were not German. Eureka was made up almost entirely of German-Russians, whose first language in the home was German. The first day of German class in ninth grade, Professor Lenz handed out books for the students. Keva opened his book to the first page of the first chapter. That's when Mr. Lenz said, "Because you all know German already, we will skip the first seven chapters of this book. Open your books to chapter eight." Keva voiced no objection, as Professor Lenz, also the manual training instructor, was known for his

[145]Recollections of Fanny (Miller) Brudnoy; Joseph Bender Recollections; Bender, *From the Prairies to the Beaches*. This incident occurred around 1925, when the Ku Klux Klan was beginning to spread its hateful message against Jews and Catholics in North Dakota.

Joseph Bender, Mayor, Eureka, SD, 1929–1930. *Author files.*

method of disciplining a student who didn't follow instructions in his shop class—throwing a wooden clamp at the offender.[146]

As Keva grew older, he found ways to fill his time when he was not needed in his parents' store. Several men in town, including his dad, had been instrumental in building a nine-hole golf course with sand greens. If Keva was lucky, he could caddy for ten cents a round. Keva had informal golf lessons from Dave Bauer, who was training his two daughters, Alice and Marlene, to become professional golfers. Alice and Marlene would hit over four hundred balls a day—spring, summer, and fall. Dave taught Keva about grip and follow-through, to never look up, and to keep his eye on the ball.

[146]Bender, *From the Prairies to the Beaches*, 2005.

By the time Keva was sixteen, he was shooting par or below on the Eureka course. He held the Eureka course record of five below par, a thirty-one, for many years.

* * *

The year before Keva was going to graduate from Eureka High School, the Bender family experienced great joy and then great sadness. The second Bender boy, David, was born at the new hospital in Eureka. The whole family was thrilled, but no one more than Keva, who now had a brother. But within a short time, their beloved Grandma Becky passed away when visiting her sister in Minneapolis. Keva continued putting on teffilin, facing east every morning, picturing her with him.

Keva graduated fourth in his class of twenty-two students and was the male recipient of the Citizenship Award. In the same month and year that Keva received this award in Eureka, South Dakota, in Germany, Adolph Hitler ordered the writings of Jewish and other "un-German" authors to be burned, and thousands of students at universities throughout Germany complied. The largest bonfire occurred in Berlin at its Opera House in May, 1933, where forty thousand people listened to a speech by Nazi propaganda minister Joseph Goebbels declaring, "Jewish intellectualism is dead."[147]

The motto of Keva's Eureka High School Class of 1933 was "Tonight we launch. Where do we anchor?" In light of the building tensions in the world and graduating in the midst of the Great Depression, the words were apropos. With over 25 percent of able-bodied Americans unemployed, Franklin Roosevelt was inaugurated as president on March 4, 1933. Twenty-seven days later, as part of

---

[147]Leonidas E. Hill, "The Nazi Attack on 'un-German' Literature 1933–45," in Jonathan Rose, Ed., *The Holocaust and the Book: Destruction and Preservation* (Amherst: University of Massachusetts Press, 2001), p. 9–46. Jewish poet Heinrich Heine's books were among those burned. In 1822, Heine had written, "Where they burn books, they will, in the end, burn human beings too." This was the beginning of the Nazis' attempts to destroy Jewish culture from Germany. Stephen J. Whitfield, "Where They Burn Books . . . " Modern Judaism 22, no. 3 (2002): 213–33.

his New Deal programs geared to end the Depression, he signed the Emergency Conservation Work Act, creating a "peacetime army" called the Civilian Conservation Corps (CCC). Three members of Keva's twenty-two-member graduating class, who were also on Keva's basketball team, were absent from the graduation ceremony, as they had already joined the CCC at thirty dollars per month plus room and board. They, along with three million other unemployed young men, were put to work in this project initiated by President Franklin Roosevelt to plant millions of trees, curb soil erosion, fight forest fires, stock rivers and lakes with fish, restore historic battlefields, and build bridges, canals, campground facilities, water storage basins, and wildlife refuges, while simultaneously helping to jump-start the economy.[148]

Keva recognized how fortunate he was to be able to continue his education, rather than going right to work. His mother had to leave school to work after sixth grade and his father had never had the opportunity to continue his studies once in the United States. Keva knew that his parents had scrimped and saved to give their children this opportunity. He vowed to work hard to make the most of his schooling. His sister Frances was already attending the University of Minnesota, and Keva followed in her footsteps. As Keva was only ten hours from home while at college, he was still able to participate in his younger siblings' lives — attending musical and acting performances by Sara Lee and Bernice, and even seeing his little brother play Sneezy the dwarf to his sister Bernice's Snow White in the school play.

During his first year in college, Keva stayed in a home on campus and received his board and two home-cooked meals daily. After one year, he moved to Pioneer Hall, a men's residential dormitory, where he studied diligently while also becoming the dorm Checkers and Ping-Pong champion. Kevin McCarthy, who later received an Academy Award nomination for his role as Biff in the 1951 film

---

[148]National Park Service, *The Civilian Conservation Corps and the National Park Service, 1933–1942: An Administrative History*, www.ccclegacy.org; *Into the Woods: The First Year of the CCC*, www.archives.gov.

Death of a Salesman, answered the phones at Pioneer Hall "because of his melodious voice."[149]

* * *

After two years of attending college, Keva told his parents he'd like to go to law school. He had done well in the declamation contests in Eureka. In his senior year in high school, he had recited by heart the Robert Benchley essay, "The Tortures of Weekend Visiting," and won first prize. Keva also liked standing up for the less fortunate, so his parents thought that law school would be a perfect fit for their eldest son.

Keva took the law school admissions test and was accepted. He knew that he was embarking on an even more challenging course of study, and he felt lucky to get one of the Pioneer Hall fourth floor "attic" rooms. They were less expensive than the lower rooms, and Keva could spend hours uninterrupted, carefully briefing all the cases he was assigned to read, with the court holding, dicta, and reasoning. With his portable typewriter, he typed all the information on onionskin paper and pasted the onionskin into volumes and volumes of leather books for each subject. It was not unusual for Keva to study until he realized that he had fallen asleep sitting up, in his attic room.

On the first day of classes for Keva's first year in law school, Dean Fraser, a Harvard Law School graduate, told the incoming students:

> Look to the right of you and look to the left of you. Only one of the three of you will actually graduate from this institution. The remaining two will be asked to leave. At the time of graduation, there will be two-thirds less people than there are sitting here with us today. And that's the way it should be. Because being a lawyer is challenging, and law school should be too.

So when Keva received a message that Dean Fraser wanted to see him, when the first year class had not yet received the results from their midterms, he was obviously concerned. Keva walked into

---

[149]Bender, *From the Prairies to the Beaches.*

Dean Fraser's office with his heart pounding. "Good morning, Dean Fraser," Keva said. Dean Fraser skipped the pleasantries and got right down to business.

He said, "Mr. Bender, we have a problem here. You have done too well on your midterm exams."

"Too well, sir?" Keva inquired.

"Yes, too well," continued the dean. "I have compared your aptitude tests which were part of your application to this law school, with these midterm grades and they do not correlate. There is no explanation that I am aware of for how a gentleman such as yourself could score so poorly on aptitude tests and then do so well in law school. Do you have any explanation for this, Mr. Bender?" queried the dean.

Keva paused for a moment and then stated, "I believe I know why the two do not correlate, sir."

"And, do share your theory with me," said Dean Fraser.

"Sir," Keva said, "there is nothing in those aptitude tests that measures determination."

The dean looked at Keva and said nothing. Then he rose, looked out his office window and repeated the word as if it was a newly discovered phenomenon: "Determination. Hmm. How do you like that? Determination." He then turned to Keva and said, "Keep up the good work, Mr. Bender. Thank you for taking the time to talk with me."[150]

* * *

Keva graduated from the University of Minnesota Law School in 1939 near the top of his class, and he took and passed the bar exams in both Minnesota and South Dakota. Keva applied for any jobs in and near Minneapolis that came to his attention. Some of the jobs advertised were looking for someone to work for nothing, just to gain the experience. That wouldn't work for Keva. At several of the

---

[150]Bender, *From the Prairies to the Beaches.*

interviews, Keva was asked what church he or his family belonged to. When Keva mentioned that he was Jewish and attended a synagogue, those interviews ended abruptly. Similar to his father not being aware of the climate challenges for farmers in North Dakota prior to immigrating to America, Keva, coming from Eureka, was not aware of a different type of climate challenge that existed as he was attempting to gain employment. Minneapolis, at the time, had the unfortunate distinction of being known as the "Anti-Semitic Capital of America." Well-known journalist Carey McWilliams referred to "an iron curtain," which separated Jews from non-Jews from the 1930s through the 1940s.[151]

Jews, McWilliams said, were excluded from employment in banking and insurance, and were limited in their employment in other fields that involved dealing with members of the public. Ads in the paper for apartments oftentimes stated, "Gentiles only," or "Christians preferred," or prohibited subleasing to "Semitic people." Jews were also excluded from living in a significant number of residential neighborhoods in Minneapolis due to restrictive covenants, including South Minneapolis. Unlike in any other city in America, service clubs — including Kiwanis, Rotary, Lions, and Toastmasters, and even AAA, the American Automobile Association in Minneapolis — would not admit Jewish members.

In 1938, the year before Keva graduated from Law School, in the Minnesota governor race, there was an underlying smear campaign against Governor Elmer Benson due to his alleged "Jewish affiliation," i.e., having some Jewish advisors on his campaign. A cartoon widely circulated in Minnesota showed Governor Benson's "triumvarite" of named Jewish advisors ignoring "the forgotten man" and leading Governor Benson to ruin.[152]

---

[151]"Common Council for American Unity," *Common Ground,* VII, no. 1 (Princeton University Press: Autumn 1946). Other contributors to *Common Ground* over the years include Woody Guthrie, Langston Hughes, William Saroyan, and Eleanor Roosevelt.

[152]Laura E. Weber, "Gentiles Preferred, Minneapolis Jews and Employment, 1920–1950," www.collections.mnhs.org, Minnesota History 52, no. 5 (Spring 1991): 166–82.

Two popular Minneapolis pastors, one at the First Baptist Church and one at the River-Lake Gospel Tabernacle, used their pulpits to spread their anti-Jewish sentiments every Sunday. A hate group called the Silver Shirts spoke of "defeating Jewish communism," first at the ballot box, but if that didn't work, with bullets. The Daytons Department Store would not hire Jews, and Minnesota Mining and Manufacturing (3M) would not hire any Jews whose jobs would involve dealing with the public. Country clubs were restricted as well. The Calhoun Beach Club in Minneapolis had a sign on its door: "No Jews, peddlers or dogs allowed."[153]

From 1933–1939, while Keva Bender was an undergraduate and law student at the University of Minnesota, he was unaware of some significant occurrences on campus. In 1935, Hitler's ambassador to the United States, Hans Luther, was hosted at a tea in Shevlin Hall on campus, with hardly an objection from faculty or administration. The Nurenberg Laws had been passed by the Third Reich shortly before the visit, which had, *inter alia*, removed German Jews' citizenship, purged German universities of Jewish students, and forbad Christian-Jewish weddings in order to achieve a "racially pure" Germany. University of Minnesota students who wanted to ask the ambassador questions about Nazi policies were barred from the tea and the campus police were called.[154]

Also in 1935, the YMCA on the University of Minnesota campus assembled a group of students with a variety of religious and political backgrounds. They signed a petition to boycott the 1936 Berlin Olympics due to actions against the Jews in Germany. This multi-religious group tried to send their petition to University of Minnesota students to vote for or against it, but they were stopped by the university postmaster, supported by Dean of Students Edward

---

[153]Ibid.; Alan Saeks, "When Law Firms Wouldn't Hire Jewish Lawyers," *American Jewish World*, July 31, 2015.

[154]Riv-Ellen Prell and Sarah Atwood, *A Campus Divided: Progressives, Anti-Communists, Racism, and Anti-Semitism at the University of Minnesota, 1930–1942*, acampusdivided.umn.edu.

Nicholson, who was involved with monitoring students perceived as "radicals."[155]

1935 was also the year that Keva Bender would have been included on a list he knew nothing about. University President Lotus Coffman, through an aide, had notified the director of Health Services that he wanted to keep a record of the number of "Negroes and Jews" enrolled at the university. Health Services Director Ruth Boynton complied, providing the president with the numbers of new students falling into those categories in 1933–1935 from records obtained during students' enrollment physicals. On October 28, 1936, at a meeting of the Administrative Committee of the Senate in the Regent's Room, "President Coffman referred to the large increase in non-resident Negro and Jewish enrollment" and requested the University Senate to track data regarding these groups. The number of Black students had risen from nine to forty between 1925–1936. The number of Jewish students had risen from sixty to 132 from 1925–1936. This was at a time when about three thousand students were enrolled at the University of Minnesota, so blacks were making up 1 percent and Jews between 3 and 4 percent of the student body, which President Coffman felt was worthy of his concern.

Only ten years earlier, also on President Coffman's watch, boardinghouses for students at the university would have their ratings lowered if they were providing housing to too many students of Jewish descent. Three Jewish students in the Dental Hygiene program in 1923 were urged to leave after the first month of classes. They were "helpfully" told there was no reason to continue, as they would never have jobs in any school system, would not be hired by non-Jewish dentists, and no Jewish dentist would ever hire a Jewish dental hygienist, for fear of over-balance with his gentile patients.[156]

By contrast to the blatant and whispered anti-Semitism prevalent in Minneapolis in Keva's University of Minnesota Law School graduation year (1939), North Dakota Governor William Langer

---

[155]Ibid.

[156]Ibid.

wrote a proclamation the same year entitled, "The American Hebrew." He stated, in part:

> I can testify that the Jewish citizens of my state have always played a particularly conspicuous part in building up its very prosperity — they preserve and maintain the loftiest conception of human relations and traditions, for which our nation was conceived — by their tenacity and industry, they have become successful farmers at Gackle, Williston, Devils Lake, Lehr, Ashley and other places.

And:

> The Jews in this state have not shrunk from the tremendous work and the heavy sacrifices required of them.[157]

As Keva did not have success in finding employment as a Jewish University of Minnesota law student with the non-Jewish firms interviewing on campus, he then interviewed for work at the few Twin Cities Jewish law firms. With these firms, he was asked who his contacts were and what business he could bring into the firms. Keva told the interviewers that he was willing to knock on doors to try to bring in business, but being from South Dakota, he did not have Minnesota business connections. One interviewer suggested to Keva that he should try to find a job in South Dakota, as even with his good grades and a good reputation he could not get hired in Minneapolis. Keva took the man's advice and got an attorney position working with a sole practitioner in Rapid City, South Dakota.

---

[157]One of Keva's first cousins, Sarah and Noah Schlasinger's daughter, Marcella, held the position of secretary to North Dakota Governor Langer for a number of years. In 1938, Marcella's sister Ethel was chosen as North Dakota's State Director of the American Guide Series—*North Dakota: A Guide to the Northern Prairie State*—which was part of the Federal Writers' Project of the Works Progress Administration, files housed at the State Historical Society of North Dakota, Bismarck, ND, #30522; Jerry Mangione, *The Dream and the Deal: The Federal Writers Project, 1935–1943* (Syracuse University Press, 1996), pp. 87-8. The Schlasinger sisters' experiences were evidence that some talented Jewish young people were given high-profile opportunities in North Dakota.

CHAPTER 8
Rapid City, SD, November 1940

WHILE GOING TO LAW SCHOOL and then working in South Dakota, Keva became well aware of the political turmoil in the world. The Nazis invaded and soon after occupied Poland, France, Belgium, Luxembourg, and the Netherlands. Then Adolph Hitler set his sights on England, with air raids and bombing offensives. At the same time, Italy was invading Albania and leaving the League of Nations.

In addition to Hitler's aggressive plan of expansion, he was orchestrating the dehumanization of Germany's Jews. Jewish children were expelled from schools, propaganda against Jews was published and distributed by the Nazis, Jews were forced to register their property, and then they were declared to no longer be worthy of German citizenship. In 1938, the newspaper and radio reports in the United States relayed a significant change in Nazi policies in Germany. No longer were the Nazis content with the repressive policies against German Jews. Now they were advocating blatant violence against them and their property. Starting in the late hours of November 9, 1938, and through the next day, more than one hundred Jews were murdered, hundreds of synagogues were torched and destroyed, and thousands of Jewish homes, cemeteries, schools, and businesses were destroyed by German Stormtroopers, Nazi party members, Hitler youth, and mobs that joined in. The broken glass that littered the streets after this unchecked vandalism resulted in these two days becoming known as Kristallnacht (Night of Broken Glass). With these disturbing events occurring, Keva believed that there would soon be a draft to get men into America's armed forces. Keva did not wish to be drafted. He wanted to represent his country voluntarily. In November 1940, he gave notice to his employer in Rapid City and returned to Eureka to volunteer for the army.

Keva was the first army volunteer for World War II from McPherson County, South Dakota.[158] McPherson County's first draft requirement was set at two, and Keva and his friend, Benny Haag, voluntarily filled the first quota for "one year of military training under the Selective Service Act." With war looming and having been raised to love America and its freedoms, Keva believed that it was his duty to offer his services to his country. He spoke with his parents and sisters, who gave him their blessings. But he wanted his eight-year-old brother David to accept his decision, as well. Keva asked to talk to David alone, in the sunroom of the Bender home. Keva explained the options to his little brother, who idolized him, and that just like in the movies, there came a time when the good guys had to fight the bad guys. By the end of the conversation, David agreed that in light of the situation in the world, his big brother's enlisting was the only acceptable choice.[159]

Keva also made another decision prior to enlisting. Over the years, when people would see his name, some of them assumed it was a female name. Keva frequently received letters addressed to "Miss Bender." When law school professors had called on him from their class seating charts, they would oftentimes ask a question of "Miss Bender." To avoid such confusion, Keva changed his first name and volunteered for the army as Kenneth M. Bender.

---

[158]Eureka, South Dakota Selective Service Board Records, Emanuel Heilman, Director, Conversation between Lester Heilman and author (Eureka, 2005); Eureka Centennial Chronology (1887–1987); Northwest Blade excerpts compiled by Elsie Heilman.

[159]David Bender recollections; Bender, *From the Prairie to the Beaches.*

Keva waved to his family as he boarded the train in Eureka on a very cold November day. He transferred at Aberdeen for the direct run to Fort Snelling, Minnesota, some three hundred miles away. The following morning, carrying one piece of luggage, Kenneth and the rest of the new arrivals were met by army soldiers and loaded into the rear of an army two-and-one-half-ton truck for transport to Fort Snelling. Attorney Bender was now Private Bender. The barracks was an old brick building. The men were told that they were now members of the 3rd Infantry Regiment, with about three thousand men. They were also informed that during the Revolutionary War, the 3rd Infantry Regiment had fought under the command of George Washington at Valley Forge.

Next, they were fitted with uniforms. Kenneth was surprised that many of the uniforms, though new, were of World War I vintage. He and his fellow soldiers had orders not to wear the outdated uniforms on pass when leaving the post, because of a potentially negative impression for America's armed forces. The jackets were wool with high neck collars. The supply sergeant told the men, "If you can still talk with the jacket on, then it is not choking you too much and it fits." The leather shoes issued were six inches high, going above the ankle, worn with leggings that tightened on the side with a heavy laced shoestring. The rifles assigned were also from World War I — 1903 Springfields, bolt action. The training consisted of attending classes on military courtesy, close and extended order drill, long marches, bayonet training, and military tactics. Kenneth was assigned to Company E, a rifle company with approximately two hundred men. They all learned to perform KP duty — washing dishes and scrubbing floors — and guard duty. The private pay scale was twenty-one dollars per month, so purchases at the PX on the base were limited.

Upon arriving at Fort Snelling, Kenneth had decided that he would do his best, work hard, obey orders, and attempt to get a promotion. After two months, the 1st Sergeant called him into the orderly room and told him that because of his good work and attitude,

Kenneth Bender in basic training at Fort Snelling and in Eureka on leave with his brother, David, circa 1941. *Author files.*

he was being promoted to Private 1st Class. This meant an increase of pay to thirty dollars per month and one stripe on his shirtsleeve.

After four and one-half months at Fort Snelling, Kenneth was promoted to "buck" sergeant, three stripes. In this capacity, he was the assistant to the squad leader, who was a staff sergeant. Kenneth's shooting scores on the range were very high, which he owed to hunting pheasants, ducks, and rabbits with his dad.

A few weeks after being promoted to sergeant, Kenneth was ordered to report to Battalion Headquarters. Two commissioned officers asked him if he had an interest in attending Officer Candidate School at Fort Benning, Georgia. If successful, Kenneth was told, he would become a Second Lieutenant. Kenneth accepted the challenge and appeared before a board of officers for an interview. After being asked many questions, Kenneth was one of only two soldiers from his regiment selected to attend the Infantry Officer Candidate School at Fort Benning.

Nine months after entering the service, in August, 1941, Kenneth Bender arrived at Fort Benning in Chattahoochee County, Georgia. Among the pine trees and sand, he was being trained as a "90 day wonder," to become an officer in ninety days. Every minute was accounted for. All of the soldiers fired all of the infantry weapons: the bolt action rifle, carbine, Browning automatic rifle, and machine guns and mortars. They were also trained with the bayonet. Map reading and use of the compass were also emphasized. There were many marches. A soldier who didn't perform was "washed out."

Kenneth Bender graduated and was commissioned as a Second Lieutenant on November 6, 1941. Approximately 25 percent of Lieutenant Bender's class did not graduate. Kenneth was in the second Officer Candidate School class, graduating one week after the first class, and almost exactly one month before the day President Roosevelt referred to as "the day which will live in infamy": the attack by Japan on the United States at Pearl Harbor, Hawaii. That attack changed the course of history for the world, and also for Kenneth personally.

Kenneth's Fort Benning officer graduation class was provided a copy of the commencement address given to the first class of graduating officers by General George C. Marshall, Chief of Staff. Kenneth was moved and inspired by General Marshall's words:

> You are about to assume the most important duty that our officers are called upon to perform — the direct command of combat units of American soldiers. To succeed requires two fundamental qualifications — thorough professional knowledge and a capacity for leadership. The schools have done all that can be done in the limited time available to equip you professionally, and your technique of weapons and tactics should rapidly improve with further study and actual practice. However, they cannot provide you with qualities of leadership — that courage and evident high purpose which command the respect and loyalty of American soldiers.
>
> You were selected as officer candidates because you gave evidence of possessing these qualifications. Modern battles are fought by platoon leaders. The carefully prepared plans of higher commanders can do no more than project you to the line of departure at the proper time and place, in proper formation, and start you off in the right direction. Thereafter, the responsibility for results is almost entirely yours.
>
> You will be responsible for a unit in the Army of the United States in this great emergency. Its quality, its discipline, its training will depend upon your leadership. Whatever deficiencies there are must be charged to your failure or incapacity. Remember that: the truly great leader overcomes all difficulties, and campaigns and battles are nothing but a long series of difficulties to be overcome. The lack of equipment, the lack of food, the lack of this or that are only excuses; the real leader displays his quality in his triumphs over adversity, however great it may be.
>
> Good luck to you. We expect great things of you.

Kenneth's first assignment was as Second Lieutenant in the Second Infantry Division at Fort Sam Houston, Texas, as a member of Company E, 38th Infantry. He was told he would be a platoon leader in a rifle company, commanding about forty men. Second Lieutenant

Bender led his unit in regular infantry training — long marches, bayonet training, firing rifles and machine guns, and military tactics. The unit also engaged in airborne (military parachutist) and glider training (gliders attached to towing aircraft) for practice dropping into enemy territory. While on maneuvers — walking and sleeping in the hot Texas fields thirty miles west of San Antonio — the men were oftentimes covered with ticks and chiggers. One soldier in Kenneth's unit, Sergeant Carl Patterson, eating his morning oatmeal before the sun came up, noticed the crunchiness of the raisins in his cereal, only to learn that the crunch came from the large number of ticks in his breakfast bowl.[160]

After the training with his men at and near Fort Sam Houston, Kenneth was promoted to First Lieutenant and received orders that the entire Second Infantry Division, approximately fifteen thousand men, was moving to Camp McCoy, Wisconsin, for further training. The Second Division was preparing for the invasion of Norway, occupied by Germany. Kenneth learned that Temple Beth-El, the syn agogue near the base in San Antonio, was having a Sabbath prayer service for the Jewish soldiers prior to their leaving the area for further training. The service included the singing of "America the Beautiful," "Fear Not, O Israel," sung by the choir, and an address by Lt. General Krueger, Commanding General, Third Army. There was also a bass solo, entitled "Arm, Arm, Ye Brave" from Handel's oratorio *Judas Maccabeus*. The selection is significant, because Judah Maccabee is considered one of the greatest freedom fighters in Jewish history.[161]

Thirty-eight years after Kiva and Yosef Bendersky heard Theodor Herzl speak at a synagogue in Odessa, Russia, of the new age of Maccabees that was arising, Captain Kenneth Bender and the Jewish men of the Second Infantry Division were being inspired in America to go fight for freedom in the spirit of the Maccabees.

---

[160]Carl Patterson, in *I Remember B Company, 38th Infantry Regiment, 2nd Infantry Division* (Leawood, Kansas: Leathers Publishing 2000).

[161]Program from San Antonio, Texas, Synagogue Prayer Service, 1941, Temple Beth-El Synagogue, author files.

****

Kenneth was soon advised that he would be part of the special advance units, to be sent for training to the Upper Peninsula in Northern Michigan near Iron Mountain. Once he dropped his gear at Camp McCoy, he was sent about 250 miles north to "the UP." There he learned to ski, snowshoe, and survive the bitter cold from soldiers in the 10th Mountain Division units, as well as some Norwegian ski instructors. Several of the army's Norwegian ski teachers had won Olympic medals at the 1936 Olympics in Bavaria, Germany. The actual temperatures in the UP dropped to between twenty and forty below zero at night, but they all fought through it.

After returning to Camp McCoy, Kenneth was told that the following winter, 1942–1943, he would be returning for six weeks to Northern Michigan with approximately fifty men under his command to teach them the winter tactics and survival methods he had learned. Almost all of the men from Company E were from southern states and had never seen snow before. The Regimental Commanding Officer feared a large number of AWOLs once the men encountered the extreme cold, due to the expected low morale of the company. He made it clear that he held the officers responsible. Hearing this, Lieutenant Bender assembled the men for a pep talk.

He told them that the weather probably wouldn't be so cold, that they had the best equipment, clothing, and the famous dehydrated mountain rations. He further emphasized that this was going to be a real adventure with terrific scenery, hills, woods, and lakes. Lieutenant Bender concluded by stating how lucky they were, "that Uncle Sam is actually paying us for this vacation and there are many big, fat executives all over the USA in stuffy offices, who would give a thousand bucks to make this maneuver."

Upon arriving in Northern Michigan, Lieutenant Bender's men left the warm railroad coaches and were hit with a blast of below zero air. They also saw over four feet of snow and heard the howling wind. Kenneth and First Sergeant Poulten led the men in a column of twos on the road, each man carrying his skis or snowshoes. The entire

Kenneth Bender's first trip to Michigan's Upper Peninsula, training for Norway invasion, 1942. *Author files.*

column was silent. Kenneth wondered if they could live through the weather. As they arrived at their assigned bivouac area—a field of snow, 200 by 300 yards—Kenneth stepped from the road and found himself in a ditch with snow up to his hips.

Two of the men pulled him out. He didn't dare look to the rear. He made an attempt to hurdle the ditch, but with heavy clothing, skis, ski poles, carbine, and a forty-five-pound rucksack, his attempt was a failure. As he struggled to his feet, Kenneth heard a soldier say in a southern drawl, "I sure do feel sorry for the big, fat executives who couldn't make this maneuver."

Kenneth's unit survived the frigid temperatures, including bedding down in the snow in double down sleeping bags and eating cold K-rations. The soldiers learned how to pack up snowbanks and use reflector fires to keep warm. Some men received medical attention for frostbite, including one tall soldier who lost an ear, as his sleeping bag was not long enough to protect him. The UP training was not solely to determine whether the men could survive in the extreme temperatures. Lieutenant Bender also led them in maneuvers to prepare for combat. In one of these, the men set up sixty yards of barbed wire. They were then told to crawl and pull themselves on their stomachs through the snow under the barbed wire, while two other members of the Company fired machine guns thirty-six inches over their heads. There were no AWOLs in Company B, 38th Regiment.

Upon returning to Camp McCoy, Kenneth Bender was promoted to Captain and assumed command of Company B of the 38th Regiment on January 1, 1943. Kenneth called all the men together for a meeting, telling them he was their new Company Commander and would work very hard to do his best. He then asked the two hundred men to form a line, and he shook hands with each of them as they told him their names and where they were from.

One of the men Kenneth Bender shook hands with was a cook in the unit, who introduced himself as Wong Thew, born in Kwangtung, China, and living in San Francisco, California. He stated his two names in the order typically said in China, with the family name (Wong) first. Several weeks after Captain Bender had introduced himself to the men, the mess sergeant came to tell him that one of the men under his command was refusing to take a few days off on furlough — Wong Thew. Bender asked the sergeant to send him to Company Headquarters. Private Wong came to see Captain Bender. Kenneth explained to Thew that he should take a few days off, that it was important for soldiers to take a break when they were able, and that many of the men liked going to Sparta, Wisconsin, approximately twenty miles away, for a little vacation. Private Wong said he didn't know anyone around the area of the base and didn't want to leave. Kenneth told him that he had been to Sparta, and that he saw a number of Chinese restaurants in the city, suggesting that Thew could visit them and introduce himself. Private Wong reluctantly agreed. Captain Bender asked him to report back after his furlough.

In a few days, Private Wong came to see Captain Bender and "was all smiles." He told Kenneth that he had a wonderful time meeting the Chinese people who lived in Sparta, that they went out of their way to show him the best time and would not accept money for their hospitality. Captain Bender shook hands with Private Wong and told him how happy he was that he had a good time. At the end of the conversation, Private First Class Thew Yuk Wong said, "When can I go again, Captain?" From that day, through the rest of the time Company B was stationed at Camp McCoy, Private Wong would come to ask permission to go back to Sparta every week.

Company B continued training in Wisconsin for ten months. In October, 1943, just under three years after Kenneth had volunteered to fight for his country, Company B, 38th Infantry Regiment, Second Infantry Division, boarded a passenger train from Camp McCoy, Wisconsin, heading to Camp Shanks, New York, under the leadership of Captain Kenneth Bender. They spent five days of additional training, including practicing using rope ladders to disembark a ship in strong winds, while carrying heavy equipment. The men then boarded the *U.S.S. Florence Nightingale*, one of thirty ships in a convoy to take them across the Atlantic to the Port of Belfast, and then for further training in Newry, Northern Ireland. The ship had a forty-degree list at times. Despite this, Company B members were honored to be selected as the Guard Company during the eight-day crossing, making certain that complete black-out conditions prevailed at all times at sixty different stations on the *Florence Nightingale*. Several destroyers served as escorts, weaving in and out of the convoy, dropping depth charges and mines to destroy any enemy submarines along the route.

CHAPTER 9
Near Cardiff, Wales, June 1944

IT WAS TWO A.M. WHEN Kenneth heard an unexpected knock on the door of his barracks. "Captain Bender, Sir!" There was some urgency in the messenger's voice.

Captain Bender had been training in Newry, Northern Ireland, with the two hundred men in his unit for a few months. Company B's barracks were on the second floor of an old abandoned concrete mill. The men practiced hand-to-hand combat drills in a greyhound dog racing enclosure and hiked up and down Camlough Mountain, where even the big rocks they walked on sank into the boggy ground with just one step. They were continuing their preparation to invade Norway. The Irish people had been warm and welcoming. As the American troops did their daily marches through the little towns, the citizens ran out to greet them. Captain Bender and his men would give them the chocolate bars from their K-ration kits. The Irish children would jump up and down and wave and smile.

But Bender and the men of the 38th knew there was nothing to celebrate. It was like having a party before going in for life-threatening surgery. The anticipation hung over all of them like a heavy, dark cloud. This was no vacation. It was a mere diversion from the enormity of the task ahead — to do their part to save the world. If Norway remained in the hands of the Nazis, there was concern that Germany would have the ice-free harbors it needed to control the North Atlantic and would have a ready source of iron ore from Sweden.

Bender's focus and the focus of the men under his command had been Norway for almost two years. They had trained outside in the Upper Peninsula of Michigan. They had tested clothing and sleeping bags for the Army, to see if soldiers could survive outside in the Norwegian climate with the inevitable frostbite. Then the plans abruptly changed. Norway surrendered to the Nazis in June of 1940, so Norway was no longer a destination for the Second Infantry Division, and the entire division had been relocated to Wales. Bender had been told of the new mission—training for an amphibious invasion of Europe to fight the Nazis on the ground. He had been informed of the timetable and the plan to leave for Omaha Beach within the week, but the knock on the door of the barracks woke him with a start. "Captain Bender, Sir!" said the messenger again. "I have a message from headquarters."

Were they changing the time for the crossing? What was this about? Kenneth Bender got out of bed and opened the door. He knew not to ask questions but instead to listen and obey. Then the message got even stranger. "Sir, you and all the men in your unit who are Hebrews are supposed to get dressed and come to the officers' tent in fifteen minutes."

"Thank you, private," said Captain Bender.

Bender quickly dressed, grabbed the list of two hundred soldiers under his command, and walked swiftly to the enlisted men's barracks. He walked in and yelled, "Attention!" The men all stood by their bunks at attention. Captain Bender continued, "I will now call out names of some men, and I want you to get dressed and meet me outside the officers' tent in ten minutes." He started calling out the names of the Jewish soldiers. "The rest of you can go back to sleep. That is all."

Captain Bender went to the officers' tent and waited outside for his men. Standing in the coolness of the Welsh night, he thought back about telling his family that he knew volunteering as a private in the infantry was the right thing to do, even though he had graduated from law school just two years before and was working as a lawyer in Rapid City. But why were the Jewish soldiers in his unit being singled out? He had not felt any prejudice as a Jew since he enlisted in 1940. When Bender had worked hard and achieved, he had been rewarded with graduation from OCS and, now, the rank of captain. His Judaism was never mentioned by anyone.

The Jewish men of his unit had lined up silently behind Captain Bender. The Captain led them into the tent. "Captain Bender reporting, Sir."

"At ease, men," said the officer. The officer broke the anxious silence:

> Gentlemen, we have been sent by Company Commander, Captain Keith Schmedeman. Captain Schmedeman has learned reliable information from the front lines, in North Africa and Italy, about how Hebrews, people of the Jewish faith, are being treated by the enemy once they are captured. The Axis are not taking the Hebrews as prisoners of war. They are shooting them on the spot. This has come down from high up. If they see that your dog tags have an "H" for Hebrew, they will kill you or torture you until you die.
>
> The Lieutenant here has a machine that can change your dog tags—you can either switch them from H, to P for Protestant or C for Catholic. When you change your dog tags, you will have a better chance of surviving the war. Now, line up behind Captain Bender to get your dog tags changed. Captain Bender, tell the Lieutenant if you want a C or a P on your tags. Once you have completed this process, you are dismissed.

Captain Bender moved up across from the Lieutenant sitting with the machine, who had his hand out to take the Captain's dog tags. Kenneth's twenty-eight years of life passed before him, as is supposed to happen when you see a car heading straight towards you on the road. But Kenneth Bender didn't see headlights. He saw his grandma Becky's face—stern, wise, and warm all at once. "You are born a Jew, and you will die a Jew." He knew what she meant. No matter what happens in between, once you are born as a Jew, you are who you are. You carry the joys and responsibilities of your religion. You carry the history of your people.

Each soldier had two metal tags around his neck, listing next of kin and religion. One of the tags had tape on it, so the enemy could not hear the American soldiers approaching due to the clanging of the two tags. If a soldier was killed, one tag would be removed and the other would remain with the body. Kenneth pictured the next of kin he had listed — his father, Joseph Bender — who had just sent him a package of a dozen pairs of warm winter gloves from Benders' General Store. The letter enclosed said that they should be distributed to the men who needed them most and ended with his dad's usual closing: "God bless you." If Keva were killed, it was Joseph who would be sent his son's dog tag in Eureka. He would see the C or P and wonder what happened.

"P or C ?" The Lieutenant's words brought him back to the moment. In the quiet of the tent, Captain Bender felt his words come from deep inside of himself, calm and confident.

"Sir, I will not make the change." Captain Bender then told the men assembled that they had the option to do as they wished, and he started to walk towards the exit of the tent. That's when he heard Private Feldman, "Sir, I will not make the change"; then Private First Class Skurmann, "Sir, I will not make the change"; and on and on, like a rolling echo in a tent covered with burlap, that would not naturally lead to the phenomenon of an echo. These were man-made echoes. These were echoes that came from thousands of years of faith. Captain Bender walked back to his barracks knowing he had made the right decision and proud that he had been a good example for the Jews in B Company.

A few days earlier, when Kenneth had received word that the entire Second Infantry Division would participate in the invasion at Normandy, France, Chaplain Nee — the Catholic Chaplain of the 38th Infantry Regiment who had become a good friend of Kenneth's — told him he had something for him. He handed Kenneth a copy of the Jewish Holy Scriptures, published by the United States Army.

Kenneth M. Bender's dog tags. *Author files.*

On the first page, prior to the Readings from the Holy Scriptures, the little brown book included the following letter:

> *The White House*
> *Washington*
> *March 6, 1941*
>
> *To the Members of the Army:*
>
> *As Commander-In-Chief I take pleasure in commending the reading of the Bible to all who serve in the armed forces of the United States. Throughout the centuries men of many faiths and diverse origins have found in the Sacred Book words of wisdom, counsel and inspiration. It is a fountain of strength and now, as always an aid in attaining the highest aspirations of the human soul.*
>
> *Very sincerely yours,*
> *Franklin D. Roosevelt*

As Kenneth read through portions of the prayer book, he turned down the corner of one page, with a psalm that particularly spoke to his circumstance, Psalm 27, entitled "A Psalm of Confidence":

> The Lord is my light and my salvation; whom shall I fear?
> The Lord is the stronghold of my life; of whom shall I be afraid?
> When evil-doers came upon me to eat up my flesh,
> Even mine adversaries and my foes, they stumbled and fell.
> Though a host should encamp against me,
> My heart shall not fear;
> Though war should rise up against me,
> Even then will I be confident.
> Teach me Thy way, O Lord;
> And lead me in an even path,
> Because of them that lie in wait for me.
> Wait for the Lord;
> Be strong, and let thy heart take courage;
> Yea, wait thou for the Lord.

Kenneth Bender realized that not only was he born a Jew and would die a Jew, but that he was born and would die an American as well. He, of course, hoped that he would die in America after living a long life and after having the opportunity to be married and have a family.

On the Tuesday night before the unit's transatlantic trip, after dinner, a 38th Infantry, First Platoon Private First Class from South Dakota named Irwin Ristow asked permission to talk with Kenneth privately. He told his Captain his problem. "Sir, the men are picking on me, calling me a German, because my parents are immigrants from Germany. Sir, I am an American and proud to be an American. What can I do to make them stop?"

Captain Bender told Private Ristow, "You are a good soldier and you are an American. I am proud to have you in our unit. Leave it to me." Later that night, Captain Bender called the First Platoon together. He told them:

> The matter that I need to discuss with you is of the utmost importance. A unit of men who do not respect one another will not fight together and will not do their jobs together. The more we respect each other,

> the greater likelihood that more of us will come out of this alive. I don't care if your parents or grandparents come from Ireland, Germany, Russia or Yugoslavia. I don't care if you're Protestant, Catholic, or Jewish. We are all Americans. We are all fighting for America. If we don't fight together as Americans, we will die alone as Americans. If I hear that anyone in this unit is not treating anyone else with the utmost respect, as a fellow fighting American, that person or persons will be disciplined. Are there any questions?

The solders were silent. Private Ristow did not inform Captain Bender of any more issues with his fellow soldiers.[162]

While stationed in Ireland, after normal duty hours, Kenneth had another set of duties besides studying German battle strategy. He was assigned to handle court martial cases, both on the prosecution and defense side, as he had also done after hours at Camp McCoy. While in the army, Kenneth handled over two hundred cases in his spare time. In Kenneth's last assigned case, before his unit was transferred to Wales, an American private was accused of getting into a brawl with an Irish citizen in a bar. The army was very sensitive to not having its men causing trouble in their guest countries. The charges were assault and battery of a citizen, with possible punishment or dishonorable discharge.

When Captain Bender first observed the soldier he was to defend, the private was crying in the corner of his cell. After Kenneth quieted him down a bit, the man said, "I'm going to spend my life in prison instead of helping my unit. It's all over. Don't waste your time with me."

Captain Bender calmly told the private to tell him what had happened. The private said he had been drinking in a bar in the town of Newry during the evening when the fight broke out, and he made a big mistake in not just walking away. "I know I'm guilty, they might as well lock me up for good now; I threw the first punch."

"Are you the kind of guy who starts fights with other people on a regular basis?" Captain Bender asked him.

---

[162]Conversations between Irvin and Margaret Ristow and author, St. Louis Park, Minnesota, 1998; Bender, *From the Prairies to the Beaches.*

"Absolutely not," said the private. "I've never been in a fight before in my life."

Kenneth inquired further. "Why were you angry?"

"Because of the things he said," said the private.

"What did he say?" asked Kenneth.

"The Irish man in the bar had been drinking a lot and was saying that Americans were no good, that they were too lazy and stupid to win the war and that America would soon be a German colony and Hitler would be president," replied the incarcerated soldier.

"Take it easy," said Captain Bender. "I'll be back later tonight." Captain Bender reported his interview with the soldier to Regimental Headquarters, saying, "If you punish this private, you will be punishing him for being a good American and for standing up for America." They agreed with Captain Bender completely. The charges against the private were dropped.

* * *

Kenneth kept his family and his town close in his thoughts as his unit continued to prepare for its encounter with the enemy. His letter to the editor of the *Northwest Blade*, the Eureka newspaper, was published under the heading "Captain Keva Bender Writes" on April 6, 1944:

> March 9, 1944
> England
>
> Dear Mr. Shankland:
>
> Hope your all getting along okay back in the Dakotas. Have been receiving the Blade recently and it is a welcome item — it really means more to one than you can imagine.
>
> I'm feeling fine and really in good health. I've commanded my dough boy, rifle company for some time and do really know my outfit pretty well. I'm sure you Eurekans would rate them tops. Everyone agrees that the ground forces will play an important part in our victory over the Nazis and there's no doubt that the war won't end until the allies march through Berlin. And my team hopes to have its little piece to say before it's all over. And we'll

> give 'em h— for many people—and especially for you in the Dakotas.
>
> I want to wish all my buddies in the services the best of luck—
>
> Best wishes to you all from
>
> Capt. Keva Bender

Two months to the day after his letter's publication, on June 6, 1944, more than nine hours into the greatest amphibious landing in American military history, an official dispatch from the Allied command was sent by military courier in a red and white striped pouch from General Eisenhower's London headquarters to the Associated Press' London office. Within one minute, it was sent by teletype to member newspapers and broadcast on United States radio stations: "Under the command of General Eisenhower, Allied naval forces, supported by strong air forces, began landing Allied armies on the northern coast of France."

It was such a powerful and pithy sentence, saying everything that needed to be and could be said in twenty-four words devoid of all emotion.

Church bells pealed and fire sirens blared from coast to coast to alert Americans to the Allied invasion. Many churches and synagogues also opened for prayers. Eleven-year-old David Bender had trouble concentrating on his job of candling eggs at Benders' General Store that day.[163]

Prior to the European invasion, Kenneth Bender, as an officer, was given a code name that could be used to identify him and his unit. Kenneth was told his code name would be "Chief," after the famous baseball pitcher in the Major Leagues named "Chief" Bender.[164]

---

[163] Candling involves holding each egg to the light to see if it is fertilized or rotten. Bernice Bender Ellison recollections, in Grenz, Anderson, and Straub. "If These Walls Could Talk: Eureka Family Dental Clinic," *Northwest Blade*, NDSU Germans from Russia Heritage Collection.

[164] The baseball playing Charles Albert Bender was from the Chippewa tribe, won over two hundred games in the Majors, and pitched three complete games in one World Series in 1911 for the Philadelphia Athletics. National Baseball Hall of Fame.

The Second Infantry Division Company Commander "Chief" Bender and the two hundred men in his unit left Cardiff, Wales, shortly after one a.m. for the three-hour trip to Omaha Beach, Normandy, France, as part of Operation Overlord on June 7, 1944, D Day +1. While Captain Bender oversaw Company B loading men and supplies onto the boat transports in Cardiff, it was still June 6, 1944, in Washington D.C., six hours earlier due to the time zone difference. President Franklin Delano Roosevelt addressed the nation, asking the American people to join him in prayer:

> With Thy blessing, we shall prevail over the unholy forces of our enemy. Help us to conquer the apostles of greed and racial arrogances. Lead us to the saving of our country, and with our sister nations into a world unity that will spell a sure peace — a peace invulnerable to the scheming of unworthy men. And a peace that will let all of men live in freedom, reaping the just rewards of their honest toil. Thy will be done, Almighty God. Amen."

Joe, Mary, and David Bender listened to the president's radio address together that evening in the sunroom at their home in Eureka, on their four-foot radio with an analogue dial. As Joe listened, he bit his cigar a bit more frequently and harder. They sensed Keva was somewhere in the midst of the throng invading France, though they didn't know where he was and whether he was safe. Then the radio station played a song sung by Kate Smith:

> Goodnight, wherever you are . . .
> If only one little wish that I wish comes true
> I know that the angels will watch over you.[165]

Kenneth Bender and the men of Rifle Company B, 38th Regiment, Second Infantry Division did not hear the president's message prayer, but they were well aware of the importance of their mission and the support of their country.

---

[165]Written by Al Hoffman, Dick Robertson, Weldon Frank, Copyright with Lyrics, used by permission, Carlin America, Inc., Shapiro Bernstein & Co., Inc., Hal Leonard Publishing. The subsequent rise of "Goodnight , Wherever You Are" up the Billboard charts, which at the time monitored radio play, sheet music sales, and jukebox coins, showed that this song's lyrics captured the feelings of many families across America. The Billboard (Nielsen Business Media, Inc., July 1, 1944).

CHAPTER 10
Normandy, France, June 1944

SEVERAL HUNDRED YARDS FROM OMAHA Beach, two hundred members of Company B went over the side of the larger boat transport and slid down rope ladders onto a smaller landing craft. They moved slowly, closer and closer to shore, with the waves rocking them, as nearly every emotion known to man was felt by some man on that boat. The Army Air Forces were very active overhead, artillery fire roared, and the men could hear shells hitting the beach area where they were headed. There was also overhead fire from the U.S. Navy ships, including battleships. Private First Class Skurmann, one of the Jewish soldiers, tapped Chief Bender on the shoulder and yelled over the deafening noise, "I'm glad we didn't change our dog tags, Captain!" He and Captain Bender shook hands with a firm squeeze.

About forty yards from shore, the landing craft boat stopped. Captain Bender shouted the slogan — which was "Follow me!" — of the Infantry School in Fort Benning. He yelled this at the top of his voice as he jumped over the side of the landing craft. He was the first in his Company to hit the water.

Once in the water, he immediately realized there was a problem. The water went almost up to Captain Bender's neck, and he was six feet tall. He knew there were men in the Company who were much shorter. Bender yelled to the Navy Ensign officer, above the roar of the artillery fire from the battleship and overhead aircraft, to move the boat closer to the beach. The ensign yelled back, "This is as far as I'm going to go!"

Captain Bender shouted back, "You better get closer to the shore, or some of my men will drown." The ensign did not respond. Captain Bender yelled again, "If you don't move closer to the shore, I will have the men shoot you!" After this remark, there was silence; then the engine started up and the ensign started moving the boat closer to shore. Bender and Boudra, Captain Bender's runner, in the water, moved toward the beach. Every one of the Company made it out of the water, near St. Laurent-sur-Mer.

What they encountered was horrific. There were dead bodies and wreckage all over the beach. Named the "Easy Red" section of Omaha Beach in the calm of generals' strategy sessions, upon arrival it was obvious that nothing was going to be easy in this campaign. Captain Bender saw one deceased American soldier who had a Colt .45 caliber pistol visible. Though Bender had his carbine, he believed that an additional weapon would help in attacking the Nazis or defending himself in close quarters and put it in his inside pocket. Even if he were captured, Kenneth felt he might be able to kill one of the enemy so one less American soldier would die after him.

Bender and his runner ran in different directions on the beach, shouting and looking for Bender's Commanding Officer, Colonel Mildren. Bender finally found him. "Colonel Mildren, Sir, you previously gave us orders to go to Ceresy Forest, a few miles inland, to assemble there. Are these still our orders, Sir?" inquired Captain Bender.

"Conditions do not look good, Captain. Our battalion will be pushed back in the water. We will all be killed!" replied the colonel.

Bender persisted, "Then what are the orders *now*, sir?"

Colonel Mildren, whose code name was Buck, paused and then repeated, "We will all be pushed back in the water and be killed."

Captain Bender then said, "Sir, before we are all pushed back in the water and killed, what are our orders?"

Buck paused and then gave the new orders: "Push inland, south, as fast and as far as you are able, to make room for other landing troops which are coming." Buck also said that Captain Bender's Company, Company B, a rifle company, was ordered to be the lead company in this advance. There was no artillery or tank support for Company B. Company D of the First Battalion had a machine gun unit attached to Company B as long as B was the lead company. Companies A and C were ordered to follow Company B, in a column.

Bender gave the new orders to his four platoon leaders and sergeants, who told the men. With planes overhead and artillery blasting, it was beyond a nightmare. Within less than one half hour after stepping foot on the beach, Captain Bender gave the orders for Company B to start to push inland. The first mission was to get over the cliff, which had been cleared of mines. Areas cleared were identified by markers placed by the engineers on the ground. The men proceeded in a column of twos, ever vigilant to stay in the marked area.

Once above the cliff, they arrived in the hedgerow country. The hedges had to be crossed over. They were located about every thirty to fifty yards and were made up of thick vegetation on top of dirt and rock walls, about two to three feet tall. The farmers of Normandy had bordered their fields with hedgerows since Roman times. Now the hedgerows acted as natural fortresses for the enemy, making the Nazis' defense of the area easier. The American soldiers had no way of knowing when the enemy would be behind a hedge, waiting until the Americans got closer to them to open fire.

In an attempt to limit casualties, Bender ordered the men in one squad to count off "one, two, three, four," and then repeat and then repeat again. Each soldier would know if he was an odd or even number. On command, the odd-numbered men would advance over the hedgerow with the even-numbered firing overhead or to the side to keep the enemy down. When the odd-numbered men reached the next hedgerow, the even numbers would jump over the starting hedgerow and join the odd-numbered men. This procedure continued hedgerow after hedgerow.

It was such a nerve-wracking process that Captain Bender decided he should be out in front to instill the confidence of the men. He would, therefore, on occasion, jump over the hedgerows with the first group. He would then hear the cry go back from the front of the unit to the rear: "Bender's over!" "Bender's over!" The riflemen, light machine guns, and 60mm Mortars worked as a team, and together they made good progress.

***

Though Captain Bender did not consider himself an extremely observant Jew, he did feel a strong connection with God. From the day he entered the service through all the days of combat, even if he had only one or two hours of sleep, he would pray to God. In France, he would pray that Company B would have few casualties, if any, and that they would be successful in their mission. He would also pray for his family and for America.

A typical June in Normandy, France, would have been idyllic, with its azure blue skies, temperature in the low seventies, and crisp, invigorating air from the English Channel. But these were not days to appreciate the oceanic climate. As Company B advanced, they saw American paratroopers hanging from branches on the trees with their parachutes open, having been killed by the enemy before they ever touched the ground. Company B also experienced its first casualties, a private and a platoon leader, both thought of highly. Each night, Chief would go back to Battalion Headquarters to receive orders for the next day and then return to the unit.

Later in the afternoon on June 14, 1944, it appeared that the enemy resistance was less, and Company B advanced more rapidly. After almost a three-mile advance, Company B arrived at the outskirts of the French village of St. George D'Elle. After several skirmishes with the enemy, Company B reached the village. Captain Bender sent a runner to determine the location of the other companies, Able and Charlie. No contact could be made. The other Companies had not kept up with Company B as they had been ordered to do.

Captain Bender radioed back to Colonel Mildren to indicate his unit's location and to tell him there was no contact with Companies A or C. Buck checked the map and said, "You're surrounded. Enemy troops are between Company B and the rest of the Batallion. If you want to surrender, that's fine, because it is doubtful you can make it back and all of you will be killed."

Captain Bender answered, "Colonel, we will make it back." Bender calmly called the platoon leaders and lieutenants together from the sunken road where they were situated. He told them of his plan:

> Upon darkness, Company B's movement will start to the rear, in a column of twos. Everyone will remove his steel helmet and will carry it, so the enemy will have more difficulty in identifying us as enemy troops. Even in the darkness, the silhouettes of the American soldiers' helmets are noticeably different from the Nazis'. Private Skurmann, as you can speak German fluently, you along with the automatic riflemen and I, with my compass, will direct the retreat.

After darkness, the advance to the rear began. The men spoke only in whispers, and walked slowly. As they were walking, Captain Bender saw a German machine gun crew quietly moving its gun up the road where Company B was located and placing it in position about forty yards from the men. He calmly moved two automatic riflemen up near him and directed their fire on the enemy crew, putting the gun out of action. Bender took many compass readings to make sure the direction was exactly accurate. On two occasions, the enemy approached the Company to try to determine if they were friend or foe. Private Skurrman took up the conversation in German, and with Browning automatic riflemen, the Company B infantrymen eliminated the enemy. After a number of additional firefights — a long ten hours later — the advance units of Company B reached the First Battalion Headquarters at seven a.m. Everyone was exhausted.

Colonel Mildren was overjoyed and surprised that the entire unit had made it back safely. Captain Bender told him that their success was the result of a team effort by all members of Company B. The next day, Bender wrote up recommendations for Bronze Stars for heroic achievement in a combat zone for Skurrman, the two Browning automatic riflemen and First Sergeant Charlie Poulten, who had carried a wounded fellow member of Company B over his shoulder all the way back, for over nine hours. All of these recommended awards were approved.

Colonel Mildren recommended Kenneth Bender for the Silver Star. For military action on June 14, 1944, the Division's Commanding Officer, General Walter Robertson, personally awarded the Silver Star for gallantry to Captain Kenneth Bender on July 20, 1944. The citation read, in part: "The competence, leadership and intrepid actions of this officer to infuse courage in his troops is in keeping with the highest traditions of armed forces of the United States."

After General Robertson pinned on the medal, he said, "Captain, you and your Company have been doing a magnificent job."

Breaching protocol by not saying, "Yes, Sir, General," Bender instead said, "General, Sir, we are doing our best."

The General responded, "That is all I can ask for, Captain."

* * *

The war continued for the Second Infantry Division, medals or no medals. It was an increasing challenge for Bender to go each night to Battalion Headquarters with his runner, his compass as his guide, to obtain orders for the next day's attack, and then return to the Company. Company B had limited artillery support, which increased the Company's casualties. The orders from Buck were to continue going as far and as fast as they were able. This placed Company B, at times, "out in front" of the battalion, even after the experience at St. George D'Elle.

During the evening of July 10, 1944, in Normandy, Kenneth received orders to report to the First Battalion Command Post. Upon arriving there, along with the commanders of Able, Charlie, and Dog Companies, they were escorted into an old French farmhouse.

General Walter Robertson pinning the Silver Star on Captain Bender. *Author files.*

The officers knew they were there to receive orders to attack Hill 192 which was an enemy stronghold that had to be taken. It was called Hill 192, because it was 192 meters above sea level. The unit that controlled this hill would have a great advantage. It was considered the best observation point in the St. Lo sector, a point from which one could observe troop movement from all directions.

Before the meeting started, Captain Bender went to the Battalion Commanding Officer, Colonel Mildren, and requested a private meeting with him. The request was granted. The two of them went into a little room. The Colonel looked at the Captain and asked the purpose of this request. Captain Bender told Colonel Mildren that he knew they were going to attack Hill 192. He also stated that Company B had been the lead company in the attack during the last several days and that, in fairness to the men of Company B, he felt they should be in reserve for the initial attack on the Hill. Colonel Mildren hesitated a few seconds, looked at Captain Bender, and then said, "I agree. Your Company will be the reserve Company." Captain Bender was pleased that there would be more equal sharing of the lead position among the companies.

The orders for the attack were issued. Company A would attack the right portion of the hill (west section), Company C would attack on the left (eastern section), and Company B would be the reserve Company. Early the following morning, Companies A and C attacked with supporting artillery fire. The attack was not successful. At about 1300 hours, Captain Bender was ordered to the Battalion Command Post and taken into a separate room. General Van Fleet was there. He was the second in command to General Robertson.

Colonel Mildren issued the order, "Company B will pass through the area of Company A, continue the attack and take the right half or western section of the Hill." The Colonel then wished Captain Bender and his men good luck. Captain Bender left the Command Post with questions going through his mind. Captain Bender returned to Company B and saw his second in Command, Lt. McArtor. (The original second in command, Lt. Miniutti, had been wounded and evacuated). Bender told McArtor about Colonel Mildren's orders and told him to alert the Company to stay where they were. Bender decided to make a reconnaissance in the Company A sector before proceeding. Together with his runner, they arrived in Company A to evaluate the situation. Company A had only been able to advance a very short distance since the early morning attack. Bender asked to see the replacement Company A Commander. Captain Ward, the original Company A Commander, had been killed.

When Bender observed the replacement Captain, he was digging a foxhole. It was waist deep, and he was still digging. Captain Bender realized that he was struggling with the situation. Bender addressed the Captain: "Sir, Company B is going to continue the attack started this morning by Company C. Where is the enemy, what is their strength, and what other information can you give me to lead Company B?"

The new Company A Captain responded, "You will never make it—there are too many enemy. You will never make it. There are too many enemy." He continued digging his foxhole. Bender left him and proceeded to talk to the Company A Sergeant, who was the most forward of the Company. The Sergeant confirmed what Captain Bender already knew about Company A's heavy casualties and inability to advance.

Captain Bender then made the decision not to pass through the Company A sector, but rather to continue his reconnaissance of the Hill. Though he knew this was against orders, he felt it was the only thing to do. Months earlier, Captain Bender had read about enemy tactics. He had learned that when defending a hill, the enemy would defend the sides of the hill and not the most elevated area. Therefore, Captain Bender went to the lower middle of the hill with his runner and started upwards. To his surprise, he found it was not defended. Captain Bender and Boudra continued advancing over the hedgerows. After advancing about a third of the way up Hill 192, Bender sent Boudra back to Company B, with orders for the second in command, Lt. McArtor, to bring the rest of the Company up Hill 192, in a column of twos.

Company B proceeded up the center of the hill, through the hedgerows. When the crest was reached, Bender sent one column to the left and one to the right. He gave orders not to proceed down the forward slope of the hill. Bender believed that just over the crest of 192, they would have better observation and were in an excellent defensive position as well. Captain Bender also ordered the men not to open fire on the enemy, as the enemy would perhaps then hit them with artillery and other weapons. Finally, Bender ordered the men to fire at the enemy when its friendly artillery hit the ground in the enemy sector. This was the plan to conceal Company B's position. After a while, from the forward slope of 192, Company B could see the enemy retreating. They could see the Nazi vehicles on the main highway. The Hill had been taken. An artillery observer who arrived in their sector ordered artillery fire on the enemy, and it imposed severe casualties.

The following morning, at the Company B Command Post, General Van Fleet looked for Captain Bender and complimented Company B, through Captain Bender, for their superior attack. Captain Bender felt that it was a blessing that his Company did not suffer one casualty. Bender felt that Company B should have been cited for a superior attack by Colonel Mildren. That did not happen. The new Company A Captain and his Company received the compliments. But Company B had no casualties and had the knowledge that they were instrumental in helping the Americans take the Hill.

After Hill 192, the general orders for Company B were to continue inland. During the evening on July 26, 1944, during a hedgerow battle, Captain Bender was hit by metal shrapnel in his hands and both legs. Though bleeding, he walked to the battalion aide station in the rear. Captain Bender was told he was being sent to England for treatment. Bender objected. He requested treatment at the battalion aide station because he didn't wish to leave his company. He knew there was already a shortage of men and officers, and believed that his leaving would harm the morale of the Company he had trained.

An argument ensued, with Captain Bender winning. Surgery was performed on the spot, and some of the larger shrapnel pieces removed. For this injury, he was written up to receive a Purple Heart medal. Shortly thereafter, around seven a.m., once Joseph had already left for his workday at Benders' General Store, Mary was cleaning up the breakfast dishes when there was a knock on the door. She opened the screen door and saw Luke Fisher, the railway station agent, who received the Western Union telegrams for Eureka. When he walked out of the railway building, everyone who saw him got frightened, wondering what direction he would go, and fearing that the telegram would say, "We regret to inform you that ______ was killed in action on ______."[166] Mr. Fisher handed Mary an envelope and told her it was from the War Department. Mary ripped open the envelope and read the telegram that provided brief news of Keva's injuries and his Purple Heart. She ran the several blocks to Benders' General Store to show Joseph, not hearing her neighbors who called out to her along the way, "Good morning, Mary!" Joseph and Mary embraced and prayed together.[167] By the time the telegram had been received in Eureka, Captain Bender had since rejoined his men—the very next day after his surgery.

As the men of Company B advanced, they arrived at a stream that they had to cross to continue. The tank, which was to assist the advance, stopped in front of the water. Captain Bender took his rifle and went to the rear of the tank and pounded on the tank until the tank commander opened the top. Captain Bender asked him why he was not continuing the advance. The tank commander said that he was concerned that there were mines in the stream.

Bender told him that he would walk in front of the tank if the tank commander would follow, as there was no other way to proceed. The tank commander agreed and told Captain Bender to walk ten to fifteen feet ahead of the tank. Captain Bender entered the stream and proceeded to cross it, moving the arm with his rifle down and up, hitting the stock of the rifle on the streambed and bringing it back up and around him as he walked. The stream was approximately three

[166]Conversation between David Bender and author, November 2017.

[167]Joseph and Mary Bender recollections, told to author's parents, Eureka, 1946 and Minneapolis 1957.

feet deep. Captain Bender was the only one in front of the tank. After crossing over half of the stream, the tank hit a mine, resulting in a huge explosion. Captain Bender was thrown in the water and saw the tank rear back and smash back in the water.

The rest of the unit was unable to help the men in the tank, who were all killed instantly in the explosion. The weight of the tank had set off the mines, though Captain Bender's weight had not. Captain Bender was dizzy from the explosion and felt terrible that the men in the tank had been lost. After a short time, Company B continued its advance.

On August 14, Company B was approaching Tinchebray, France. They had broken through the main enemy lines. A platoon lieutenant and his men from Company B were advancing south. They became surrounded and the platoon became isolated. Then Captain Bender received an order from the Battalion that his unit was to advance to the East. The platoon lieutenant was a walking wounded and came to the Company area to inform Captain Bender as to his location. Bender made the decision to get to the platoon to bring it back. With his runner, he proceeded in that direction. As he was nearing the unit, while running across an open field, Captain Bender felt a burning, stinging sensation and realized a bullet had gone through his upper left arm. The shot knocked him down and he was "bleeding heavily."[168] Boudra, his runner, patched Captain Bender up with bandages, but he was in bad pain. Bender was told he was being sent to the rear to the Regimental Aid station. Prior to leaving Company B, Captain Bender called Lt. McArtor and told him, "McArtor, you are going to have to take over; you are now the Company Commander of Company B."[169]

✲✲✲

[168]William S. McArtor in *I Remember B Company*.

[169]Ibid.; Kenneth Bender, *From the Prairies to the Beaches*.

There was a knock on the Benders' door in Eureka. It was Luke Fisher with a second telegram.[170] This time, it was after Benders' General Store had closed for the day, and the sun was almost on the horizon. Mary was in the kitchen, taking cinnamon *kmishbroit* out of the oven.[171] Joseph answered the door, accepted the envelope, and silently walked outside as the courier left to make his other deliveries. Joseph leaned against the conifer tree and read:

> Joseph Bender
> Eureka S.D.
>
> Deeply regret to inform you that your son Captain Kenneth M Bender was slightly wounded in action in France fourteen August period progress reports will be forwarded as received.
>
> Ulio
> The Adjutant General

Joseph knew of families who had received the "slightly wounded" telegram only to be followed by the news of their loved-one's death. Joseph's sister Sarah had just received news that her youngest son, Larry, Keva's first cousin, had died of injuries sustained in Cherbourg, Normandy. Joseph wiped his eyes, prayed, and headed back inside to tell Mary.

After Captain Bender called Lt. McArtor, the next thing he remembered was being in an army hospital in England. The doctor said that the bullet went three inches from his heart, he had lost a lot of blood, and they hoped they could save his arm.

On August 16, Captain Bender, aware that his family in Eureka would be visited by the Western Union man any day, sent the following letter to his parents:

> Dear Folks:
>
> Hope you are all okay. I am just fine and getting along okay. I do not know War Department Policy, so I will

[170]This was Captain Bender's third wound in action, though it was his second Purple Heart. He had refused to be written up for a Purple Heart for one of his injuries, so as not to alarm his family with another telegram. Conversation with David Bender and author, 2017.

[171]Kmishbroit is a sweet bread loaf, similar to, but oftentimes softer than, biscottis.

> give you the latest news. You may have or you may in the future receive a telegram from the War Department, that I was wounded slightly on the 14th of August.
>
> Please believe me when I say it is only a slight wound and in about ten days I will probably be back with my company.
>
> I was hit by a single rifle shot and the bullet went completely through my left arm[.] I can move my arm okay and my hand is only slightly sore. I feel that I was very lucky.
>
> I am in a nice hospital here. Have nice clean sheets and hot meals and pleasant nurses.
>
> Please don't worry. Keep smiling. Hello to Sneezy. Will write again tomorrow.
>
> Love, Ke

Though Kenneth tried to reassure his parents, he knew the severity of his injury. He remained in England in the hospital getting care and therapy for almost five months until returning to France on January 1, 1945. Due to his disability, Captain Bender was assigned to headquarters, Ninth U.S. Army in France, until the war was over.

General Robertson, the Second Infantry Division Commanding Officer, had said that being a Rifle Company Commander was the most difficult job in the army. This was a sentiment echoed by others with experience: "Rifle companies in World War II did most of the close-in fighting. Consequently, they suffered most of the casualties."[172] In an infantry division, such as the Second Infantry Division, there were three regiments: the Ninth, the Twenty-third, and the Thirty-eighth. Each had nine Company Commanders, making a total of twenty-seven Rifle Company Commanders. At the time that Kenneth was hit, he was the twenty-sixth of the original twenty-seven Rifle Company Commanders to be put out of action due to death, capture, or significant injury.

While overseas, Captain Bender received many wonderful letters from his family. His dad wrote on September 25, 1944:

[172]Captain William S. McArtor, in *I Remember B Company*.

Dear Keva:

Everything is o.k. here — was out yesterday with David hunting, we had our limit, also was in Bowdle and played a few holes of golf, but I sure would like to have you with us . . . so let us hope with God's help to see you home soon, and victory will come soon as possible, don't trust them [the Nazis] an inch, as we read in the papers they are not to be trusted, and we all hope God will be with you. Well be good Keva, take care of yourself and God Bless you.

Your Dad, Joe Bender

Kenneth's mother wrote on September 12, 1944:

Dearest Son Keva,

Happy New Year to you my dear son. God help us to win this war soon and you come back safe and well, that's all we pray for. The weather is a lot cooler now. The farmers are busy threshing. We are going to Aberdeen for the holidays and David will be bar mitzvahed. God bring you through this war safely and home. Amen.

Love to you from all.

Mother[173]

One letter from Keva's brother, David, sent a couple of years later, referred to an assignment David had in school, to write about an American hero. He made his oral presentation in class, entitled "True Patriotism." David told of a soldier who had "an average upbringing in a small town," and who rose to the challenge of war overseas in sixty-eight continuous days of combat, and then stated, "He had spent the five best years of his life in the army. He isn't bitter about it for he feels he fought for a cause which will bring everlasting peace to the world. It is men such as he, ready to die for their country, that have kept the U.S. at its top world position."

It wasn't until the last line of his story when David divulged that the hero he was referring to was his brother. David wrote to his

[173]Mary Bender is referring to the Jewish New Year, which occurs in September or October, depending upon the Jewish calendar.

brother that his English teacher in Eureka gasped when he read the concluding lines from his essay: "Who is he? What is this patriot's name? His name is Kenneth Bender, he is my brother."

Based upon his actions while in combat, together with the time he served as Army Captain, David Bender's brother was promoted to Major. In addition to the Silver Star, Major Bender was also awarded two Purple Hearts; five Bronze Service Stars for the Normandy, Northern France, Rhineland, Central Europe and Ardennes Campaigns; the Bronze Star Medal; the Combat Infantryman Badge; European African Middle Eastern Ribbon and medal; and the French Jubilee of Liberty Medal.

Better than any medal was the fact that he made it through the war and did his part, like so many others, to help the Allies achieve victory.

Kenneth Bender's army compass. *Author files.*

Major Kenneth M. Bender, circa 1945–1946. *Author files.*

CHAPTER 11

Eureka, SD, 1946

ON JANUARY 2, 1946, ALMOST four months after World War II ended in both the European and Pacific theaters, Major Kenneth Bender received his honorable discharge papers from Fort Blanding, Florida. Kenneth was scheduled to take a train from Minneapolis to Eureka, South Dakota, but decided to visit the University of Minnesota campus to surprise his youngest sister, Bernice, before boarding the train.

When Kenneth arrived on campus, the crowd was very dense. There was a Snow Days Parade, and he wondered how he could locate his sister. While observing the parade, a convertible with Snow Queen candidates was moving closer towards him. He looked up and couldn't believe his eyes.

One of the candidates was Bernice! Keva had not seen her in over five years. He was so moved to see her after all this time. He ran over to the convertible and yelled her name. She looked at her brother in utter amazement. They arranged to meet after the parade and had a visit with hugs and tears.[174]

Then Keva took the train to Eureka. It was a wonderful reunion with his parents and brother. Joe and Mary both said, "Thank God you're home." David hugged his brother and did not want to let go.

[174]Bernice Bender Ellison conversation with author, *From the Prairies to the Beaches.*

When Keva returned to his family's home, he was particularly surprised by the size of their yard. When he used to mow the lawn, it had seemed so large. Walking with the push mower seemed like an endless task. "What is he doing?" Mary asked Joe, looking through the window, as Keva stood in the small backyard and watched the gleeful children pouring out of the brick school across the street. "He's getting used to being a civilian, Mary," said Joe.

During Kenneth's homecoming, he was sad to learn that his first cousin, Larry Schlasinger, who was in the 28th Infantry Division in Normandy and had been raised close by in Streeter, North Dako-

Eureka High School basketball team with Keva Bender (second row far right), Edwin Spitzer (second row, third from left), and Harvey Strobel (second row, second from left), 1933. *Eureka Pioneer Museum Collection, Northern State University Archives & Special Collections, Williams Library, Aberdeen, SD, NSUdigital.org.*

ta, had died of wounds sustained in the war. Kenneth also was told that two members of his 1933 basketball team had made the ultimate sacrifice: Edwin Spitzer, the team captain, from wounds in action on Manus Island in the Pacific Theater, and Harvey Strobel, a guard on the team, in Belgium. Kenneth heard that Eureka had lost many other fine young men, too, which made his return bittersweet.

Shortly after returning to Eureka, the mailman told Kenneth that he had some mail for him. Among the letters was one from Oklahoma. Stokes Baggett had been a Lieutenant in Company B and commanded the First Platoon in the Company. Within a few weeks after landing on Normandy, as the Company was advancing inland over the hedgerows, a member of Lieutenant Baggett's platoon came to Kenneth and said, "Our Lieutenant Baggett has been killed." Kenneth asked the soldier to take him to the location.

When they arrived in the woods, there were a few people standing around the lieutenant. Captain Bender asked one of the men where Lieutenant Baggett had been hit. He told Bender that Baggett had been shot in the face and the bullet had exited on the side of his ear. Captain Bender knelt down and saw the entry and exit points of the bullet, but there was no blood. Captain Bender told the men to improvise a litter and to take him back to the aid station on the beach.[175]

One of the men said to Captain Bender, "Captain, why bother? Baggett is gone." Bender was more angry at the soldier's lack of compassion for a fellow soldier than for his disobeying an order and said, "Either you men take him to the beach or you will be court martialed." They then proceeded to carry Lieutenant Baggett in the direction of the beach. A few days later, a battalion doctor told Bender that Baggett was preliminarily treated at the Aid Station and flown to England. Though there was a chance that the Lieutenant would make it, the doctor felt the odds were not good.

Kenneth had not heard anything else about Stokes Baggett until he received a letter, two years later, in Eureka. The letter stated:

---

[175]Two men would take their rifles and wrap raincoats around them to form the litter.

> Captain Bender:
>
> I hope this letter finds you well. I am back home in Oklahoma and am getting along pretty good. I learned that you started the process for my evacuation when I was shot in the face by ordering the men to take me to the aid station. Had you not done this I would not be here today.
>
> What you do not know is that my family is quite wealthy—owning lots of oil wells in Oklahoma. My father is thankful that I made it back and would like to reward you for what you have done. I have enclosed a return envelope. Write down any amount of money that you would like my family to pay you, and send it back to me. I will see that you get it.
>
> Stokes

Kenneth wrote back immediately:

> Stokes:
>
> I am so thrilled to receive your letter. I will not accept anything from you. What I did for you, you would have done for me. I thank God that you made it through the war.
>
> Kenneth

Kenneth realized how lucky he was also—after being wounded three times—to be back home. He also realized how lucky his ancestors were, to have taken the leap to get on ships to leave Russia. While in Eureka, Kenneth learned that approximately two weeks before he was commissioned as an officer at Fort Benning, Georgia, in late October 1941 in his father's former residence of Odessa, Russia, the Romanians—Nazi allies—rounded up approximately twenty thousand Jews. They either shot the Jews or poured gasoline on them and burned them alive. The remaining ten thousand Jews from the Odessa area were sent to concentration camps; few survived. Kenneth was angry and disappointed that the Allies had not gotten to them sooner. At the same time, he felt thankful that the war had been won. Though these Russian Jews were far away from Eureka, as were the American soldiers who had died, Kenneth felt all of their souls with him as he walked Eureka's quiet streets.

Company B officers in Ireland, before the Normandy invasion. Standing left to right: Lieutenant McArtor, Captain Bender, Lieutenant Howe. Front row, left to right: Lieutenant Baggett, Lieutenant Miniutti, 1944. *Author files.*

One morning, Joseph told Kenneth that his army footlocker with his personal effects had been delivered. Kenneth brought it into his old room and sat down on his bed. He first took out the paper French francs, signed on the fronts and backs by every man in his unit on the crossing before the invasion. Starting with pilots making transoceanic flights, this process had become a custom for troops heading overseas. Kenneth touched the signatures of those men who he knew had died in service for America as he pictured each of their faces. He silently praised them and prayed for their families. Having just returned home, there were many men whose fate Kenneth did not yet know.

In the peacefulness of the Bender home, in the room where he had dreamed a child's dreams, he was suddenly overwhelmed. He had come from this serene place, and had gone so far away to fight for America's very life.

***

When Kenneth received letters from members of Company B over the years, he felt the highest compliment that could be paid to him was their saying that he was a good leader or that they would never forget him. He was so proud of them and knew he would never forget them, either.

Kenneth was offered a job in the FBI by J. Edgar Hoover, but turned it down, as he was looking forward to settling down and raising a family after over five years in the service. A friend in the FBI told Kenneth that being an agent and expecting a reasonable home life was unrealistic. Kenneth worked for the Veterans Administration in St. Paul for a while as an attorney in their claims division, and he then transferred to their Seattle office. While in Seattle, he enjoyed being close to his mother's sister Henrietta, her husband—former Minneapolis boxer Frank "Frankie" Gilman—and their two children. However, Kenneth didn't find the work very challenging. He decided to look at other options.

In 1947, Minneapolis Mayor Hubert Humphrey—who grew up in Doland, South Dakota, about two hours from Eureka—successfully advocated for a city ordinance that would lead to fines and jail sentences if companies discriminated in hiring based upon religion or race. He also appointed Amos Deinard, a blind Jewish lawyer, the year before, to the Mayor's Fair Employment Practices Commission, to, among other tasks, meet with CEOs of Minneapolis corporations as part of the Commission's efforts to end discrimination in the city. The concept of human rights was being discussed in Minneapolis and across the country. In 1948, at the Democratic National Convention, the future vice-president of the United States, Hubert Humphrey, supported the minority plank for the party's strong civil-rights agenda, urging fellow Democrats "to get out of the shadow of states' rights and walk forthrightly into the bright sunshine of human rights." The plank passed. The Southern states walked out.[176]

In 1949, Kenneth Bender moved to Minneapolis from Seattle after making contact with a friend who was with the Butler Brothers wholesale organization. They had a large warehouse in Minneapolis and approximately two hundred franchised Federated Stores. Kenneth heard they had an opening for a franchise on West Broadway in North Minneapolis and signed the papers. He figured this would be an exciting opportunity for him for the time being, and it would make a place for Joe to mingle with customers, which he so enjoyed doing. Joseph and Mary were planning on selling their general store in Eureka after David graduated from Eureka High School in 1949 and began attending classes at the University of Minnesota. Being closer to his parents and younger brother created a strong incentive for Kenneth to move to Minneapolis.

The Federated Stores supplied clothing for the whole family, plus domestic items such as fabric yardage on bolts, patterns, yarn, and sewing and knitting notions. Kenneth also provided uniforms

[176]www.findagrave.com, Amos Spencer Deinard; Iric Nathanson, MinnPost, "Into the Bright Sunshine—Hubert Humphrey's civil-rights agenda," www.minnpost.com (May 23, 2011); Alan Saeks, "When Law Firms Wouldn't Hire Jewish Lawyers," *American Jewish World* (July 31, 2015).

for neighboring religious schools and would measure and supply residents at the Veterans Home and other nursing homes to meet their clothing needs. Kenneth would happily drive the more than one-and-a-half-hour round trip to satisfy the veterans' requests, even if just for a small sale.

There were times during the winter at the Federated, because of the snow and cold weather, when the traffic along West Broadway, "The Avenue," was slight, and few customers came in. Kenneth would keep his spirits up by saying to himself, "Don't complain, Kenneth. At least there's no one shooting at you."

In 1954, Kenneth and a date attended the wedding of his date's friend, Evelyn. At the wedding, Kenneth met a captivating blue-eyed girl, who was a friend of his date and a very good dancer. Kenneth asked Frima Gordon to dance. They never went out with their wedding dates again.

Frima Gordon, high school graduation, 1947. *Author files.*

Within three months after cantaloupe a la mode at the St. Clair Sweet Shoppe in Frima's Highland Park neighborhood in St. Paul, coffee grogs and dancing at the Waikiki Room at the Nicollet Hotel in downtown Minneapolis, and long walks and talks, Kenneth and Frima were engaged.

Frima was a Jewish girl from a patriotic, hardworking, and warm family in St. Paul. Her father was a veteran of World War I and the son of Reverend Jacob Gordon, Minneapolis *shochet* and *moel*.[177]

Frima's father's brother, Rabbi Harold H. Gordon, was a different type of Jewish pioneer. Known as the Flying Jewish Chaplain during World War II, he had brought the Torah, sometimes on a dogsled, to American troops serving in remote regions of the world.[178] Frima's mother's family had changed their own last name at Ellis Island from Burch to Goldberg to sound more Jewish. They wanted fellow Jews to know who they were in their new homeland.[179]

Kenneth and Frima had a lot in common, including optimism, the ability to see humor in everyday life, dedication to family, patriotism, pride in their Judaism, love of each other, and appreciation of the little things — from a breathtaking sunset, to a perfectly ripe ear of sweet corn; from an amusing story that makes everyone laugh, to the radiant glow of the Sabbath candles on Friday night.

The boy from Eureka and the girl from St. Paul stood under the chupa together on August 15, 1954.

---

[177] A shochet is trained in humane killing of animals for food and a moel is trained in circumcision.

[178] Harold Gordon, *Chaplain on Wings: The Wartime Memoirs of Rabbi Harold H. Gordon* (Shengold 1981).

[179] Conversation between Minnie Goldberg Gordon and author.

Frima and Kenneth, wedding picture, August 1954. *Author files.*

CHAPTER 12
St. Louis Park, MN, 1969

I AM THE SECOND OF Kenneth and Frima Bender's two children. My name, Rebecca Ellen, "Rivka Esther" in Hebrew, is after my dad's two grandmas: Grandma Becky and Grandma Esther. I went right from being born at Midway Hospital in St. Paul to our newly built house in St. Louis Park, a suburb of Minneapolis. It was called "St. Jewish Park" by some, in and outside of Minnesota, due to the then disproportionate number of Jews living there.

Our dad was one of the few people in town granted a license to shoot muskrats within the city limits. Muskrats were St. Louis Park's bothersome, digging equivalent to South Dakota's gophers. Even though over the years we frequently had muskrat holes in our backyard abutting a pond, interestingly, our sharpshooting, decorated army veteran never shot one. He much preferred to invite my sister, Nancy, and me to watch him experiment with his woods and irons in the summer and fall as this former golf "luminary" hit old golf balls across — or into — Twin Lakes pond after a long day at the store.[180]

While growing up, I enjoyed reading, writing poetry, singing, playing piano and violin, and putting on plays with my sister at senior citizens' homes. The play performances involved the whole family, with our dad being the roadie, disassembling and assembling

[180] *Bismarck Tribune*, August 28, 1937, referencing Missouri Slope Golf Tournament.

props, and our mom packing costumes and helping us memorize scripts. The Torah teaches: "You shall rise before the aged and show deference to the old" (Leviticus 19:32). We were taught this principle early on, whether respecting and appreciating the wisdom of our family elders, or wanting to do a mitzvah (a good deed) for an older person we had never met.

I also tap danced and sang for the Christmas shows at the Minneapolis Shriners Children's Home and the Masonic Home for the Aged. My tap dancing teacher, Dick Erhardt, a former vaudevillian who used to be on the Orpheum Circuit with Bill "Bojangles" Robinson, was a Shrine Merrymaker. He organized the shows and invited his students to perform. The title of the shows didn't matter to me. I felt good knowing I was making people happy and thereby doing a mitzvah.

We celebrated all the major Jewish holidays as a family. For Rosh Hashanah (the Jewish New Year), my mom followed her mother's tradition of always having those assembled dip cut pieces of apple in honey and say a special prayer for everyone to have a Shana M'tukah (sweet year). Nancy and I had the privilege of picking the apples from our Haralson apple tree in the backyard. Rosh Hashanah begins the Ten Days of Repentance for Jews, during which time we are given the task of taking care of all of our sins that have affected others. I was taught that it isn't enough to pray to God regarding these matters or merely to ask a person for forgiveness. One must take affirmative steps to attempt to remedy the situation. With respect to sins against God, we are to repent, pray, and do charitable acts to avert the severity of God's decree.

The *machzor* (High Holiday prayerbook) that I grew up with paints picturesque images of God sitting on a throne and reviewing everyone's actions over the last year, and God being like a shepherd, watching his sheep pass one by one before him on the Day of Judgment. We recite in Hebrew, "*B'rosh Hashanah yikatevun, uv'yom tzom kippur yechatemun* [On Rosh Hashanah, it is written, and on Yom Kippur, it is sealed — our fate for the next year]." On Yom Kippur, from the time we are thirteen years old, we do not work and are to practice self-denial, which means no eating or drinking for twenty-four hours, from the sundown that begins the holiday to the sundown that ends it. There are many reasons given for fasting: it's part of the process of repentance for our sins, it helps us to connect with those less fortunate, it allows us to get closer to God, etc.

When I was growing up, I was impressed with the elderly members of my synagogue who took this direction to fast, found in Leviticus, so seriously. Prior to the High Holidays, the rabbis at our synagogue announced from the pulpit that if, for health reasons, a person could not physically fast, they should not. However, each year there was between one and three elderly congregants who fainted at my synagogue in the midst of the service due to their insistence on following this passage of the Bible despite warnings. After audible gasps from fellow worshipers, paramedics quietly arrived and took the fainters away in ambulances to get them hydrated. It was a dramatic show of faith to everyone, but especially to a young child.

Another memorable occurrence for me in later years demonstrated the close connection between Jewish tradition and love of family. I overheard a conversation between my mom and her dad, my zada Sam, on Yom Kippur. Our zada was living with us at the time.[181] After services, my mom was preparing lunch for her dad, who needed to eat food with some of his medications on this fast day. I heard him say, "Frim, I feel bad that you are having to make me food when you are fasting."

My mom responded, "Do you remember when I was little and we would go to Yom Kippur services at Bucka Hall in St. Paul?"

"Sure," said my zada.

"Do you remember taking me down the street to get a malt at the drugstore because I was too young to fast, and sitting with me while I drank it, and you were fasting?"

"Yes," said my zada.

"Well," my mom continued, "I never got to really thank you for that before today." Then I saw them hug each other.

---

[181]Baba is grandmother in Yiddish, and Zada is grandfather. I always called my grandparents on my dad's side Grandpa (Joe) and Grandma (Mary), and my grandparents on my mom's side, Zada (Sam) and Baba (Minnie).

When the holiday of Chanukah (the Festival of Lights) occurred, from a young age, Nancy and I would take turns picking out which colored candles we wanted to place in the menorah.[182] We would stand before the dancing flames with our arms around each other and our parents, reciting the blessings over the candles and then singing Chanukah songs. We played the *dreydle* (a spinning top) game, which is traditional for this holiday. When the Greek Syrians occupied Israel over two thousand years ago (165 BCE), defiled the Temple in Jerusalem, and passed laws outlawing the study of Torah, the Jewish children—who continued their learning despite the ban—would have small tops ready to play with. When patrols would come around to check adherence to the law, after hiding their Bible texts, the children would show them their dreydles. These tops were used by the children to try to convince the patrols that they were just playing, not receiving Bible instruction.

Though Chanukah occurred during the same season as Christmas, and gift-giving became a part of the Chanukah holiday for many Jewish families, our family was not into the material gifts that much. I recall my favorite gift from my sister was the royal blue and lime-green slippers made out of washcloths with yarn pom-poms that she had made in her seventh grade home economics class. I also recall my favorite Chanukah present from my baba and zada when I was a little girl was a baby doll that looked like me. In high percentage Swedish and Scandinavian Minnesota in the late 1950s and early 1960s, it was difficult to find a baby doll that had brown eyes and brown hair. I was convinced my baba and zada could move mountains when I opened the box, lifted up the doll and her brown eyes opened.

On one Chanukah, my mom—the high score holder and most-games-over-200 winner in the Adath Jeshurun Synagogue (our synagogue) Couples Bowling League—was surprised when she was given a personalized turquoise and white swirly bowling ball by her

[182]What some refer to as the Chanukah menorah is also called a Hanukiah. It is a candelabra with places for eight candles, one for each night of Chanukah, and one additional place for a shamash (a candle used to light the other candles).

partner, my dad. Unfortunately, our house was burglarized a few years later, and the only thing of value taken by the burglar was my mom's personalized ball. We tried to make the best of the situation, chuckling together at the image of a burly man going to bowl with his friends and taking out his turquoise ball with the name "Frima" engraved in gold. Frima never wanted another bowling ball, despite my dad's offer to buy her another one. She said, "There are plenty of bowling balls at the alley that I can use."

Hands-down, my favorite Jewish holiday was and is Passover. The themes of freedom and new beginnings, mixed with good food and family, make a perfect eight days. We had Passover Seders the first two nights of the holiday. We, together with family, told the story of the Israelites' exodus from slavery in Egypt, reading from the Hagadah, the book that tells the story. Seder means order, and the dinner has a particular order for explaining the meaning of the holiday to those assembled.

The youngest person at the Seder table who could learn Hebrew always got the honor of chanting the four questions in Hebrew. The chant begins with the question, "What makes this night different from all other nights?" Nancy and I loved learning the Hebrew and recited it proudly when we were little. At the end of the meal, the head of the household hid the Afikomen, the middle matzah from a stack on the table. The children would then all go looking for it, as the leader needed everyone to have a piece of this middle matzah before concluding the meal and saying the Grace After Meals. When the Seders were at my baba and zada's house or at our parents', all children shared equally in the reward of finding the Afikomen. At my parents' home, those rewarded usually received his or her own box of Kosher for Passover fruit slices or chocolate lollipops. At my baba's and zada's, the reward was always a new, crisp dollar bill, which my zada Sam had procured at the bank as a prized gift for each of his grandchildren.

On Passover, our mom packed special lunches for us to eat at grade school, as we couldn't eat any food with yeast that had risen.

This tradition recalled the haste with which the Israelites had to flee Egyptian slavery, so when they made bread along the way for sustenance, they did not take time for it to rise prior to baking. The eight-egg, fluffy-on-top and *gedicht*-on-the-bottom Passover popovers were delicious with anything, be it tuna salad, chicken salad, hard cheese, etc.[183] Our mom also poured boiling Passover jello and pudding in white Styrofoam cups for us to eat at school in our lunch. It seemed magical to me, that I would take the aluminum foil off the cup, and inside was my special Passover treat. But best of all was the note from our mom that she placed in our brown paper bags. It was a bit of a let-down to go back to the school lunches when the eight days of Passover were over.

Our family's annual weeklong family car trips in the summer were carefully planned by our mom, with the aid of AAA motel guides—an attached coffee shop and an outdoor pool were a winning combination—and numerous brochures. It wasn't unusual for our dad, on his vacation from the long hours at the Federated Store, to happily drive five hundred or six hundred miles a day so we could see the sights. We learned all the lyrics to one of our dad's old army marching songs, "This is the Army, Mr. Jones," by Irving Berlin, on one such car trip:

> This is the Army, Mr. Jones!
> No private rooms or telephones
> You had your breakfast in bed before
> But you won't have it there anymore
>
> Do what the buglers command
> They're in the army and not in a band[184]

Nancy and I visited the mountains and glaciers of Banff, Canada, where our parents had honeymooned twelve years earlier, and rode the repainted World War II amphibious Army Ducks in the Wisconsin Dells, originally used at Normandy to move troops in

[183]Gedicht is a Yiddish word for a dense food

[184]"This Is The Army, Mr. Jones" by Irving Berlin © Copyright 1942 by Irving Berlin © Copyright Renewed © Copyright Assigned the Trustees of the God Bless America Fund International Copyright Secured All Rights Reserved Reprinted by Permission

1944, and in 1965, when I was seven, traveled for the first time to our dad's hometown of Eureka, South Dakota, and the Jewish Homesteaders Cemetery in Ashley, North Dakota, which left a lasting impression on me.

There was a common denominator with all of our trips over the years. No matter where we went, we would always bring back a little souvenir or treat for our grandparents, for the clerks at the Federated Store, and for my dad's friend Jim Nelson, who were "holding down the fort at the Store" so our dad could vacation with us. Witnessing our parents thinking of others became such an ingrained part of Nancy's and my lives that—like a route that is taken so often on an unpaved road—our wheels still naturally move right back to those familiar grooves.

In 1969, something happened that took us off our typical path. One of my dad's mother's six sisters, Aunt Claire, had worked in the

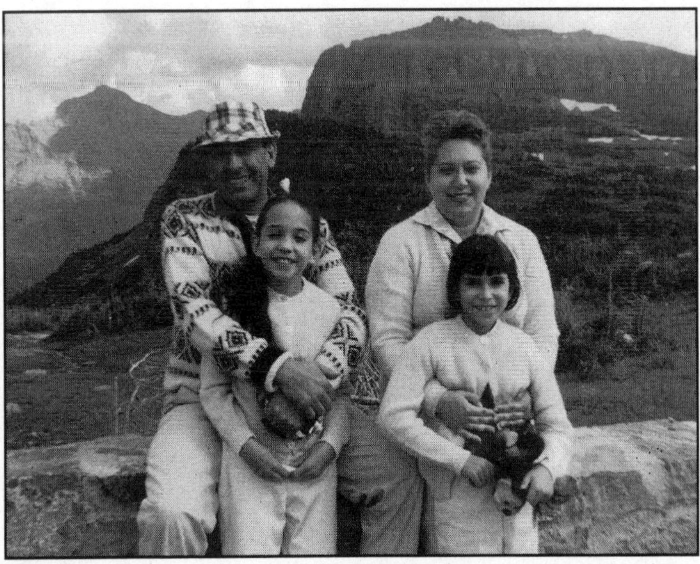

Kenneth and Frima, Nancy (at left) and Rebecca at Banff, Alberta, Canada, 1966. *Author files.*

movie industry in Hollywood for years. She had been particularly involved with assisting in developing the careers of actors Freddie Bartholomew (best known for his lead roles in Little Lord Fauntleroy and Captains Courageous) and Deana Durban (an actress who started her career as a child star, well known for her amazing soprano vocal range). Aunt Claire heard of Nancy's and my performing experience and one day called our dad long-distance with a question. At that time, she was the personal secretary to Universal Pictures producer Ross Hunter. "Keva, would your girls be interested in trying out for a movie being filmed in Minneapolis?" she asked. "I sure think they would, but let me ask them, and I'll call you back," my dad replied.

"If they are, Mr. Hunter will be in Minneapolis scouting out locations next week. I told him about Nancy and Rebecca and he would like to meet them. They would play two sisters, Robbie and Libby Bakersfield, who are Burt Lancaster's character's daughters," Aunt Claire continued.

Needless to say, we were excited. We met Ross Hunter at the Curtis Hotel, and he asked us about our hobbies and our pet turtle. Aunt Claire called that night: "Keva, they got the parts! Ross was very impressed with them. I will let you know when their scenes will be filmed. George Seaton, who directed *Miracle on 34th Street* will be directing the picture. The name of the movie is *Airport*."

We soon read in the newspaper that the crew for *Airport* was in town. Then our dad got a call from Aunt Claire one evening, when he had just gotten home from work. "Keva, bad news. All the scenes at the Minneapolis airport are being filmed from 10 p.m. until morning, when there aren't many people around the airport. We just learned that Minnesota's child labor laws are not favorable for child actors. Children under eighteen are not allowed to work during these hours. We are going to have to recast their parts, and shoot the scenes in Hollywood with California actresses. I'm so sorry."[185]

Our mom and dad gave us hugs and told us they knew we would have done a great job in the movie. Though we were disappointed, it

[185]The girl who was cast in "my" part was Lisa Gerritsen, who ended up playing the character of "Bess," "Phyllis's daughter" on the Mary Tyler Moore Show.

was an early lesson in how even minor potential fame can be fleeting. Our family was right there with us, offering support as usual. We returned to our school homework and our childhood activities — from piano lessons (always preceded by a homemade snack) with Fanny Miller Brudnoy, our dad's first cousin who grew up in Hillsview, South Dakota, to ballet and tap, Nancy's and my respective favorite dance lessons.

Summers at White Bear Lake, where my grandparents Baba Minnie and Zada Sam Gordon had a seasonal cottage, were greatly anticipated after working hard on our studies during the school year. White Bear Lake for us was synonymous with love, fun, patriotism and Judaism — all combined. Nancy and I would spend time with our first cousins — Sandee, David, and Jimmy — choreographing swim routines between races in the lake, fishing from the wooden rowboat or the dock with droplines and worms we'd dig up from the yard, looking for interesting rocks on the shore, and singing songs from a huge pile of sheet music, accompanied by our mom or baba on the slightly out-of-tune piano. Our chores of taking off the shutters in the spring and putting them back on in the fall, sweeping the steps, weeding the gardens, or bailing out the rowboat with a big yellow sponge and an old coffee can on a yardstick never really seemed like work. The neighbors' stories of summers before we were born were always a source of entertainment for us, too — "We would go to your grandparents' cottage to get your mother whenever anyone lost anything in the lake. Your mom would change into her bathing suit and dive for it until she found it — from a child's dropped shoe to a wedding ring!"

When we stayed overnight at the cottage, our dad would drive an hour one way to come out after work and leave before dawn to get back to work so we could have dinner and time together. In addition to our dad's sleep sacrifice to spend as much time as possible with family, we saw our grandparents and mom working hard cleaning and fixing up the old cottage and the rowboat and cleaning and frying up the fish we caught, so we could all have a good time. We observed altruism in action, as our zada would come over and turn

Clockwise from Rebecca (the girl with the braids), Cousins Sandra and David, Zada Sam, Nancy, and Cousin Jim at White Bear Lake, 1966. *Author files.*

on a lamp for us while we were reading or push up a footstool when we were sitting or lead us with an industrial flashlight if we were walking from the cottage to the car at night, always with the same valediction, "Drive carefully! Give us a call when you get home" (though this request meant he would have to stay up an hour more to go to sleep).

Homemade cheese knishes made by my baba in the tiny kitchen never tasted as good as they did at the lake.[186] When Shabbat (Hebrew for Sabbath) came along on Friday night, it was always observed with homemade *challah* (bread), *gefilte* fish made from fish we had

[186]A cheese knish is a farmers cheese and onion mixture covered with a sour cream dough, baked, and oftentimes served with sour cream on top.

caught, and traditional blessings over the candles, grape juice, and bread.[187] If the adults didn't want the children to hear something they were discussing, they would speak in Yiddish. But as Nancy and I got older, we started to pick up on some key phrases: *makhn zikh nisht visndik* (ignore what is happening), *giv a keek* (take a look), and *fabissen* (a sour person). We kids even joined in our baba and zada's favorite Yiddish expression: *Ess gezunterhai*t (Eat in good health)!

Our baba and zada's attitude was always the more the merrier, and when aunts, uncles, and cousins from both sides of the family would come to visit, we'd squeeze onto the long white benches of the oversized picnic table and eat and laugh together. There was always enough food in storage for whoever would appear. Carefully labeled aluminum foil wrapped goodies—from homemade beef *prachas* (cabbage rolls) to *kugels* (noodle puddings)—were quickly defrosted and ready to be served. Jars of home-canned pickles, pickled beets, and cinnamon applesauce were opened and instantly devoured. Our baba and zada, Civil Defense Neighborhood captains during World War II, had a sizable Victory Garden next to their house in St. Paul during the war years. Through the shortages experienced during this time period, they had learned the art of growing a variety of vegetables and fruits and canning them successfully.

Our Baba Minnie had also become the go-to first-aid expert at the lake for injuries large and small. With rubbing alcohol and sterilized tweezers, she could remove a portion of an old fishing hook or a wood dock splinter from anyone's heel with nary an infection on her watch. If you were under twelve years old, she would let you wind her 1920s musical metal powderpuff box and listen to the tinkling music during the operation.

Fourth of July at White Bear Lake started with our zada, who was Commander of Jewish War Veterans Post #162, getting out the large American flag from the house and carrying it up the many steps to display it near the road. Then was the little Birchwood parade, a parade that allowed in any child or adult before or during the

[187]Gefilte fish is ground, deboned fish, mixed with eggs, matzoh meal, and various seasonings, boiled in fish stock, and oftentimes served with horseradish and carrots.

Frima with Baba Minnie working in the Victory Garden in their St. Paul yard, 1944. *Author files.*

parade. Dinner was kosher hamburgers expertly barbecued by our uncle Bob to each person's specifications in the old stone barbeque pit, followed by my mom's sister Josephine Berg's traditional, ornately-decorated firecracker cake. We would watch fireworks across the lake from the community dock and our cousins' "private display" in the backyard. July fifth was the traditional counting of the most mosquito bites.

When Nancy and I would catch bullheads at the lake (almost always under the dock as dusk fell), we knew that they were bullheads even before we pulled them out of the water. They would strike suddenly on our droplines, and then feel like an inanimate heavy winter boot as we started to pull up our lines. We also knew they were not kosher and would not be accepted by our baba for cooking, but we came to know who in the neighborhood would like them. Our dad used to call the area of cottages where our baba and zada lived "a little United Nations." The Henry Ruchies (pronounced "Rooshe") were first generation Italian. Mr. Ruchie was a gifted woodworker, whose steps leading up to his home were adorned with his wooden creations—from children, to birds, to pinwheels—that all moved and danced with the wind. Mrs. Wilkinson was first generation Scottish, with a brogue thicker than fog over White Bear Lake in the early morning. They were our best customers for the bullheads. Mrs. Wilkinson would always thank us for bringing a bullhead to her, and as she went to get her pliers to take the fish off the hook she'd always say, "Fry them in butter; it's like the finest steak." Mr. Ruchie would call to his wife, saying, "*I nipoti Gordon ci ha portato la cena* [The Gordon grandchildren brought us dinner]," and then he would tell us to give regards to our baba and zada.

But once there was a fish issue of biblical proportions. Our Uncle Bob and Cousin David saw a huge fish floating in the lake. It had apparently been hit by a boat propeller, but appeared clean and fresh. They proudly brought it up to the cottage, so our Baba Minnie could prepare it for dinner. Minnie pulled out a large piece of aluminum foil and set the fish on top of the foil on the kitchen table. She examined it carefully on one side, and then flipped it to the other side for further inspection. She then lowered her glasses down on her nose, to study the fish without the aid of her glasses, and then reset her glasses where they had been. "I need to speak with Zada about this," she said, and left Uncle Bob and David puzzled in the kitchen. She and my zada then discussed whether a fish discovered dead, the victim of a boat motor, was considered kosher under Jewish law.

They turned to their worn cottage copy of the Tanakh (Five Books of Moses, Prophets and other Writings) and opened to the book of Leviticus, which lists the prohibitions regarding eating certain foods. Leviticus 22:8 provides: "That which dies of itself, or is torn of beasts, he shall not eat to defile himself therewith: I am the Lord." My zada said, "It clearly died before it was caught, so I believe this passage applies and we can't eat it."

My baba said, "But it didn't die of itself; it was killed by a boat motor of a person." After some more analysis, they reached the decision that the fish should not be eaten and should be buried at the bottom of the yard. They went back to explain the decision to Uncle Bob and David, who accepted it, got a shovel, and together headed down to the bottom of the yard to follow Baba and Zada's instructions.

No one thought more of it until the following morning. We were all eating breakfast when our Jewish neighbor Mr. Sobol appeared at the screen door, and as he entered, said, "Good morning, everyone!"

"Good morning, Mr. Sobol," said my baba and zada. (Every adult at the lake in the 1960s, even neighbors, were always referred to as Mr. and Mrs., rather than by their first names.)

"I had a wonderful meal last night, and I will again tonight," said Mr. Sobol.

"Good for you, neighbor!" said my zada.

Mr. Sobol continued, "I had the best fish I've ever had."

"We're happy for you!" said my baba, a little perplexed. Mr. Sobol continued with a story worthy of Sholem Aleichem.[188]

"I overheard your discussion about the fine fish you found floating in the lake while I was mowing my lawn. I watched you bury the

---

[188]Solomon Naumovich Rabinovich, known as Sholem Aleichem, was a well-known Yiddish humorist, who wrote stories and plays. His tale, "Tevye the Dairyman," was the basis for the play *Fiddler on the Roof.*

fish at the bottom of your yard and waited for you to go back up to your cottage. I brought a shovel down, dug up the fish, washed it off and prepared it for dinner. It was delicious, and we have enough left over for tonight. It was foolish of you to throw away such a fine fish."

"We are glad you enjoyed it," said my zada. After Mr. Sobol left, there was silence. Then my baba simply stated, "He interpreted the Bible differently," and we continued eating our breakfast.

I was more fortunate than many, as I had doting grandparents on both sides whom I loved dearly and admired. My sweet grandma Mary Bender had a gentle manner that disguised how strong and tough she could be, a quality my dad inherited. She would happi-

Baba Minnie and Zada Sam Gordon taking time out from repairing the cement around the summer cottage to dance to Lawrence Welk band music coming from the TV, 1973. *Author files.*

ly read stacks and stacks of books of our choice to Nancy and me while babysitting. When I was three years old, she bought us the soaring Percy Faith instrumental "Theme From A Summer Place" on a 45 record to play on our little silver metal record player. When Grandma Mary was knocked down by a robber while walking home from the downtown Minneapolis bus and her purse was stolen with the proceeds of her cashed Social Security check, she didn't let this incident stop her. She continued to take the bus downtown to purchase matching dresses for Nancy and me, oftentimes in yellow, her favorite color, "like the sunshine."

Though my grandma Mary passed away when I was young and in the fourth grade—while I was working on a "stained glass window" with different colors of thin tissue paper so the sunshine could shine through—I still remember the feeling of being near her, the peaceful calm. My grandma's death was my first experience with forever losing the physical presence of someone I loved. Near the end of her life, when she was in a nursing home, Nancy and I would visit to sing and recite poems for her, and every Sunday afternoon my dad would pick her up and bring her to our house for cheese blintzes.

After the funeral, as is Jewish custom, we returned to my grandma Mary and grandpa Joe's home to sit Shiva, where caring family and friends had prepared food for the immediate family. Though cheese blintzes with sour cream had always been one of my favorite foods, as well as one of my grandma's, when everyone sat down to eat, I refused to eat and went to sit on the radiator, facing away from the table. I was angry with the people I didn't know who were smiling and laughing. Didn't they realize that my grandma should have been at that table?

My mom saw me and asked me if I was going to the table to eat. I told her that I wasn't hungry, that I didn't want to eat, and that everyone should be sad, instead of smiling and happy. She explained to me that part of Judaism is focusing on life and the living. "We are sad now, and that is OK, but the reason why the family is brought a meal is to remember that Grandma Mary would want you to go on, to eat, to smile again. She knows that she will always be in your heart,

Nancy, Rebecca, Kenneth, and Grandpa Joe at Passover Seder, 1967.
Author files.

but she wants you to keep enjoying life and doing good deeds. Think back to how her seeing you happy could make her smile."

My mom gently took my hand and we sat at the table together and ate cheese blintzes. And I gave a little smile. Though it has been over fifty years since my grandma passed away, when I happen to hear "Theme From A Summer Place" on the radio, I immediately think of her.

I also have strong and fond memories from my youth of listening to my grandpa Joe Bender, with his Russian accent, talking to my dad in the front seat of our car while I was riding in the back. I always found listening to them talk much more interesting than listening to the radio. I learned about my grandpa Joe's meeting Gorky in the Odessa bakery, shaking hands with Herzl, being stranded in Antwerp, and farming in North Dakota from these precious rides. He more specifically referred to his homestead as being in "Nort Dakota," as the "th" sound is not found in Russian, Yiddish, or Hebrew.

* * *

A new building in St. Louis Park was built to house the Talmud Torah (Hebrew School) in the 1970s. Several years after Grandma Mary passed away, Grandpa Joe married Rae Feldman, a widowed housemother at a Jewish fraternity on the University of Minnesota campus, and they moved to St. Louis Park. Lucky for me, their condominium was right across the parking lot from the new Hebrew School. This provided me with a great opportunity to see Grandpa Joe for regular, albeit brief, visits. When I was attending Talmud Torah after school and on Sundays, we had a ten-minute break between the first and second hour of classes.

I would take off at high speed as soon as the bell rang, running out the door, across the parking lot, up the half-circle drive of the condo, to buzz my grandpa to open the door. He, Rae, and I would visit for about five minutes, have a little snack together for three minutes, give each other a quick hug, and I would run back to Hebrew School with my grandpa Joe's admonition to "learn a lot!" and *"Go Gezunterhait* [Go in good health]!" still fresh in my ears. If I was slightly late on a couple of occasions, I told the teacher I was visiting my grandfather across the parking lot, and that was always an excused tardy. I came back to class extolling the virtues of my little visits so much that several of my girlfriends, whose grandparents had passed away or lived out of town, requested to go with me to visit Grandpa and Rae.

Growing up, I was also blessed with a wonderful sister and role model. Nancy, two years older, never focused on what she could do that I could not. Instead, she respected and appreciated what I could do (including making her laugh) and supported my interests, even when they diverged from her own. As I grew, she took me to my new schools and showed me around, helped me pick classes and told me which teachers to seek and which to avoid, and found the same enjoyment that I did in our endless violin and flute duets. She and I had matching good taste in television shows: first the *Patty Duke Show*, then *Gidget*, then *Bewitched*, *The Flying Nun*, and the best of them all, *That Girl*, with Marlo Thomas. We both enjoyed taking our miniature turtles for walks in the grass of our yard and feeding them lettuce and kosher hamburger in their yellow plastic home, complete with palm tree. Nancy worked harder than anyone I ever knew of our age in school and Hebrew School, and her A pluses and Alef pluses (the equivalent of an A plus for Hebrew School, as Alef is the first letter of the Hebrew alphabet) were living proof of the theory that hard work pays off. If there was one cookie or piece of cake left, we always tried to give the other sister the larger piece once it was divided. It was (and is) a mutual admiration society between us, fostered by our parents, who cherished both of us. When Nancy married Barry Kelner years later, it was kindness and support squared.

Nancy and I were also blessed with loving aunts, uncles, great-aunts, great-uncles, and many cousins. Our sixteen first cousins, whom we would visit or who would visit us, shared in special simchas or everyday fun: the St. Paul Bergs; the Saskatoon, Saskatchewan, Bernbaums; and the California Benders, Ellisons, and Plachtes. Our parents enjoyed having the family over for our mom's multi-course, traditional Jewish meals. In between dusting our mom's china teacup collection prior to the guests' arrival, Nancy and I would take repeat trips into our pink and turquoise kitchen to enjoy the special snack of hot *gribenes* — right out of the frying pan —little pieces of chicken skin fried in oniony *schmaltz* (rendered chicken fat).

When I was growing up, there was a wide range of observance levels in the Twin Cities Jewish community. They could be easily seen by anyone perusing the pages of the *American Jewish World (AJW)*, the 11 x 14 inch, 25-plus-page weekly newspaper primarily for Jews living in Minneapolis, St. Paul, and suburbs. Around Rosh Hashanah, Chanukah, or Passover, the Jewish and non-Jewish ad-

Nancy and Barry's pre-wedding photo, under chuppah at Adath Jeshurun Synagogue, Minneapolis, MN, 1980.
Copyright Al's Photography, Allen Wuori.

vertisers increased, all wishing Hag Sameach (Happy Holiday) to "our friends and patrons." But while some, like Brochins Delicatessen, advertised kosher products — schmaltz, *kishka* (stuffed mixture of flour, onions, carrots, and chicken fat in beef casings), and corned beef — others like Farnhams Coffee House in St. Paul, boasted its "golden-tender shrimp," though shellfish is forbidden to be eaten by observant Jews. Even at our synagogue on Shabbat, different levels of observance could be seen. Our family and most others drove to services, about five miles from our home, while others who lived closer, or even the same distance, walked.[189] And no one at the time seemed to mind this diversity within our faith.

The political views expressed in editorials and letters to the editor in the 1960s were generally much more uniform, with support for equal rights for all races and religions, concern about the treatment of fellow Jews in Russia, vigilance against anti-Semitism, and remembrance of those who perished in the Holocaust.

No matter one's level of observance, Jewish families in Minnesota seemed to all submit information regarding their family's milestones — births, bar and bat mitzvahs, graduations, weddings, and deaths — to the *AJW.* And we all took note of these events and talked about them. Reading the *Jewish World* in my early years gave my suburban neighborhood a modern day shtetl-feel.

When you add in to all of this — Nancy and I going to drive-in movies in the back seat of our parents' car in pajamas, waiting on the step that led up to our front door in our matching red canvas tennis shoes with white rubber toes to get an orange push-up from the ice cream man's truck that frequented our big baby-boomer-population neighborhood, running after fireflies in our lawn at night, and my sister's and my stand (infamous in our neighborhood, though not particularly successful), selling lemonade as well as salamanders

---

[189]The Bible forbids doing work on the Sabbath (Commandment eight of the Ten Commandments, Leviticus 23:3, etc.) or lighting a fire, e.g. sparking and/or burning fuel (Exodus 35:3). These admonitions, alone or together, result in Orthodox Jews and some Conservative Jews walking to services on the Sabbath or a Holy Day, rather than driving their cars.

that fell into our window wells—it would rightfully seem like an almost entirely blissful childhood. It would probably even be difficult to imagine a challenge that would have arisen in my life during that time.

However, there was an early challenge of faith that I faced.

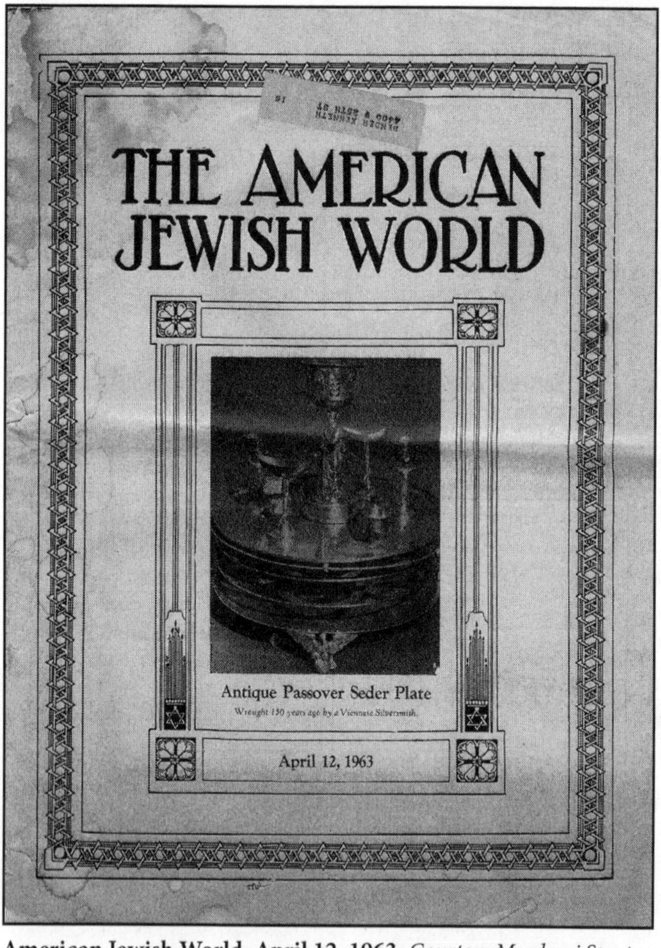

American Jewish World, April 12, 1963. *Courtesy Mordecai Spector, AJW Editor and Publisher, author files.*

CHAPTER 13
St. Louis Park, MN, 1971

THE EARLIER GENERATIONS OF immigrants from any country, let alone those fleeing the murders of their people and those fighting in a World War, obviously have the more dramatic and life-altering experiences. The Jewish immigrants were no exception to this general rule. However, some may say that the pressures of assimilation that are consciously and subconsciously felt by the subsequent generations, interacting regularly with more people of different faiths, make maintaining Jewish identity and living a Jewish life in a modern society even more challenging.

There was a sense among many Eastern European Jewish immigrants in the early 1900s that maintaining one's religion and culture was important, though being a true American meant learning to quickly speak and write English rather than Yiddish. There was also a practical aspect to this desire, as obtaining jobs and encouraging children to succeed in school required that English be learned. Though over two million Jews immigrated to the United States between 1880 and 1924 with a rich Jewish culture of Yiddish language, music, books, and plays, "[they] were among the fastest of all immigrant groups to drop their native tongue." In the 1940 Census, the government attempted to measure the numbers of both second and third generation immigrants speaking their Old World language. Of eighteen different immigrant populations, Yiddish did not fare well; it was fifteenth out of eighteen.[190]

The challenges to my faith and desire to live a Jewish life while growing up were clearly nothing compared to the life and death situations faced by my ancestors. Only in hindsight do I recognize that significant changes were occurring and that pressures to assimilate existed. I was too young and then too busy living my life to analyze it critically as it was happening. I didn't understand most of the Yiddish my grandparents occasionally spoke, but I didn't sense that the culture associated with that language was slipping away. Yiddish was not a class offered at the Hebrew School that Nancy and I attended, and I was not aware of any discussion regarding its inclusion.

I saw the stacks of 78 records with Yiddish songs sitting unused in my grandparents' record cabinet. But my baba and zada were not often cranking up the old Victrola phonograph to play their older American records on the green felt turntable, either. The difference was that Yiddish music at the time could only be heard on these old records, unless one happened to attend a concert where Yiddish music was performed. On the other hand, we were hearing American popular music, old and new, on radio stations and on television every day.

Though the Eastern European Yiddish cultural influences were fading, thanks to our parents and grandparents my sister Nancy and I grew up immersed in Jewish learning and Jewish traditions in America. We prayed at the synagogue, celebrated Jewish holidays, had Sabbath meals together with our family, attended Hebrew School after school and on Sundays, prepared and ate Jewish foods, kept kosher, played Jewish songs on the piano, read books with Jewish topics, went to the synagogue to recite prayers to honor the memories of family members who had passed away, etc. We also were typical young girls in America, proud of our country, celebrating American holidays—Halloween, Veterans Day, Thanksgiving, New Year's Eve,

---

[190]Miriam Weinstein, Yiddish: A Nation of Words (South Royalton, Vt: Steerforth Press, 2001), cited in Sherry Mayrent, "Why Listen to Scratchy Old 78s?" 2016, klezmeracademy.com/blog/2016/9/23/why-listen-to-scratchy-old-78s.

Abraham Lincoln's birthday, Valentine's Day, George Washington's birthday, the 4th of July—watching popular TV shows, singing with songs on the radio, and attending public school in the St. Louis Park school district.

The night of Thanksgiving, after our family get-together, Nancy and I also enjoyed bundling up in coats, hats, scarves, and mittens to walk with the throngs viewing the annual Christmas windows at Dayton's Department Store in downtown Minneapolis. We were fascinated by the mechanical moving figures in the North Pole workshop and the reindeer landing on the rooftops, and we thoroughly discussed with each other the rationale for our individual favorite window-picks. The fact that we didn't share the religious beliefs of most of our fellow fog-breathing observers seemed irrelevant. If a stranger greeted us with "Merry Christmas," we knew it was coming from a warm place, and responded reciprocally, "Merry Christmas." Our attendance at this Christmas-themed event had no impact on our beliefs, and we never would have considered bringing any Christmas decorations into our home.

In 1973, when I was about fifteen years old, the daughter of one of my mother's first cousins was marrying a fellow who was not born Jewish. Some older family members would not attend, even though the groom had converted to Judaism, fearing that the children would not be raised Jewish. Our parents told us that though Jews do not seek out non-Jews to convert, as long as this fellow had done this of his own free will, we would attend to support the bride, the marriage, and the family. After the ceremony at the synagogue and a dinner in the social hall, a band started playing for dancing. The twenty-year-old brother of the groom promptly walked over to our table to ask me to dance, and I found myself dancing with him as the rest of my table (including my parents) pretended to focus on eating their chocolate *rugelach*.[191] When the groom's brother called to ask me out after the wedding, I told him the truth, which was that I didn't go out on dates yet. In hindsight, my exposure to this Christian boy at

[191] Rugelach is a traditional Jewish pastry with a triangle of dough wrapped around fruit or other ingredients, forming a crescent shape.

a family wedding at that age would probably not have even occurred several generations before.

Researchers have attempted to gather statistical evidence of the pressures of maintaining Jewish identity through analyzing the ever-increasing assimilation rates by Jews in the United States (a product of marriage outside of the faith, people not feeling that they are Jewish though they were born Jewish, people not raising their children Jewish, etc.). In 1970, only 17 percent of Jews married outside the faith. The Pew Research Center's Religion and Public Life Project in 2013 found that as of that date, thirty-three years later, 58 percent of all Jews intermarry, two-thirds do not belong to a synagogue, one-fourth do not believe in God, and one-third had a Christmas tree in their home. The Pew Study also found that though 4.2 million American adults say their religion is Judaism, about 1.1 million more say that though they were raised Jewish or have a Jewish parent, they're atheist, agnostic, or "nothing in particular." The study concluded that this was a significant increase of unaffiliated Jews from the time of the National Jewish Population Survey in 2000.[192]

Though not directly related to my Judaism, the first personal challenge of faith I recall did test my Jewish compass. It came upon me in an unusual time and place: Fern Hill Grade School, during the 1969–1970 school year. Fern Hill was one of those many red brick grade schools that popped up around the country in the early 1950s, when the baby boomers were ready for kindergarten. Over seven hundred students in twenty-one classrooms attended Fern Hill in St. Louis Park, Minnesota, whose playground was on filled-in

---

[192]Pew Research Center, "Portrait of Jewish Americans" (September 30, 2013). For every survey taken, there are proclaimed flaws with the research, and the Pew Study is no exception. In J.J. Goldberg, "Pew Survey About Jewish America Got it All Wrong" (October 18, 2013), the author, inter alia, explains that in 2000, the National Jewish Population Survey did not include interviewees with "weak Jewish connections," resulting in a disappearance in that study of Jews who claimed they did not follow a religion. As the Pew Study in 2013 included these previously excluded persons, it then looked as if many people considered Jewish were abandoning their religion at an astonishing rate. As respondents to the United States Census may not be asked questions about their religion, the bottom line is that survey numbers on religion are always going to be extrapolated estimates.

swampland, with the usual fare of teeter-totters, slides, painted lines on the tar for hopscotch, and primary-colored swinging aluminum cast horses. I attended Fern Hill since kindergarten as a member of Mrs. Nelson's class, who got home just in time to watch *Lunch with Casey* on our black-and-white TV as I ate my cream cheese on white bread sandwich. (Casey was a railroad engineer who sang songs with Roundhouse Rodney and showed the Mighty Hercules cartoons.)

At Fern Hill, I was a Brownie (junior Girl Scout) with the neighborhood girls as we proudly wore our paper-bag-colored brown dresses with dark brown accenting belt and short orange ties and beanies on meeting days. At school, we students all shared the gleeful experience of seeing the "AV Man" wheel the projector in and hand a large reel of 16 mm film of an unknown subject to our teacher, meaning we were going to see a movie about something that day.

I received an A+ for my fifth-grade required bug collection at Fern Hill, making good use of one of my grandpa Joe Bender's old wooden cigar boxes, after running through the neighborhood with my classmates and our homemade pillowcase butterfly nets. There I also participated in the talent show in third grade, reciting Henry Wadsworth Longfellow's "Hiawatha's Childhood" by heart and then harmonizing with classmate Rachel on "Blowin' in the Wind," going up one major third on the second syllable of "answer" in the chorus.

My mom had been a room mother with my classmate Loren's mother in fourth grade. Loren's brother had graduated from St. Louis Park Schools and was a United States Marine killed in Vietnam. I remember when Loren returned to class after the funeral and was wearing a ripped black ribbon pinned to his shirt, following the Jewish tradition of Keriah, tearing one's garments after the death of a close family member as Jacob, David, and Job did in ancient times. Though I had never met Loren's brother, I remember crying when I heard the news.

I was in one of the three sixth-grade classrooms in 1969. My teacher, Mr. Nash, was one of the few male teachers in the school. He enjoyed acting out the poem, "Casey at the Bat," for our class, as if it was more intense than a Shakespearean soliloquy. That year, a new music teacher started. When the music teacher with bright red hair entered our classroom, Mr. Nash left the room for a break. A couple of the girls in my class started making fun of the new teacher, first with whispers and then right out loud. They didn't like her clothes, her haircut, the way she talked or looked. It snowballed until everyone in my class had joined forces with the same common goal: to not sing. They refused to respect her and decided they were better than she was. There was one student who would not follow the crowd down a path she knew was wrong: me. Despite our years of shared history, I intentionally separated myself from my classmates.

When the teacher wanted our class to sing, I sang. The teacher and I sang duets all year long. Hearing only the teacher's and my voice on "Water Come a Me Eye," even with the teacher strongly strumming on the autoharp, sounded very thin in the big classroom. When the principal came to check on our class, suddenly there was a huge crescendo and the class became a choir, but when he left, it was again the duet of the music teacher and I singing "The Sidewalks of New York" or "Born Free." In March of 1970, the music teacher asked to talk with me after school. Though she assumed that the students in my class would all sing at the upcoming Spring Concert once their parents were in the audience, she wanted to reward me for being the only student who sang in my class throughout the year. She wanted me to sing a solo at the concert. I had loved to sing for as long as I could remember.

Shortly after the music teacher's request of me, a classmate heard me practicing in the gym after school and asked what I was doing. I told him that I was going to sing a solo in the Spring Concert. Within a couple of days, a petition was being circulated, seeking to prohibit me from singing the solo. Many students thought it wasn't right that parents should have to sit and listen to one person sing, instead of the whole class. A number of teachers in the school also signed the petition. I ignored it as best I could, though it was hard to do. Walking home from school was oftentimes a challenge, with students blocking my way or throwing stones or snowballs. I tried to focus on the future, meeting new kids in seventh grade at the junior high.

About a week before the concert, the principal, Mr. Keeton, called my parents into his office. He asked them if they were aware of the petition. They told him they were. He urged them to tell me not to sing the solo. He commented, "Your allowing Rebecca to sing this solo could affect her for the rest of her life." Frima and Kenneth told Mr. Keeton that it would be up to me to decide.

I chose to sing. My parents bought me a new dress—white with bright flowers, a ruffle at the bottom, and a deep purple satin sash. I sang "Where is Love?" from the musical *Oliver!*, the very question that I had asked myself through this experience. My voice at the concert was weak at first, but then became stronger as I found my inner strength.

Afterwards, we went to the Lincoln Del, a family-owned Jewish neighborhood delicatessen in St. Louis Park, where I ordered one of my favorite desserts, hot apple pie a la mode, with cinnamon ice cream. While we were waiting for our treats, I remember that my Great-Uncle George Gordon, visiting from California, inquired if he could ask me a question. I agreed. Then he took a heavy gold pen out of his sport coat pocket, handed it to me, and asked if he could have the privilege of having me autograph his Spring Concert program. I proudly obliged.

The Fern Hill principal was right about one thing: my singing at the concert affected me the rest of my life. My standing strong—literally alone with a spotlight on me—when I knew in my heart that I was doing the right thing was a moment that gave my early life direction.

***

My grandpa Joe had a saying: "When you meet Johnny on the street, remember that you are no better than Johnny."[193] I never tolerated anything less from my own or others' behavior. This wasn't just a saying for my grandpa Joe. He walked the walk, too.

[193]Ellis Ellison taped interview with Joseph Bender (Phoenix, Arizona, 1970).

When I was about twelve years old, Nancy and I went to the downtown Minneapolis library with our mom to check out our weekly books. When I handed the librarian my library card to check out, he stated my name out loud, "Rebecca Bender," as if it were something miraculous. Then he looked up and said, "Are you related to Joe Bender?" I told the librarian that Joe Bender is my grandfather. "The Joe Bender who lived on Xerxes North?" he continued.

"Yes," I said. "1314 Xerxes." The gentleman motioned the people waiting behind us in line to another open line and reached under his desk to pull up his "Closed" sign on top of his desk.

"Do you have a minute?" he asked Nancy, my mom, and me. We all agreed that we did. He began to tell us a story.

"When I was a young boy, growing up on the Northside in the '50s and early '60s, my friends and I had trouble finding work. People didn't want to hire us because of our skin color. Your grandfather," he said, pointing at Nancy and me, "wanted to help us earn a little money to help our families. He was the first one who would hire us to caddie at the Jewish golf course, Brookview. Not only did he offer us the chance to caddy, he would pick up three or four of us, we would caddy at the club, and then he would bring us home. We earned some good money and were treated well. The non-Jewish country clubs didn't want anything to do with us. Pretty soon, I worked my way up to answering the phones at the club. When I graduated from North High, I went to college and became a librarian. So you see why I had to close my lane. Your grandfather is a great man. When you see him, tell him that Willie from the Northside who used to caddie for him is working at the library."[194] We promised we would and all gave him hugs.

***

[194]The predominantly Jewish Brookview Country Club was incorporated in 1947. Though people of any faith could join, it was formed because Jews were intentionally excluded from the other country clubs in town.

My strength as part of the Bender family was tested again several years after my decision to sing the solo. Our neighborhood was all beige and white houses, with an occasional red brick. My mom loved the colors in a sunset and the subtle shade differences found in roses. From an early age, under her tutelage, Nancy and I were referring to the color of the sky as cerulean blue and the sun as cadmium yellow. She was unique among many housewives in the Midwest in the 1950s in that she was reading magazines about what types and colors of homes people were building on the coasts. Our dad, having lived in Seattle after the war, had seen many walkout ramblers being built. Together, they designed and built their walkout rambler dream home, which was pink with purple shutters, overlooking a serene pond, with geese, ducks, and egrets. Our mom planted perennial bulbs and bushes to complement the colors in our home. Also, unlike most in the neighborhood, she weeded her gardens, planted the carefully selected flowers, and pruned her evergreens on her own.

Kenneth Bender did not sweat the small stuff. He had faced the big stuff as a young man in World War II. But shortly after the painter had finished putting a new coat of the pink paint on our home and the purple paint on the shutters, a letter arrived with no postage and numerous signatures. It was placed in our mail slot, and it fell right onto our cork den floor. It demanded that we change the color of our home. Our dad was mildly upset. Now to make it clear, these were not non-Jews who were seeking uniformity and control in their neighborhood. Almost all of our neighbors at the time were Jewish. Also, not all of our neighbors, Jewish or non-Jewish, signed the petition.

Our dad called a family meeting one night after dinner. He pointed out that Nancy and I were being taunted going to and from school because of the color of the house. I was sometimes forced to use my violin case as a battering ram when classmates blocked my path home. (Nancy's small flute and piccolo cases did not have the same defensive effect). He also reminded us of the number of times he and Mom had scrubbed off the raw eggs and shaving cream from our house on Halloween. He suggested that we take an anonymous vote on the question whether to keep or change the color. All four family members completed our ballots.

Kenneth started reading off the votes in his dramatic Eureka, South Dakota, declamation contest winner voice: "Vote number 1: keep the pink. Vote number 2: keep the pink. Vote number 3: keep the pink. Vote number 4: keep the pink. It's unanimous. We are keeping the pink!" We all hugged each other. It was more than agreeing to keep the pink. It was agreeing to be uncommon and creative, to not bow to pressure from others. It was an important lesson for Nancy and me.

I also refused to bow to a less obvious type of pressure at our Conservative synagogue in Minneapolis, the Adath Jeshurun, a

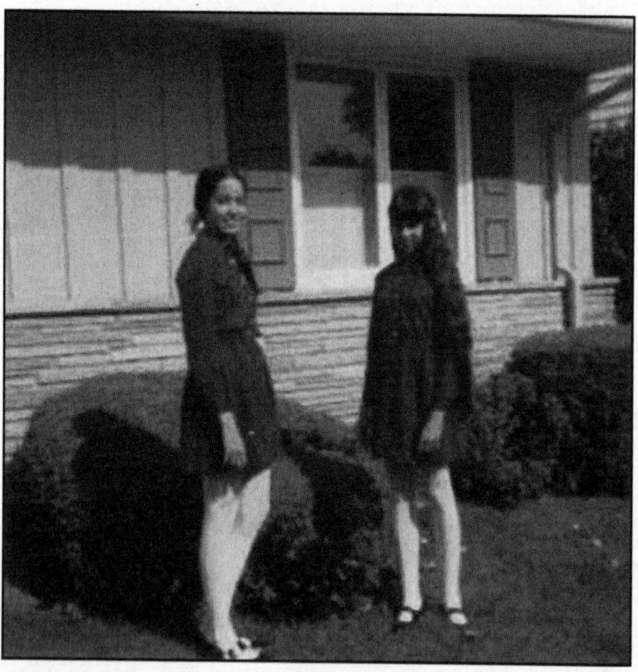

Nancy (at left) and Rebecca in front of the rambler house in St. Louis Park and one of Frima's rosebushes, 1972. *Author files.*

pressure within my own religion. There are three main branches or denominations of Judaism among Ashkenazi Jews: Reform (least traditional, making up around 35–38 percent of American Jews), Conservative (middle-ground traditional, making up around 18–33 percent of American Jews), and Orthodox (most traditional, making up around 10–22 percent of American Jews).[195] My great-grandparents on both sides considered themselves Orthodox, though my grandparents, parents, and I have identified with the Conservative movement and belonged to Conservative congregations.[196] Contrary to popular belief (probably even among many Jews), the naming of these different denominations does not go back far in Ashkenazi Jewish history—only to the 1800s.

HaAretz, a popular newspaper in Israel, recently cited an often-told joke meant to poke fun at how parochial many of us can get with regard to our selected house of worship: A Jewish person who had been stranded alone on a desert island for a long time is finally discovered. He volunteers to show his rescuers around the island before leaving. "And here are the two synagogues I built," he says.

"Why two?" his rescuers inquire.

"This is the one I attend, and this is the one I refuse to attend," he responds.[197]

Prior to the labeling of the levels of observance, Jews were either "more observant" or "less observant," and it seems the rigid lines of identification drawn today were more malleable. For example, Eastern European Jews generally attended synagogues close to where they lived or with others of their profession, or where their families had attended, or where they were comfortable with the service or

[195] Ashkenazic Jews are descendants of Jews from France, Germany, and Eastern Europe, and make up most of the American Jewish population. Sephardic Jews are descended from Spain, Portugal, North Africa, and the Middle East. Tracy R. Rich, Jewfaq.org; Pew Research Center, "Portrait of Jewish Americans," 2013, Berkley Center for Religion, Peace, and World Affairs; Religious Institute, Georgetown University, "Demographics of Judaism."

[196] The Jewish Conservative movement has no relationship to the political group that is called conservative.

[197] www.haaretz.com/jewish/.premium-1.533097

the rabbi or cantor. In the United States, my great uncle Rabbi Harold H. Gordon was the executive director of the New York Board of Rabbis for many years after World War II, a cross-denominational Jewish organization with Reform, Conservative, and Orthodox rabbis as members with a goal "to foster fellowship, provide educational enrichment, and rise above theological differences to strengthen and defend the Jewish community advancing its educational, religious, and social values."[198]

The Reform movement, the most liberal branch of Judaism, began as part of the *haskalah*, or enlightenment movement, in Germany in the early 1800s. Reform Judaism changed or abandoned many traditional Jewish religious observances, believing that the laws and rituals proclaimed in the Bible needed to be adapted to the modern world. The Orthodox movement was officially formed around 1850 in Europe in reaction to the changes to tradition introduced by the Reform Judaism movement and provided a home to those who wanted to continue the traditional, strict interpretation of the biblical texts. Many say that the Orthodox branch, though not named as such, exemplifies the traditional way that Judaism was practiced for thousands of years. The Conservative movement of Judaism began around 1880, shortly after the Orthodox movement was named, as a moderate alternative to the Orthodox and Reform branches. Conservative Jews generally believe that though Judaism could be adapted to modern ways of thought, traditional elements of Jewish law should be preserved. Changes proposed in the Conservative movement are based on traditional halakhic decision-making by Conservative rabbis.[199]

---

[198]Alvin Kass, *Watchman for The Community: A History of the New York Board of Rabbis*, pages 9–22 in *The American Rabbi: A Tribute on The Occasion Of The Bicentennial Of The United States And The Ninety-Fifth Birthday of The New York Board Of Rabbis*, ed. Gilbert S. Rosenthal (New York: KTAV Publishing House, Inc. 1977).

[199]The Halakha is made up of the written law (the Torah, or five books of Moses) and the oral law, called the Talmud—made up of the Mishnah and the Gemorrah—laws , statutes and legal interpretations handed down from ancient times, but not contained within the Torah. Together, these laws and interpretations constitute the Jewish "code of conduct." http://www.jewfaq.org/movement.htm, Tracy R. Rich.

Part of my beginning the process of preparing for my bat mitzvah at a Conservative congregation in Minneapolis involved taking classes on Saturday mornings at the synagogue. There were some required courses, such as learning the prayers and memorizing the notes for chanting the Haftorah (reading from the Prophets). There was also a time slot for an elective. The girls all took "Jewish Home," and the boys all took "Torah Reading." I came home and told my mom that I already knew about how to have a Jewish home. Our family kept kosher, we lit the candles on the Sabbath, said the prayers over the candles, bread, and "fruit of the vine," and celebrated the other Jewish holidays in our home and at the synagogue.

I wanted to learn to read from the Torah. My mom, daughter of St. Paul's first female to attend St. Paul's Hebrew School, encouraged me to take whichever course I wanted.[200] The next Saturday, when it was time for the elective course, I went to the room for Torah study. Though some of my peers told me that I was in the wrong room, the male, teenage Torah reading teacher never said a word. He taught me as he taught the rest of the class.

On Saturday mornings, it had been the tradition at the Adath Jeshurun Congregation, a Conservative synagogue, for bar and bat mitzvah candidates to chant their Haftorah, the blessings before and after the Haftorah, the Maftir (conclusion of the Torah service), to lead some prayers, and to give a speech. Some boys, who had learned to chant the Torah trope (notes) and knew the text well, would also read portions from the Torah. The remainder of the Torah sections they had not learned would then be read by the Regulars, a group of mostly older men, who had been reading Torah for years.

After much hard work in my Saturday morning class and at home, I learned my entire Torah portion and chanted it for my teacher. He gave some helpful corrections and then said that he was certain I would be ready for my bat mitzvah. He recommended to our synagogue's rabbi that I read the entire Torah portion. Rabbi Arnold Goodman agreed.

---

[200]My mom's grandfather, A. B. Goldberg, had been one of the founders of the first St. Paul Hebrew School. His daughter, my grandmother Minnie, was the first female attendee.

I selected my invitations with my mom, dad, and sister—light pink with gold writing and a picture of a Torah on the front.[201] We also went to the main post office in downtown Minneapolis to purchase a stamp that would be worthy of the event. We chose a stamp honoring the landing of the Pilgrims in 1620 (a six-cent stamp). Then began the lengthy process of my mom, Nancy, and I handwriting all the envelopes with our special gold pen, putting the tissue paper correctly over the reply envelope, and embossing our address on the back flap with the embosser purchased two years before for Nancy's bat mitzvah. After a salad, everyone would dine on the traditional roasted chicken and *kischke*, with fresh fruit, followed by a *pareve* chocolate mousse dessert.[202]

At the practice before my bat mitzvah in the sanctuary, a group of four of the regulars showed up. They were very upset. They said that a woman should not be reading from the Torah at all, let alone an entire Torah portion. "Lightning will strike the synagogue if you let her do this!" they said. "It's a *shunda* [a disgrace]!" said another. The Torah reading teacher politely asked them to leave, and I continued my practice.

On Saturday, May 8, 1971, I chanted the complete Torah portion for that Sabbath from the Torah, the first woman to do so at my synagogue. Lightning did not strike.

***

I felt the strength from my great-grandmother Rebecka Bender and generations past. I saw my dad wipe away a tear when I walked down the aisle carrying the decorated Torah. He knew that without his service and the service of countless other men and women, that moment would never have taken place. He also knew that had his

---

[201] At the time, it was more customary for girls to pick a picture of Sabbath candles to adorn their invitations, as this was in line with the traditional role of the female to bless the candles.

[202] Pareve denotes a food that could be eaten with a meat or milk meal, as it is made without any dairy "milchik" products.

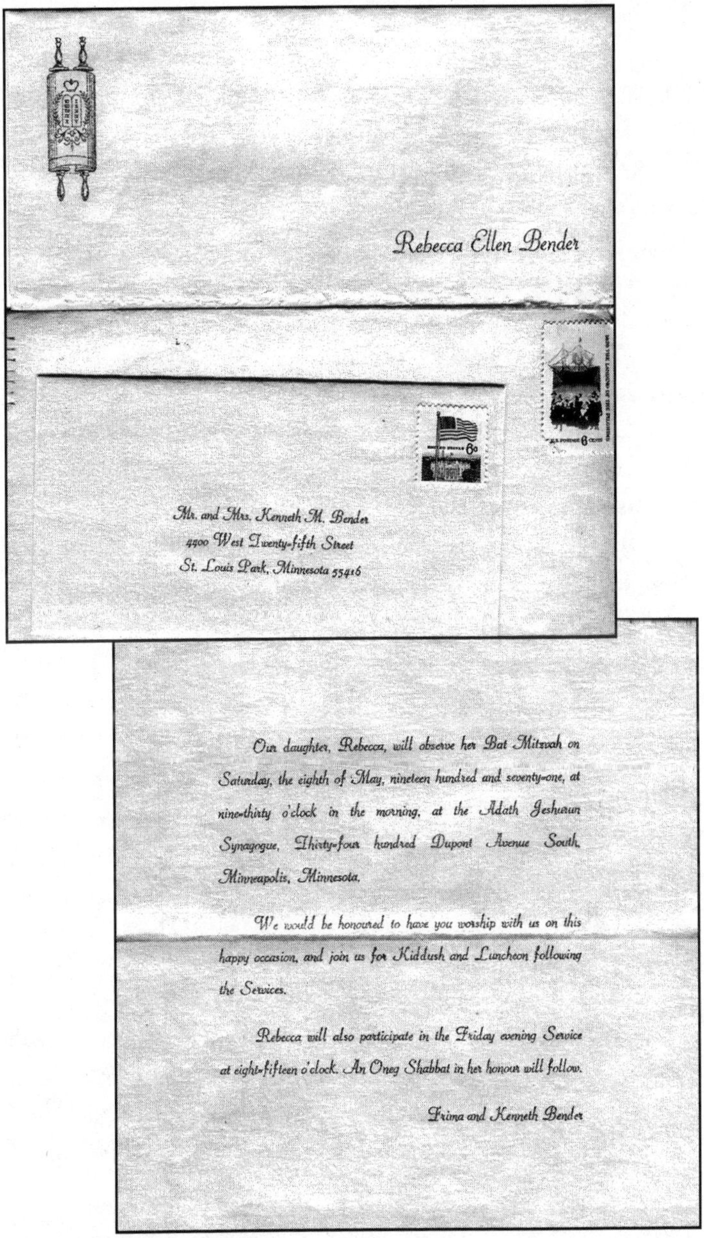

Rebecca Ellen Bender

Mr. and Mrs. Kenneth M. Bender
4400 West Twenty-fifth Street
St. Louis Park, Minnesota 55416

Our daughter, Rebecca, will observe her Bat Mitzvah on Saturday, the eighth of May, nineteen hundred and seventy-one, at nine-thirty o'clock in the morning, at the Adath Jeshurun Synagogue, Thirty-four hundred Dupont Avenue South, Minneapolis, Minnesota.

We would be honoured to have you worship with us on this happy occasion, and join us for Kiddush and Luncheon following the Services.

Rebecca will also participate in the Friday evening Service at eight-fifteen o'clock. An Oneg Shabbat in her honour will follow.

Frima and Kenneth Bender

My bat mitzvah invitation, 1971, and Pilgrims Commemorative stamp. *Author files.*

grandparents and father not taken the leap to America, that moment was also unlikely. My Torah reading teacher gave me a book for my bat mitzvah about Israeli Prime Minister Golda Meir, with a note: "Here is a story about another strong woman. Mazel Tov."

As sometimes happens with historical events, some of the people witnessing the reading seemed unaware of its historic import. I think that the Oneg Shabbat held after the Friday night service for my bat mitzvah was the subject of more discussion at the synagogue at the time than my Torah reading had been.[203] Family members had started baking months before my bat mitzvah. My parents had purchased a large standing freezer, which they placed downstairs at our house to hold the many family and friend bakery contributions for Nancy's bat mitzvah. It came in handy two years later as my bat mitzvah drew closer.

At the Adath, it was understood that the mother of the bar or bat mitzvah was responsible to ensure that the products brought for her child's simcha were baked in accordance with the laws of kashrut (kosher practices). For example, no pork products such as lard or traditional gelatin or even products that might contain lard, such as graham crackers or marshmallows, were allowed. In addition, the mother was also required to coordinate who was baking which sweet. In other words, a person wouldn't want to end up with a whole Oneg of pink daisy spritz cookies, or Russian tea cakes, or lemon squares, or thumbprint cookies with chocolate centers, or even marzipan strawberries (my aunt Josephine's specialty). The one item that made Nancy's and my bat mizvah Onegs different from most other bar or bat mitzvah Onegs, was the *shtrudel*. This was not any shtrudel. This was my baba Minnie's time-intensive, made-from-scratch, hand-stretched dough, filled and rolled carefully with a mixture of dates, oranges, raisins, lemon, sugar, apricots, coconut, cinnamon, walnuts, and other secret ingredients and a gentle dusting of powdered sugar shtrudel.

[203]The Oneg Shabbat is a celebration with refreshments, usually at the conclusion of the Friday night Sabbath service at a Conservative synagogue.

At the Adath Jeshurun building at the time, the Friday night service took place in the main sanctuary upstairs. The Oneg Shabbats were held in the social hall on the main level. It started as a whisper, but then became noticeably louder among some non-family congregants during the concluding song of "Adon Olam" (King of the Universe). "They have shtrudel for the Oneg!" "Yes, I heard it's homemade!" "It's going to go fast!" I can still hear the sound of the wooden doors of the sanctuary being swung open with force when the last note of the service was sung.

This experience caused Nancy and me to make up a new version to the children's fingerplay, "Here is the church, here is the steeple, open the doors, and here come the people." We changed it to, "Here is the synagogue, here is the Ner Tamid, if you have homemade shtrudel, to the Oneg the people stampede."[204]

At the time I began studying for my bat-mitzvah, unbeknownst to me as an eleven-year-old, there were many discussions taking place in the Conservative movement regarding the role of women in the synagogue service. I had been born at a time when boys and girls in a Conservative congregation could study for their bar or bat mitzvah, though it had not always been the case.[205] However, at this time, females over thirteen could not be counted as part of a minyan (the ten-person quorum for reciting certain prayers). I recall as a youth that when there was a shortage for a minyan on a non-Sabbath day, the leaders of our congregation would go out into the neighborhood in South Minneapolis where the synagogue was located to find a male to fill the spot, despite having learned Jewish females present.

When, in the 1970s, girls were being allowed to routinely read a portion from the Torah for their bat mitzvahs at American Conservative synagogues, the obvious issue became how a Conservative

---

[204]The Ner Tamid is the Eternal Light, found in synagogues in different forms and symbolizing that God is everpresent.

[205]The first bat mitzvah took place at a Reconstructionist synagogue in 1922. Some Reform and Conservative congregations started the practice of a bat mitzvah in the 1930s, and it became quite widespread by the 1960s. Paula E. Hyman, "The Introduction of Bar Mitzvah in Conservative Judaism in Postwar America," *YIVO Annual* 19 (1990).

synagogue could promote the girl's participation at age twelve, and then deny the girl the right to continue reading from the Torah as she grew older, or to be considered part of a minyan. Two years after my bat mitzvah, in 1973, the Conservative movement's Jewish Theological Seminary's Committee on Jewish Laws and Standards voted to allow women to be counted in a minyan.[206]

It wasn't until 1983 that the Jewish Theological Seminary allowed women to attend its Rabbinical School, and in 1985 the first female Conservative rabbi was ordained. The rabbi of my synagogue in Minneapolis during my bat mitzvah in 1971, Rabbi Arnold Goodman, then the rabbi at an Atlanta congregation, was the president of the 1200-member Rabbinical Assembly of the Conservative Jewish movement in 1983. He stated that the Jewish Theological Seminary's faculty decision was "consistent with the position of the vast majority of the members of the Rabbinical Assembly who are on record as favoring the ordination of women."[207] Looking back, I realize that had my rabbi and my Torah reading teacher not believed in the egalitarian participation of women and men in the Conservative synagogue service, my breakthrough moment would not have happened.

* * *

It was around the time of my bat mitzvah that I first consciously analyzed my method for choosing friends. I remember verbalizing it to my parents: "I've found that the people I want to be friends with believe in something that makes them want to be good people."

I was proud that so many of my new Christian friends at junior high, including Ruth, Ann, Tami, Marie, and Sarah, attended my bat mitzvah, though many of them had never heard of this Jewish milestone before.[208] My friend Sarah was in orchestra with me. She

---

[206]Irving Spiegel, "Conservative Jews Vote for Women in Minyan," *New York Times* (September 11, 1973): 1.

[207]The first female Reform Rabbi in the United States was ordained in 1972. The Orthodox movement has not yet accepted women in its rabbinate. Charles Austin, *New York Times* (October 25, 1983).

[208]Ruth's father was a violinist with the prestigious "Golden Strings," playing for diners at the Radisson Hotel's Flame Room in downtown Minneapolis.

had a sticker on her violin case with bright pink and orange flowers on the outside and the phrase "Jesus Loves Me" at the center. Sarah and I would walk down the junior high hall together, carrying our violin cases and talking. From almost our first conversation, we realized that our moral compasses were pointing in the same direction, though our religions were different.

I have a strong memory from being ten years old at Hebrew school. My teacher was Mrs. Goloni; she was from Israel. We were learning conversational Hebrew. When the bell rang, she told us that her husband was coming to talk with us after the break. We were all excited to meet our teacher's husband.

When we returned to the class, a tall, well-dressed man in a crisp white shirt and blue tie sat in our teacher's chair in the front of the room. Mrs. Goloni had moved to the back of the room. We sat quietly. Then in the quiet of that little room, Mr. Goloni unbuttoned his shirt sleeve at the wrist and slowly rolled up his sleeve. He showed the class his left forearm, which had numbers written on it. "Does anyone know what these numbers represent?" he asked.

We were all still quiet.

"These are numbers that were placed on Jewish people's arms by the Nazis to keep track of the number of Jews who were in concentration camps." He continued quietly:

> For those of you who have never heard of the Holocaust, I know that this is a lot of information . . . The Nazis were a political group that came to power in Germany in the 1930s. Part of what they believed in was having what they called a pure Germany, without Jewish people being a part of German society. The only problem was that Jewish people had been living and working in Germany for over 1500 years. So the Nazis came up with a plan to take away the German Jews' rights. They then rounded up Jews and took them to concentration camps. These were not like summer camps. They were more like prison. Once you were in one of these camps, it was unlikely that you would come out alive. I am one of the lucky ones. Members of my family and six million Jewish people in Germany and Poland and Russia were not so lucky. They were murdered

> by the Nazis in concentration camps. Probably some of your family members or friends of your family members were among the six million killed. Does anyone have any questions?

First, there was silence. Then one boy raised his hand. "What's your name?" asked Mr. Golani.

"Daniel," said the boy.

"That's a good strong name, Daniel, yes? He prayed to God even though he knew it might mean his death. What is your question?"

"Do you want to get rid of the numbers?" asked Daniel.

Mr. Golani replied:

> That's an excellent question. When I was in the concentration camp as a little boy, I dreamed of picking up apples at the store for my mother, like I used to do, and racing my friends through the fields, with no number on me. But now that I'm alive and free, I do not want to take away the numbers, because it shows that I survived, and my living my life and getting married and having Leelac [his daughter] is my showing anyone who sees the numbers that I am still here. Now I can be counted as one who beat the Nazis. They didn't beat me.

He carefully rolled his white shirtsleeve back down and buttoned it at the wrist. When the bell rang to go home, all of our class usually ran out of the building to the buses that took us home to dinner. That day, none of us ran. I don't know who went up first to Mr. Golani and gave him a hug, I just know that soon we were all hugging him. On the way home, bumping along on the hard seats of the Talmud Torah bus with other boys and girls, I tried to picture Mr. Golani as a little boy. I wondered how anyone could put a little boy in prison when he had done nothing wrong.

Even in the secular world of public school, I was not afraid to connect with my Judaism. When I was fourteen years old and in eighth grade, I was looking for a text that touched me to enter our school's declamation contest. I had recently read a nonfiction book from the library called *Tell Me Another Morning*, by Zdena Berger. It was about a young Jewish girl who had lost her parents, but who kept a little boy's spirits up in a Nazi concentration camp by descriptively painting pictures of better days with her words. My mom helped me to adapt excerpts of the book into a serious prose piece to recite. Though it was difficult to get through the piece, I did it. I was hopefully helping fellow classmates, teachers, and judges to understand the Holocaust through the story of a girl about my age. I was thankful and proud to use my voice to bring her story to life.

I also remember a time from my youth when I felt pride in another Jewish person's accomplishments, solely because we shared the same religion. As the last days of August approached, the outdoor activities at White Bear Lake became even more precious to me, my sister, and our cousins. The swims, walks, searches for special rocks along the shore, and fishing time on the dock all got longer as the days got shorter. After lunch on Labor Day 1972, at the end of the last official weekend of summer before school began, we four grandchildren of Baba and Zada Gordon helped them load up boxes and food items to head back to the Highland Park neighborhood in St. Paul, where our grandparents, aunt, uncle, and cousins lived.

Aunty Joey (Josephine) and Uncle Bob invited us for a barbecue in their backyard, while my parents helped my grandparents unpack. After dinner, we sat down to watch the summer Olympics being held in Munich, Germany. Aunt Joey and Uncle Bob were antique collectors, and the family room where we watched the Olympic coverage on television had numerous ticking antique clocks on the shelves keeping track of every second. We were especially interested in seeing if Mark Spitz, who was Jewish, would continue winning gold medals in the swimming events. When he won his seventh gold medal that night, he was the first athlete ever to win that many medals in any Olympics, and he won each of them (individual and relay) in world record times. We cousins were all cheering.

Then I looked over at Uncle Bob, who was sitting in his reclining chair in the corner. He had served with the Army Air Corps in North Africa during World War II. As a young man of seventeen enlisting in the United States Army in early September 1942, he lied about his age so he could begin fighting for America. He was not typically a shy, retiring personality, though everyone knew he had a kind heart. I noticed he had taken off his black-framed glasses and was wiping his eyes, saying quietly, "How wonderful, just wonderful. For a Jew to accomplish this, in Germany, after the Nazis tried to eliminate the Jews. Wonderful."

We said our thank-yous and goodbyes and headed home across the Mississippi to St. Louis Park, to sleep fast before the first day of school. While Nancy and I fell asleep under pink blankets, still feeling the warmth of the White Bear Lake sun on our faces from our lengthy swim earlier in the day, a Palestinian terrorist group took eleven members of the Israeli Olympic team hostage in Munich. By nighttime on the next day, broadcaster Jim McKay reported, "They're all gone."[209] I think back now to the ticking antique clocks and how it only took a second for the great joy I felt as a young Jew to change to great sorrow.

In the late 1960s, or early 1970s, my dad was contacted by Sam Scheiner, the Executive Director of the Anti-Defamation Jewish Council based in Minneapolis. The National Anti-Defamation League (ADL) had been formed in the United States in 1913 "to stop the defamation of Jewish people and to secure justice and fair treatment for all."[210] A History graduate student at the University of Minnesota had written a thesis entitled, "Why Jews Did Not Serve in World War II." The local ADL Council had been contacted by the graduate student's advisor, a non-Jew, as he believed there was much misinformation in the piece.

Sam Scheiner contacted three of the many decorated World War II Jewish war veterans who lived in the area: my dad, Kenneth Bender—Jewish Silver Star and Purple Hearts recipient, who worked his way up from private to major with the Second Infantry Division in battles at Normandy; Si Weismann—Jewish Silver Star and Purple

---

[209]www.britannica.com/event/Munich-Massacre; latimes.com/sports/Olympics/la-sp-munich-massacre-20170906-story.html Forty-four years later, on August 3, 2016, two days before the start of the 2016 Summer Olympics, the International Olympic Committee—for the first time—officially honored the eleven Israelis killed.

[210] MNOPEDIA at mnopedia.org/group/jewish-community-relations-council-minnesota-and-dakotas, Minnesota Historical Society.

Heart recipient, who worked his way up from private to sergeant with the Third Infantry Division in battles at Anzio; and Harold (Hal) Goodman — Purple Heart recipient, who worked his way up from private to captain with the Eighth Infantry Division in battles in France, Luxembourg, and the Rhineland, liberated a concentration camp in Germany, and later served in Korea.

The three Jewish soldiers scheduled a meeting to talk with the graduate student, to tell him their personal stories and to provide him with real facts and figures from the statistics kept by the United States and Allies.[211] The truth was that around 550,000 Jewish men and women were in the armed forces during World War II. This was a higher percentage of Jewish soldiers serving in the United States armed forces in World War II (4.23 percent of all soldiers) than the percentage of Jews living in the United States, including children (3.3 percent), and around 11,000 American Jewish soldiers were killed in World War II, 40,000 wounded, and 52,000 decorated for bravery.[212]

When my dad returned from the meeting, I asked him if he had changed the student's mind. He responded, "You never know what impact you may have had. Now at least, he knows there are undisputed facts that undermine his theories." This anti-Semitic theme, that Jews would not fight for their countries, had reared its head over the course of America's history, even prompting an apology of sorts from Samuel Clemens (Mark Twain). He first fanned this falsehood in an article he wrote in *Harper's Magazine* in 1898, stating that Jewish people had an "unpatriotic disinclination to stand by the flag as

---

[211]Conversation between Kenneth Bender and author, author's conversation with Harold "Hal" Goodman.

[212]JewishVirtualLibrary.org/statistics-on-jewish-american-soldiers-in-world-war-ii citing to *American Jewish Historical Society Newsletter* (Fall/Winter 2003), based upon Bureau of War Records housed at the Society. The Bureau's final report is contained in the collection. Dr. Samuel C. Kohs, Director, Bureau of War Records; Isidor Kaufman. *American Jews in World War II: the story of 550,000 fighters for freedom* (Dial Press. 1947). Information regarding Jewish participation with Allied nations at http://www.yadvashem.org/holocaust/about/combat-resistance/jewish-soldiers. Both President Franklin Roosevelt and General Douglas MacArthur praised the fighting abilities of Jewish men and women.

a soldier."[213] After being presented with statistics from the War Department, Twain corrected his previous statement in 1904 in a postscript attached to his essay, writing:

> When I published the above article in *Harper's Monthly*, I was ignorant— like the rest of the Christian world—of the fact that the Jew had a record as a soldier. I have since seen the official statistics, and I find that he furnished soldiers and high officers to the Revolution, the War of 1812, and the Mexican War. In the Civil War he was represented in the armies and navies of both the North and the South by 10 per cent of his numerical strength — the same percentage that was furnished by the Christian populations of the two sections. This large fact means more than it seems to mean; for it means that the Jew's patriotism was not merely level with the Christians, but overpassed it. That slur upon the Jew cannot hold up its head in presence of the figures of the War Department. [214]

***

When I was thirteen years old, our synagogue youth group was going to put on a production of *The Sound of Music*. I auditioned, hoping to get the part of one of the Von Trapp children. At the audition I was asked if I could yodel. I had never yodeled before, but gave it a try, and lo and behold, I was yodeling. Apparently I was the only one who tried out who could yodel, because I was cast as Maria Von Trapp. It was a wonderful experience. Baba Minnie and Mom worked hard to alter my mom's clothes from the 1940s for "Maria," including my mom's wedding dress. Nancy, my sister, was cast as one

---

[213]Cyrus Sulzberger, philanthropist, active in many American Jewish causes, including as president of the Jewish Agricultural Society, and in whose honor the Ashley, North Dakota, Jewish farmers' cooperative was named in 1908, wrote a response to Mark Twain's *Harper's* piece. Though he complimented Twain on his "spirit of absolute fairness," he disagreed with Twain's opinion that religion did not form part of the basis for existing Anti-Semitism. Dan Vogel, *Mark Twain's Jews* (Jersey City: KTAV Publishing, 2006).

[214]Roughly 250,000 Jews fought for the United States in World War I, another 550,000 in World War II. Martin Gilbert, T.A. Bicknell, and Arthur Banks, *Atlas of Jewish History* (New York Hippocrene Books, Inc., 1976), p. 81.

of the head nuns, which meant we got to listen to "Rex Admirabilis" ("King most wonderful"), a Latin hymn, for three straight months. But that was only fair, as she had to listen to my yodeling practice for "Lonely Goatherd" over the same time period.

There was one problem with the production, which the director noticed as we neared our performance dates. The play was being performed in the sanctuary of our synagogue. The director was concerned about having the Jewish boys playing Nazis wearing *yarmulkas* (Jewish head coverings), as was required in the sanctuary. When they made their scene entrance wearing head coverings, they were not believable as Nazis. As luck would have it, one of these boys was one of the rabbi's sons. He agreed to personally ask his father if it would be acceptable for those playing Nazis to not wear yarmulkas. Rabbi Goodman agreed, stating that the messages of freedom implicit in the play were far more important than having people distracted by the yarmulkas at a non-religious event. Just as with my being allowed to read the whole Torah portion at my bat mitzvah, I found that in addition to being able to weave a sermon like the finest tailor, Rabbi Goodman was reasonable.

About two years later, when I was fifteen years old and in tenth grade, I was selected to be a St. Louis Park Parkette. This was a unique organization, as it was made up of high school girls who were the official cheerleaders for the NFL's Minnesota Vikings. The Parkettes at the time were trained in ballet, tap, show, and jazz styles, and learned over sixty full-length and one hundred short-length routines. The Parkettes were modeled after the New York City Rockettes style of dance lines and wore more fabric for their costumes than five typical NFL cheerleaders of today put together. The parents of the girls were Program Vendors, selling the NFL programs at the games, making it a true family affair.

But there was a conflict: The Minneapolis Talmud Torah (Hebrew School) had two-hour sessions three times a week—two weekdays and one Sunday class. Attendance at all three days was mandatory. Parkette practices of the whole squad were, at a minimum, two days a week for three hours, and Vikings home games were on a number of Sundays. Attendance at Parkette practices and games was also mandatory. This was not an insurmountable problem, thanks to my supportive mom and dad. After high school on Tuesdays and Thursdays, I had my Parkette practice from 3 p.m to 6 p.m. My mom would pack food and my dad would pick me up after work and bring me to Hebrew School, which started at 6:10 p.m. I would eat on the way and then be ready for my Jewish education. After Hebrew School, I would take the bus home and begin my high school homework at about 8:30 p.m.

The Sundays of Vikings games posed a more unique challenge. The bus left for the games from the St. Louis Park High School parking lot at 11:15 a.m. for the 1 p.m. games. We girls needed to be dressed and ready when we got on the bus. The first session of Hebrew School was from 9:00–11:00 a.m. Again, not a difficult problem with supportive parents. On game days, I wore my Vikings cheerleader outfit to Hebrew School (which was basically a dress with an embroidered Viking logo on the front), and learned classic Hebrew poetry from Dr. Nachshon, comparative religion from Rabbi Louis Milgrom, the fine points of Hebrew grammar from Dr. Jonathan Paradise, and Rashi interpretations from Mr. Max Weitz. Then my dad would pick me up with the lunch packed by my mom (peanut butter on bagel), and I would board the bus to the old, outdoor Metropolitan Stadium in Bloomington. The Mall of America is now on the site of the old Met, where I used to absorb the sights and sounds as fans filled up the stands before the games, Red McCloud's Vikings band tuning up, smoke wafting through the chilly air from fans' thermoses of hot beverages, the players counting down jumping jacks, and the grounds crew on its mission to make the field look good for television cameras.

I never considered not attending Hebrew School, though I was the only Parkette at the time who did. My parents lived their lives in a way that made me want to learn more about Judaism and to be connected with those before me. They went out of their way to see to it that I had a good Jewish education while still being involved in activities at high school, though it took their time and effort to make

Author's grandparents and step-grandmother at her Talmud Torah graduation. From left, Rae Bender, Sam Gordon, Rebecca Bender, Minnie Gordon, and Joe Bender, 1976. *Author files.*

it work for me. When I later tested out of thirty-seven credits of Hebrew before attending college (which allowed me to graduate college in three years) and was a teacher's aide for Hebrew at the University of Minnesota while a freshman, all the hard work and perseverance had additional, unexpected benefits.

As Nancy and I grew up, we observed the selflessness and generosity of time, spirit, money, and energy that typified our parents' lives. Without fanfare, they simply helped people when they needed help. Sometimes it was a sick relative who needed some chicken soup flavored with parsnips, a hand held, and cheering up by Frima.

Other times, it was a lonely widow of a friend of Kenneth's whom we were picking up to go out with us for dinner. I took note of the fact that after dinner, my dad would always take the extra time to go first into the lady's home to check it out and give the all-clear before she entered a dark home alone. Or it was Frima, helping Nancy and me to clear out clothes and books we "didn't really need anymore" to give to others who were going through rough times. Or a foster mother, Mrs. Graham, who couldn't quite make the last payment on one of her foster children's lay-by Christmas present, who came by bus to my dad's Federated Store on Christmas Eve to ask Kenneth to hold the toy until after Christmas. My dad went to the lay-by area and handed her the toy wrapped in brown paper, writing the notation, "Paid in Full." Then he gave her a ride home. Compassion towards family, neighbors, and strangers was expected, as taught in Exodus, Proverbs, and the Psalms. Thanks to our parents and grandparents, Nancy and I grew up not knowing any other way that people should act or live.

***

One of my earliest memories of my dad is sitting on his lap in the big blue chair with matching footstool in the corner of our den, watching the Minnesota Twins on our television in the blonde wood console. I must have been about six years old. As my dad explained to me about balls and strikes, I remember feeling bumps in his fingers and asking him what made the bumps. "Shrapnel," he said matter-of-factly.

"What's shrapnel?" I asked.

"Little pieces of metal," he replied.

"How did they get in there?" I asked.

"When Daddy was in World War II fighting for America," he said softly. And that was all I needed to know at the time.

About seven years later, on August 10, 1971, Nancy, our dad, and I were cheering for the Minnesota Twins to beat the Baltimore Orioles, diligently trying our best to keep track of balls and strikes with our mini pencils on the program scorecards. We were seated in the left field bleachers of the since demolished Met Stadium. Number 3, Harmon Killebrew, came up to the plate, and took his typical stance with wrists parallel to his shoulders. Twins fans had been waiting for fifty-nine at bats since he hit his 499th homerun for him to reach the milestone 500 career homeruns. Lo and behold, he blasted his 500th homerun right towards us. Our dad reached up to catch the ball, but it was hit with such force, it bounced off of his hands into the hands of someone else's dad behind us. The other dad and children were quickly ushered down with Twins officials to meet with Harmon Killebrew, so he could "buy back" the historic baseball with some autographs and have pictures taken to commemorate the event. Our dad apologized to us, saying he felt so bad that he had not caught the ball for us, as he knew that Harmon was one of our favorite players. Nancy and I told him that we felt bad because he felt bad, but told him we didn't feel bad about the ball. Nancy and I then checked our dad's hands and fingers to see if they were OK. The shrapnel was still there. He smiled at our concern and said he was fine.

In 1974, when I was sixteen, I was a member of Donaldson's Youth Board. Donaldson's was a big department store in Minneapolis, and students selected from area high schools participated in promotional events for the store, did charity work, and learned about the retail business. Among our assigned duties was answering letters to Santa. We were each given a stack of fifty letters to Santa that had been dropped in the store's North Pole mailbox, along with instructions to not promise anything, but to be positive and to encourage continuing good behavior. I recall spending hours and hours handwriting out responses to these Dear Santa letters, and feeling like I was doing a mitzvah.

CHAPTER 14
Minneapolis, MN, 1976

WHEN I WAS A FRESHMAN at the University of Minnesota in 1976, I was required to present an emotional speech for my Introductory Speech class. I had become aware of the plight of the Soviet Jews, who were not allowed to freely practice their religion or to leave Russia to do so. Jewish Americans who tried to bring prayer books or Jewish religious items to Russia were followed by the KGB and sometimes even arrested. I decided to present a speech on the Jews of the Soviet Union.

I recorded myself on a cassette recorder playing the moving, minor-key melody of Israel's National Anthem, "Hatikvah" ("The Hope"), on the piano and began my speech with the class listening to the recording. I explained that merely listening to Israel's national anthem in the Soviet Union could lead to a Soviet citizen being arrested and sent to the work house or Siberia. After describing the conditions for Jews living in the Soviet Union, I concluded my speech by stating that both sets of my grandparents came from areas that later were included within the Soviet Union. I explained that if they hadn't left in the early 1900s, these people being persecuted could have been me, if my family had been lucky enough to survive the Holocaust. I received ten out of ten from all of the students, though I don't believe any of them were Jewish. Once again, I found that it felt good to connect with my Judaism, even in a secular setting.

During the time I was attending the University of Minnesota, I was given the honor of standing up as a bridesmaid at my good friend Lee Ann Herbert's wedding. We had met as members of the University of Minnesota Danceline. The wedding was taking place at the Ascension Catholic Church in North Minneapolis, where my dad, owner of the Federated Store a few blocks away, had measured thousands of students every July over the years and then provided well-fitting uniforms to them before the start of school. Kenneth and the Ascension's Pastor, Monsignor Coates, had become good friends since the 1950s, when they first met.

At the practice before the wedding, Monsignor Coates told all the members of the wedding party where they would be standing during the ceremony. I was a bit concerned about how it would go, as Jewish people do not bow or kneel before a cross in a church. Then Monsignor Coates said, "At this point, after the Unity Candle is lit, all the bridesmaids will come right down here and kneel. Rebecca, I have placed you on the side, so you may walk to a pew and sit down for this portion. I know that your dad would not want you kneeling." I was relieved, and proud of the fact that the Monsignor so respected my dad and his beliefs that his respect flowed over onto me, as well.

***

Growing up, I never had any doubt that my sister and I would marry Jewish men and raise our children as Jews. This was not an elitist perspective, but rather an accepted responsibility to continue the religion through future generations. Then in 1976, though still living at home for college, I left the high-percentage Jewish population bubble of St. Louis Park for the University of Minnesota in Minneapolis, and in 1977 I met Devin (not his real name).

Devin sat next to me every day in Astronomy class at the University of Minnesota in my second year of college. The professor, Karlis Kaufmanis, had a Latvian accent and an engaging personality that made astronomy exciting and yes, romantic. He spoke of the science that deals with heavenly bodies and of how many of his students had become couples after gazing into the night sky to locate the miraculous constellations together. Perhaps with wishful thinking, I decided that Devin must be Jewish, though he never said he was. He had curly hair, and to me, looked like a good-looking version of Barry Manilow.

One day, students in a religion course at the university were conducting a survey, and we astronomy students were supposed to circle what we believed to be true. The paper I was handed contained the following question:

> I believe that Jesus . . .
>
> a)was the Messiah and son of God;
>
> b)was a wise man who started Christianity; or
>
> c) none of the above.

I was circling the letter b, when Devin picked up the survey and said, "Why do we have to do this?" and crumpled it up.

"Aha," I thought, "he must be Jewish!" I allowed myself to start falling for him as we walked to and from class together and studied together. He was smart, funny, and kind. I felt bad for what I thought was his poverty state (he had holes in his jeans prior to this being a fad and was very thin). I found reasons to tell him I had an extra apple or tuna sandwich or chips in my jean book-bag, and he took them willingly. Then Devin told me that he had visited his sister in Boston, and that she had invited him to dinner with some "Jewish friends." Nothing more needed to be said. Case closed. He clearly was not Jewish.

Devin asked me out over winter break. I found excuses to justify my accepting his invitation in talking with my parents. "He helped me in astronomy . . . it's just one date," etc. Methodist Devin picked me up in his bronze-colored Camaro and drove to the Lincoln Del — one of two Jewish delicatessens in St. Louis Park — for dinner. When I asked how he picked the restaurant, he told me that his mother told him that this was the place that Jews liked to eat. Prior to getting my cheese blintzes and sour cream, I said to Devin, "There's something I have to tell you."

"OK," he said.

"You are a very nice person, which is why this has to be our last date," I said.

"I don't understand," he said, "did I do something wrong?"

"If we were to get married," I continued, "what would our children be?"

Devin laughed and said, "I'm not asking you to marry me; I just asked you on a date."

"I know," I said firmly, "but one date could lead to another and another. Jewish people are chosen for responsibility—to be an example of the way to live, and I must pass that on to my children. It's best we just stop now."

"Can we still eat our food and go to the movie?" he asked.

"Sure," I said, "as friends." We went to a new movie that had just come out, Saturday Night Fever. I thanked him for dinner and the movie, and we said goodbye.

Two days later, on Christmas Eve, I attended the "Everything is Closed Jewish Singles Dance" at the St. Paul Jewish Community Center. In case attendees went out of the social hall, they stamped peoples' hands with a Jewish star. While I was dancing with a Jewish single to Donna Summer's "Last Dance," I was thinking of a Methodist single.

When Valentine's Day came, I read through all the Personals in the *Minnesota Daily*, the University student newspaper, and lo and behold, Devin had written one to me, asking to meet, complete with astronomy terms. Around this same time, my dear baba Minnie was diagnosed with lung cancer. My mom was staying with my baba and zada Gordon in St. Paul during the day, and my dad was driving back and forth forty-five minutes each way before and after work to drop her off and pick her up. With this new freedom, I met Devin for ice cream. He also took me out for my birthday, driving me to a dock on a big lake and lifting me into a speedboat, as I said, "Who does this belong to?" Surprisingly, he was far from poor, and his family owned an island in Lake Minnetonka, west of Minneapolis.

Devin and I started going out, and he invited me to his sister's wedding. His sister was a doctor, and in her vows, she talked about her hoping to have the same relationship in her marriage as an old Jewish man who had been her patient and had refused to take off his wedding ring before surgery. I felt accepted, for a time, but then Devin told me not to mention that I was Jewish to his German grandfather at the wedding, and then put his arm around me and said with a smile, "let's go to the buffet."

One evening when I was at Devin's home, his mother thoughtfully found his older sister's skates to lend to me so Devin and I could skate on the little ice rink by their house. Devin was an accomplished skater and hockey player, while I could only do basic skating strokes and preferred to slow down rather than ever have to stop abruptly. Nevertheless, Devin did not speed past me on the rink or try to impress me. He skated slowly with our arms in skaters' position, as I sang Johann Strauss's *The Blue Danube Waltz* under a glowing moon and he smirked, so as not to laugh out loud at my skating efforts.

Despite this and other endearing moments as time went on, it was clear that Devin's family was not thrilled with me. Though they were cordial, and his dad showed me a poem he liked, "If Once You Have Slept on an Island," by Rachel Lyman Field, I later overheard Devin's dad saying to him, "You should go out with other girls besides Rebecca. You're too young to be going out with just her." One night, shortly thereafter, I was invited to dinner at their home and pork was served, which I do not eat. I said I was fine eating the other foods served, but Devin's parents insisted that he go without me into the kitchen to make something else for me to eat. Devin later told me that his mother said to him, "I hope you won't make the same mistake as your older brother and move in with her." He thought that was so funny and showed that his mother didn't know who I was, as he knew my strong beliefs about what was not appropriate pre-marriage.

My family trusted me that Devin was a good guy, but also encouraged me to date Jewish fellows, more so the longer Devin and I went out. Nevertheless, once, when Devin was sick, I told my mom, who immediately made homemade chicken soup with matzoh balls for him, put it in a glass container she had kept from some purchased Manischewitz beet borscht, and handed it to me with a smile. (He ate the soup, and gave the matzoh balls to a Jewish friend in his dorm.)

It would be good for this story for me to say that I was strong enough in my beliefs to tell my first love directly and succinctly that it was over. Rather, in hindsight I can say that the family pressures gradually weighed on both of us, though we didn't admit it to each other. I believe that it was ultimately Devin's recognition that the person he had been dating was strong in her religious beliefs and that he was strong in his religious beliefs that ended the relationship. He said, "You are going to want to light the Chanukah candles with your children, and I am going to want to move the cows around in my mom's miniature Christmas manger with my children." Maybe his comments were a convenient way to get out of the relationship, but after all of these years I still prefer to think he cared enough to not challenge the strong faith I had, and that what I had said on our first date, ultimately led to our last date.

I remember vividly in 1980 when Neil Diamond's fourth remake of *The Jazz Singer* came out in theaters. The basic story is that of a young man who is the sixth generation of cantors (singing the liturgy in the synagogue), and who is drawn away from that traditional life to pursue his dream of singing popular music. My parents invited my aunt Alice to come with us to see the movie. After all, they said, "How many times does a movie come out about a Jewish cantor?"

I was sitting next to my great aunt Alice, two seats in, and she was on the aisle. She was my zada's little sister on my mother's side, the daughter of Reverend Jacob Gordon, a well-respected Rabbi, shochet, and *moel* for years in Minneapolis.[215] I had often heard the story that as a young girl, she used to accompany her father to perform the circumcisions at the bris ceremony for Jewish boy babies, proudly carrying his little leather black bag.

[215]A shochet is trained to kill animals for food in a humane way, and in accordance with Jewish law, and a moel performs circumcisions of Jewish baby boys in accordance with Jewish law.

We were all caught up in the music and the story, when suddenly my aunt stood up abruptly and left the theatre. I followed her out to the lobby and asked if she was OK. "I'm fine, I'll sit out here until it's done, but I just can't watch that movie anymore. He's leaving his nice wife, hurting his father, and turning his back on tradition. I don't want to see this kind of thing." I explained to my aunt that this was a fictional story, but she refused to return to the theater. When we all walked out at the end of the movie, we told our aunt that the Neil Diamond character returned to sing "Kol Nidre" at the start of the Yom Kippur service, and that his character had reconciled with his father.[216] Our aunt responded without much enthusiasm, "Well that's good to hear." My great aunt was so strong in her beliefs, she didn't even want to see a fictional account of a Jew not following the Jewish faith. I recall that it was a very quiet ride home, with my parents trying to make small talk about everything other than the movie.

My grandpa Joe Bender passed away when I was in my second year of college. Once living in the city in Minneapolis, Joe so missed being close to farm fields, he purchased a little farm in Anoka, Minnesota, that he rented to a farmer for years. He enjoyed "checking on the farm" whenever he had a chance, and he kept playing golf until shortly before he passed away, always with the trademark cigar in his mouth as he launched the ball skyward. I miss how he always spelled my name "Rebecka" in letters and postcards to me (the way his late mother had spelled her name in America), how he would squeeze Nancy's and my arms and with twinkling eyes call us *Schweinalas* (little piglets), the consistency with which he ordered hearty pumpernickel bread with his corned beef, and the fact that he was always pleased to receive a gift of golf balls or chocolate cherry cordials on special occasions. Most of all, I miss his distinctive accent, which I heard near me when we were praying in the synagogue and that pulled me in to listen more carefully to his stories. Rabbi Abelson

[216]Kol Nidre begins the prayer service for the Jewish Day of Atonement (Yom Kippur), and has a distinctive, recognizable melody when sung by cantors and then repeated by congregations.

of Beth El Synagogue, wrote the touching eulogy, which provided, in part:

> Yosef ben Akiva v'Rivkah, Joseph Bender was one of the last survivors of the pioneering generation that helped pave the way for the numerous and prosperous American Jewish communities of today . . . And he represented the Jewish people with honor and distinction, for he was a man of integrity and compassion. He earned a shem tov—a good name for his honesty, and his readiness to be helpful to those who had a bad year or suffered misfortune. As we bid a final farewell to this good man Joseph Bender, we feel the truth of Kohelet's words, "Dor Holekh"—"a generation passes with him." But we draw comfort from the knowledge that his generation serves as an inspiration to the "dor ba" to the generations that follow in its footsteps.

My grandpa Joe also prized education. As a farmer, he started taking out insurance policies to fund his children's future education and would then cash them in for tuition. For years, he proudly carried around the 1956 letter from the University of Minnesota President J. L. Morrill, congratulating him and Mary on his five children's graduations from the University of Minnesota. The lines on the paper are still visible, from the number of times he took it out to proudly show acquaintances, and then refolded it and put it in his pocket.

I absorbed the appreciation for education, an important pillar of Jewish tradition, from both of my parents and both sides of grandparents. Once, when Nancy and I were young girls and with our mom in a taxi on our way to a ballet lesson, we were hit by another car when the taxi driver didn't yield. The jolt was so strong that when I looked over at my mom, her normally bobby-pinned up auburn hair was down and flowing. The taxi company sent us a check. There was a brief discussion between our parents as to the proper use for the unexpected funds, and quick agreement. That is how Nancy and I were the fortunate recipients of the incredible 1966 World Book Encyclopedia volumes. The covers were a pebbled ivory color, with dark green and golden accents. They were a wonderful resource for school projects and a welcome companion for rainy days.

The paramount importance of education in our family was also demonstrated to me when I was trying out to be one of several child actors for the upcoming Guthrie Theater season in 1967 when I was nine years old. After reciting a prepared piece, and going through an interview, I was called back for the second round of auditions. There were ten of us kids who were told that five of us would be taking various children's roles in the upcoming season, depending upon who won this set of auditions. We were put in groups of two, and brought into a big room with a huge trunk in the corner and three adults with notepads. Inside the trunk were bits of costumes, and we were instructed to find something we liked in the trunk to make a costume and then to be seated. I was paired with a boy who picked a cowboy hat and holster. When asked who he was, he said, "I'm a cowboy." When I was asked who I was, wearing a pink feather boa, I responded, "Ethel Merman."

One man told us each to think of a song we liked to sing, but not to tell anyone. Then the woman said, "On the count of three, I want you both to start singing the song you picked as loud as you can, at the same time. So when you hear the other person singing, you just keep singing your song! . . . Go!" We began. The little boy was singing "Twinkle Twinkle Little Star." I was singing "Give My Regards to Broadway." Before I had finished the second verse, I noticed that I was the only one singing, and the boy ran out of the room crying, yelling, "She sings too loud!" My mom received a call that I had been selected to be a Guthrie child actor.

My mom's first question was, "she won't have to miss any school for this, will she?"

The lady on the phone said, "Oh yes, she will have to miss school, but we have tutors for the children."

My mom politely declined, saying, "My husband and I would not want her missing any school."

***

When my zada Sam dropped off his daughters Frima and Josephine at Mattocks Grade School, at James Avenue and Macalester in St. Paul, he frequently pointed out the saying carved above the door, “Take fast hold of instruction . . . for she is thy life” (Proverbs 4:13). He worked very hard to keep educating himself once he was working full-time, and was successful at this endeavor, as for years he was my “go-to person” to check the spelling of a word.

I graduated from the University of Minnesota Law School, like my father, sister, and brother-in-law, Barry Kelner.[217] At age twenty-four, my first job after graduation was with a securities litigation and arbitration and underwriter’s counsel boutique law firm.

When the Jewish High Holidays were approaching, I went into the law firm’s senior partner’s office to request to have the day of Yom Kippur off so I could attend services. (Rosh Hashanah that year fell on a weekend.) I told the partner that I would make sure all of my work was done prior to leaving, but that if anything new came up I would work over the weekend to complete it. The partner sat and said nothing for what seemed like an eternity. Then he said, “Why do you want Yom Kippur off?”

“Because I’m Jewish, and it’s our holiest day of the year,” I responded.

“You’re not Jewish,” he said.

“Yes, I am,” I said. Finally, he gave me approval to attend services.

I returned to my office to review some brokerage account documents, and heard the senior partner call the other firm partner and say, “John, you wouldn’t believe it. We hired a Jew. Rebecca Bender is a Jew!” I felt my heart sink. Though my dad had counseled me to specialize in a particular area of the law when choosing a firm, I wondered if I had accepted the wrong employment opportunity. At lunchtime, the senior partner invited me and the other two associates to lunch at his country club. In the car, the comments continued, “I can’t believe that you’re a Jew.”

---

[217]Our mom, Frima, was in law school until she met our dad, then withdrew from classes to get married.

Rebecca Bender in front of Northrup Hall on University of Minnesota campus before U of MN Law School graduation, 1982.
Photo by Frima Bender, author files.

During the subsequent weeks of work, I came to learn that the outspoken senior partner did not dislike Jews. To the contrary, he talked fondly of being a "Shabbos goy" while he was growing up in Memphis. The most ritually observant Jewish people, Orthodox Jews, make certain that nothing they do on the Sabbath could be considered work, which is prohibited on the Sabbath. The Shabbos goy is a person hired by Orthodox Jews to turn on or off the stove or the lights on Sabbath, as a Jewish person does not want to cause another Jewish person to violate these Sabbath work prohibitions. I worked at this law firm for over six years, learned a great deal from this former director of the Securities and Exchange Commission Division of Enforcement, and was glad I didn't have a knee-jerk reaction to his initial response to my Judaism.

One day, when all the members of the firm had finished having lunch together, we all wandered into a game store. The senior partner saw a board game called "Oy Vey!" "Becky Jo," he said. (Everyone in his office had "Jo" as a middle name, as he joked that where he grew up in Memphis, everyone's middle name was Jo.) "I've never seen a Jewish board game, would you like it?" I told him it wasn't necessary. When we exchanged gifts at Christmas time in the office, lo and behold, he picked my name and gave me the game. Though the game definitely reinforced stereotypes of Jewish mothers — the goal was to get your two sons to become doctors and to get your daughters married to doctors — I knew that his gift came from a fun-loving rather than a mean-spirited place. So I joined with the generations of Jews who have been able to laugh at ourselves in much worse situations.

My "Jewish" beliefs were tested many times over the course of my eighteen years as a lawyer, prior to my going on voluntary restricted status in order to deal with family health issues. While in my own practice, I accepted cases of people who would not have had their cases taken because the dollar amount lost was too low. I also rarely took a full third (the standard for a contingency securities litigation and arbitration case at the time) when I successfully represented a client, though I could have used the full amount. Though I was adversarial when I needed to be to represent my clients properly, I never was dishonest in representing a client.

One opposing attorney, who was not doing well in a securities arbitration against me, asked for a break in the middle of his client's cross-examination by me. The panel denied his request, as they wanted to hear what his client *really* had to say, instead of what the lawyer told him to say after a briefing. At that point, the lawyer told the panel that he hadn't wanted to disclose this fact, but he needed a break as he was diabetic. The panel, of course, granted his request, and I expressed my empathy to the lawyer for his situation as he ran out of the room.

After the break, the client who had been testifying came back, changing much of his previous testimony and stating that he hadn't understood my questions previously. Weeks later, I heard from a fellow lawyer friend that this same attorney was telling colleagues that he pulled one over on me, pretending to be diabetic to get time to brief his client. Several years later, this attorney was named a United States Federal Court Magistrate. Despite this seeming to be a situation of good things happening to bad people, it did not cause me to change the way I live my life or treat others. The amazing thing about both a compass that you hold and an inner compass is that it can direct you no matter what is happening around you. There can be thunderstorms, tornadoes, lies or deceit around you, but it still shows you the way.

***

It was around 1900 when Charles Wingate—who owned the store my dad later purchased from his heirs in 1951—and his friend George Draper Dayton made a bet as to where downtown Minneapolis would develop. Mr. Wingate believed it would develop in North Minneapolis around West Broadway and Bryant Avenue and built his department store there, after having had a successful North Minneapolis dry goods store about two miles northwest of the site.[218]

Mr. Dayton predicted he had found the correct location where downtown Minneapolis would develop around Nicollet Avenue and 7th Street and built Dayton's Department Store there.[219] Though Mr. Dayton won the bet, Kenneth felt he was the beneficiary of Mr. Wingate's decision, as he appreciated the small town feel of the West Broadway neighborhood, where he walked miles every day on the

[218]Elmer, Barton, *City of Minneapolis: A review of her growing industries and commercial development, historical and descriptive* (1889). Twentieth Avenue North was the original name for West Broadway. It was first a wagon trail that connected with the Red River Ox Cart Trail up to Canada. Old Highland Neighborhood Association, "Introduction," Minneapolis Historical, accessed November 1, 2017, http://mineapolishistorical.org/item/show/38.

[219]Story told by Mr. Wingate's widow to Kenneth Bender (1950)

wood-planked floors of the Federated Store to wait on customers and made lasting friendships.

In 2005, my dad closed the store after fifty-three years on West Broadway. During his time there, the city replaced the sidewalks and removed the horse hitching posts that had been out front since Mr. Wingate's days. Kenneth had so many memories over the years—good and bad, but as he would say, mostly good.

On December 31, 2004, the *Minneapolis Star Tribune* published an article about Kenneth Bender's influence on the neighborhood and his kindness to veterans. He was amazed at how quickly the years passed. He had nothing negative to say about his fifty-three years at the store to the reporter, Doug Grow. Kenneth said, "Most people have been good customers. It's always been my job to make sure I have the things my customers wanted."

He outlasted a Target Store in North Minneapolis, several blocks from the Federated. When Target was moving in, loyal Federated customers were concerned. "Will Target put you out of business?" they asked Kenneth. Kenneth was not worried.

"They don't know the people and the neighborhood the way I do," he confidently said, and just kept working as hard as he could. And he was right: the Target was only in business about twenty years.

CHAPTER 15

Eureka, Ashley, and Beyond, 2005

KENNETH, NANCY, HER TEN-YEAR-OLD daughter, Sage, my seven-year-old son, Lincoln, and I took a car trip to Eureka the same year Kenneth closed the Federated. After visiting with some old friends, taking a swim in Lake Eureka, seeing the former Bender home, lifting up the mats in the weight room to see the free throw lines where Keva and David stood in the old Eureka gym, and sampling some *kuchen* (the official South Dakota dessert, baked in Eureka), we all headed to the Ashley Jewish Cemetery.

This time, Kenneth held grandchildren Sage and Lincoln's hands after we parked the car on the country road and went down the little hill to the cemetery. As they looked at the monuments, Kenneth explained to his grandchildren, as he had to his children, that Jews were not allowed to own land in Russia. "It was like a dream to be able to own land in the United States, and to be able to be safe as Jews, to celebrate Jewish holidays, and to study the Torah and the prayers." We said the Mourner's Kaddish at Kiva Bender's gravesite, and returned to the car.

"I almost forgot!" I said.

"What?" asked Lincoln.

"I almost forgot that I brought one big and four little American flags to place at Kiva Bender's grave, representing the five generations of our family who have lived in America."

I hurried down the hill, placed the five little flags in the Dakota ground, and then watched as the wind made the flags dance happily.

***

In law school, I was busy trying to learn new terms and concepts. After law school, I was occupied with studying for the bar exam. After I passed the bar exam, I was focused on doing a good job at my first post-graduate job. So I didn't make or take a lot of time for socializing, and finding eligible Jewish men to date was not an easy task. Though I happened to meet some fellows at Jewish events and was fixed up by mutual friends, once I was working I relied heavily on the Jewish Dating Service in Minneapolis. The JDS was run by two Jewish ladies who considered it part of their mission in life to be matchmakers for nice Jewish singles to carry on their Jewish heri-

From left, Rebecca, Lincoln, Kenneth, and Sage at Kiva Bender's gravesite, 2005. *Author files.*

tage. Sometimes, I must admit, I wondered about their methods due to the people I encountered (who they predicted would be "perfect" for me). Their names, of course, I will not disclose here. Suffice it to say they ranged from a Monet-like painter, who on the first date told me that he may go crazy like Monet eventually did, forgetting to eat or drink because of his obsessive pursuit of perfection, and inquired as to whether I would care for him when this happened, to a doctor who was getting over his recent breakup with a woman who had chosen instead to marry a member of America's political dynasty, to an arrogant lawyer twenty years my senior, who informed me on the first date that he really didn't believe in God.

I ended up marrying two Jewish men, not at the same time, of course, and not due to the efforts of the JDS ladies. My grandparents, parents, aunts, and uncles were married over fifty years, and my sister and brother-in-law also have a lengthy marriage. So I never could have imagined not being married "forever" to the same person once I stood under the chupah. However, my first marriage lasted about six years and the second one about eight.

I met my first husband in law school, but we didn't go out until we were fixed up by a former high school classmate of mine after graduation. He was raised as a Reform Jew, had a quick wit and determination, liked "Green Onions" by Booker T. and the M.G.'s, adored his grandmothers, and asked me to marry him. I met my second husband due to his attending a Columbia College alumni picnic that my sister and brother-in-law organized. He tended to my nephew Marshall who had skinned his knee, and my brother-in-law promptly gave him my phone number. He was raised as a Reform Jew, had a quick wit and determination, was taking cello lessons, adored his grandmothers, and asked me to marry him.

The fact that the marriages ended in divorce never caused me to believe that I shouldn't have married Jewish men. Rather, I realized that the marriages failed for reasons not related to religion and that both my partners and I were responsible. I never doubted that either marriage should have taken place, as I feel I learned what was truly important to me through these experiences. I also knew that without meeting and marrying my second husband, I would never have given birth to our son, Lincoln, and had the gift of watching him grow.

I have too many wonderful memories about the person Lincoln is to fit in one hundred books. It is perhaps the occurrences that many would call minor that I treasure most. Even at a young age, Lincoln demonstrated that he took the words of the Bible to heart, happily going to visit the ill and the aged with me and speaking at his baba and gramps's funerals and his dad's dad's funeral, despite the personal losses he was feeling. Once when Lincoln was young, I had finished making his favorite macaroni and cheese dinner. I was calling him to eat, and he wasn't coming to the table. Then I found him, feeding his dog, Buddy. He said, "Mom, the Bible says you should feed your animals before you eat. I'll be there once Buddy is done."

***

Though some of my friends think I'm a bit crazy to say this following two divorces, my two weddings were among the happiest days of my life. They were times of such joy and hope, beginning a new chapter with someone I loved, surrounded by family and friends. On top of this, the Jewish wedding ceremony is so meaningful, full of connections to the past.

Prior to the wedding, a *ketubah*, or Jewish wedding contract, is signed by the bride, groom, two witnesses, and the officiating Rabbi. Though the ketubah is traditionally the document in which the husband guarantees to his wife that he will meet certain human and financial conditions of marriage, my ketubah also contained English poetic language in which the groom and I made mutual promises of love, tenderness, and faithfulness before God, and included the phrases, "May our life together be illuminated by our peoples' heritage. May our home be built on Torah and loving kindness."

It has become a modern trend for many couples to have an artist hand paint the Hebrew writing and decorate the ketubah with painted flowers and vines and sometimes pictures of things special to the couple, as well. These modern day ketubahs are oftentimes

Lincoln with Buddy (2005–2014), a.k.a. "the Greatest." *Author files.*

framed and hung in the couple's new home, as meaningful art. My ketubah with my first husband had pictures of important things to me on the right hand vine, and important things to him on the left. The first pictures on my side were the dock at White Bear Lake and a sodhouse on the prairie.

I was recently asked if Jewish life is at all similar to that depicted in the movie *Fiddler on the Roof.* I explained that it was a different time and took place in Russia, but that some of the same traditions depicted in that movie are followed today.[220] For example, at a Jewish wedding, the bride and groom stand under the chuppah to symbolize the home they will build together, reminiscent of structures in use when the Jewish people were in the desert for forty years between the time they were freed from slavery and arrived in the Promised Land. Also, as in *Fiddler*, at the conclusion of the wedding ceremony, the groom stamps on a glass (wrapped in a napkin so no one gets injured). Some Jewish people believe that this custom is to remind us of the destruction of the Temples in Jerusalem and the fact that even in times of joy we should be aware that life also includes sadness, while another interpretation is that the world is broken like the glass, and we have the power to make it whole again with acts of *tikkun olam* (repairing the world). And everyone does still yell, "Mazel Tov!" once the glass is broken.

In Conservative Jewish weddings, the bride usually walks down the aisle to traditional Jewish or Israeli music.[221] For my wedding

[220]In this matter, I defer to someone who lived through the shtetl life in Russia: Golda Meir. Meir, the first female prime minister of Israel stated: "The shtetl, reconstructed in novels and films, which has become known today in places my grandparents never even heard of, that gay, heart-warming, charming shtetl on whose roofs fiddlers eternally play sentimental music, has almost nothing to do with anything I remember. The poverty-stricken, wretched little communities in which Jews eked out a living, comforting themselves with the hope that things would somehow be better one day and with their belief that there was a point to their misery." Meron Medzini, *Golda Meir, A Political Biography* (Germany: De Gruyter Oldenbourg, 2008).

[221]Unlike at many non-Jewish weddings, "Here Comes the Bride" is rarely played at Jewish weddings as it is part of the opera *Lohengrin* by Wagner. Wagner was one of Hitler's favorite composers and a prolific writer of anti-Semitic materials.

to my second husband, a klezmer accordion player played a piece written by a European Jewish composer who had died in the Holocaust. I felt that this gave me a connection to those Jews killed in the Holocaust who never had the joy of experiencing a wedding. As part of the ceremony, the bride does *hakafot*, or seven circles around the groom, which some say is based upon the seven days of creation and the creation of a new home through the wedding ceremony. The vows are taken in Hebrew with the words: Behold, you are consecrated to me, with this ring, according to the traditions of Moses and Israel.[222]

The year before Lincoln's gramps Kenneth died, he gave Lincoln his World War II compass. Kenneth told him, "This compass is special because it helped guide me and my Company in France during World War II. But it is not the most important compass. Do you know where the most important one is?"

"No," responded seven-year-old Lincoln.

"The most important compass you have is with you all the time. It is right here," he said, placing his hand on Lincoln's heart. "If you take time to listen to your heart, you'll always be guided in the right direction." Lincoln listened to his heart when his grandparents were ill, happily serenading them on the piano and singing Hebrew prayers and American songs to them, which gave them a lift.

At Lincoln's bar mitzvah in 2011, though his baba Frima and gramps Kenneth had passed away, they were very much present in spirit. Lincoln had been fortunate to share some precious years with both of them, learning by watching. As long as they were physically able, they had not missed one of his baseball or basketball games, one piano or drum recital, one Hebrew School or public school event or concert, one birthday party, one chance to read him the library

[222]If a Conservative or Orthodox Jew seeks to get divorced, the husband is required under Jewish law to initiate the process of obtaining "the Get," a legal writ nullifying the original marriage contract. Without it, the husband and wife are still married under Jewish law, even if they have completed a civil divorce. The Jewish divorce contract is handwritten by a scribe in Hebrew, under rabbinic supervision, and with witnesses attesting to it.

books he had checked out, or one invitation to go on a Sunday adventure with him. They felt lucky for these moments, too.

Before Lincoln's bar mitzvah service began, there were a number of assigned ushers who were handing out programs to persons entering the sanctuary. None were helping with more enthusiasm than Lincoln's best friend, Justin, who had met Lincoln in first grade in St. Louis Park. Justin's family had moved back to Memphis when he was starting fifth grade, but the boys had stayed in touch. Justin had driven up with his parents from Memphis to attend the milestone ceremony for his best friend, saying "Shabbat Shalom" ("Have a peaceful Sabbath"), to all who entered. Justin's parents are both Baptist ministers who had welcomed us to their church on Christmas Eve two years before. His parents, Renita and Anthony, were thrilled to be able to witness Lincoln's coming of age ceremony and to hear the sound of the Hebrew prayers, as they were chanted in Biblical times. We appreciated the James family's realization of the importance of this day for Lincoln and taking off from work to drive over eight hundred miles one way to celebrate with us, along with the sacrifices made by other relatives and friends to attend.

In my speech to Lincoln at his bar mitzvah, I said to him:

> I am holding the Jewish prayer book that your gramps Kenneth Bender was given by a Catholic Chaplain shortly before the invasion of Normandy in June 1944. On a page that had the corner turned down by Gramps, I found this psalm that gave inspiration to him at a time when he didn't know whether he would live or die:
>
> > Wait for the Lord
> > Be strong and let thy heart take courage
> > Teach me the way O Lord
> > And lead me in an even path.
>
> In other words, Lincoln, look to the Lord for strength, courage, and guidance, even in tough times. When our family has found itself in challenging times, we have looked to God for support and guidance. I hope that you, too, will find courage and strength from God.

I had also placed an item on an easel on the *bima* (pulpit), and stated:

> Your baba Frima painted this impressionist oil painting of a path before you were born. It is a symbol of the road we choose to take in life. It is your choice. Lincoln, as you face the ups and downs along life's road, I pray that you may remember your strong roots and get strength from them, have the courage to stand for what is right and good and be guided by God to the beautiful even path.

Large displays of brightly colored hothouse flowers usually adorn the pulpit at our synagogue for bar and bat mitzvahs, donated by the families of those reaching this milestone. Lincoln and I had agreed on something different. We wanted to frame the place where Lincoln would be chanting the age-old prayers with something more meaningful to us. As Lincoln read from the Torah, chanted his Haftorah, led the Schacharit (morning) service, said the blessings and delivered his speech, the sun shone brightly through the synagogue's stain-glassed windows onto Lincoln and the long spikes of Dakota prairie grass in the vase on the pulpit.

CHAPTER 16

New York, New York, May 2013

THEY HAD TAKEN GRUELING WRITTEN tests for one and a half hours regarding the finest points of six biblical books. Then they had a short break, followed by one and a half hours more of testing. There was time for a quick bite of kosher pizza and then they went into the auditorium at Yeshiva University in New York City to hear the names announced of the semifinalists in the two different age divisions for Jewish day school and public school for the Chidon Hatanach (National Bible Contest). Once announced, the top three scorers in the four categories would sit facing the large audience and would answer more questions to determine the national winners from each of the four categories. These United States representatives would then be sent to Israel the following year to compete in the International Bible Contest in Jerusalem.

Lincoln had been studying six different books of the Bible each year for the previous three years. Each year he had received a high enough score on the regional exam to participate in the National Bible Contest in New York. The first year he made it to New York City, he did not make it onto the stage for the final round. He vowed to work hard enough to make it onto the stage the following year. The second year, he made it onto the stage and placed third in his division. He told me he was determined to learn more and win his division the third year.

Lincoln waited for the portion of the program to begin when the results would be announced, and I went outside the auditorium to get a drink from the water fountain. As I was heading back into the auditorium, I looked to see where Lincoln was sitting and I saw an inexplicable light shining on Lincoln's blue and white six-panel bar mitzvah yarmulke and nowhere else in the room. I quickly took out my camera to take a picture, thinking that no one would believe me otherwise and returned to my seat next to Lincoln. I didn't say anything about the light that was around him, but at that moment I knew he was going to win.

There was not much leg-room, sitting in the bucket seats of the Yeshiva Auditorium, and another competitor's backpack was on the ground, blocking Lincoln's way to walk to the aisle leading to the stage, if his name would be called. I asked the gentleman sitting two seats away if that was his child's backpack. He said that it was.

"Would it be OK if I put it on the seat, instead of the ground?" I asked.

"Yes, you may," he said.

"You must be quite confident that your son's name will be called, trying to clear a path for him!" I smiled and didn't respond. I didn't want to appear arrogant, but I was very confident. I knew how hard Lincoln had worked over the last year. I could no longer stump him with any question on the six books he had studied—not who said what to whom, name the place, fill in the blank, what is the law—nothing. And there was also that inexplicable glow.

* * *

Over the previous year, Lincoln had individual instruction via Skype two to three times a week with Rabbi Meir Smith, a rabbi from Minnesota. Lincoln had also studied on his own, answering the questions that Rabbi Smith sent to him via email. Lincoln had also studied with me—reading the texts, discussing the texts, answering thousands of questions. The reason why Lincoln had not been

Lincoln Bernhard waiting to hear Bible Contest results at Yeshiva University, 2013. *Photo by Rebecca Bender, author files.*

able to study with Rabbi Smith in person was that Lincoln and I had moved from St. Louis Park, Minnesota, to Eureka, South Dakota, prior to Lincoln's starting high school. Lincoln would have attended a high school with around three thousand students in St. Louis Park. Instead, he was attending a high school with around forty students and living in his late gramps's hometown. It was a unique feeling to be moving closer to our past.

A lot of planning and discussion took place before Lincoln and I decided to move. After a couple of trips to Eureka, during which we met with Kenneth's old friends, the Heilmans, and the Superintendent, K-12 Principal, and Athletic Director (all of whom happened to be the same person), everything seemed to fall into place. The town had not been the wheat capital of the world for over one hundred years, but a sign upon entering proclaimed that Eureka was the birthplace of the founder of USA Today, Al Neuharth. Those who carefully studied USA Today's weather map around this time, may have noticed that Eureka, South Dakota, population 880 people, was listed among the major cities in the United States, at the request of Mr. Neuharth.[223]

We met with the town realtor, who took us to three houses. In the first two, Lincoln could not stand up either in a doorway or a room, as he was too tall. Then the realtor said he had another idea, but it was an older home that was on the market. We walked into the house, and Lincoln had plenty of room as the old house had high ceilings. The house was on a hill overlooking Lake Eureka with lots of room for Lincoln's dog, Buddy, to run and play fetch. Then I saw a note on the wall that referred to the home as the former "Gerdes House." I asked the realtor, Mr. Krein, "which Gerdes is that, who lived in this house?"

"He was the town doctor, years ago. They used to call him 'Doc' Gerdes," said the realtor.

Stunned, I turned to Lincoln and said, "Lincoln, this is the house where your gramps was brought back to life after falling through Lake Eureka."

After a moment of silence for it all to sink in, Lincoln said, "I really like it."

"I do, too," I said.

In order to purchase the Eureka house and begin our new chapter, we had to sell our home in St. Louis Park. But I was afraid that

[223]A little over a year and a half after Mr. Neuharth passed away, the USA TODAY weather map was downsized. The little town of Eureka, that had stood uniquely and proudly among the many metropolises on the map, was no longer listed.

this meant that the home in Eureka would be gone by the time the Minnesota house was sold. My parents had given me a violin when I was in seventh grade. It was like a friend to me. The violin was made in Germany in 1934 by Fritz Heberlein. I called the violin Fritz. I was first chair in my high school orchestra, first attended the University of Minnesota as a violin performance major, and oftentimes included a violin track on original songs I recorded. I had also played my dear baba Minnie her favorite song, "Lara's Theme," from *Dr. Zhivago* on this violin less than an hour before she passed away. The violin was the only item of value I still held, other than our home, as I had sold everything else to make ends meet for Lincoln and me since the divorce.

In hopes of a new start for Lincoln and me, I sold my violin. We also received a generous gift from Marvin, a kind, former elementary school classmate of my late mom's for the remainder amount needed for a down payment on the Eureka home. The Andersons, owners of the Gerdes home—a Eureka dentist and his wife, the family and consumer science teacher—were very accommodating. They agreed not to market the Eureka home after receiving the down payment until I had a chance to sell our Minnesota home. In talking with the Eureka dentist, I also learned that the building where he had practiced dentistry in Eureka for decades was the building where Benders' General Store had been located. Though I had learned over the years not to put too much faith in signs, they were becoming too amazing to ignore.

Prior to making the decision to move to Eureka, however, I did some investigating regarding a synagogue close by. To my delight, I learned that only one hour and twenty minutes away in Aberdeen, South Dakota, was South Dakota's only Conservative synagogue. To my additional amazement, I learned that the couple who were the lay leaders of the Aberdeen synagogue for years, the Premacks, had another connection to the Bender family. When Kenneth's brother, David, was studying for his bar mitzvah, he lived with Herschel Premack's family in Aberdeen so he could study with a rabbi in town to prepare.

We sold our home in Minnesota and were on our way. When Lincoln and I pulled up to our new home in Eureka—white with John-Deere-green shutters — we experienced quiet, interrupted only occasionally by a tweeting bird or a few far off "moos."

The day of our arrival, our new neighbor, Arvilda Schaeffer, whose late brother-in-law used to work at Benders' General Store and whose late husband used to play golf with my dad and Grandpa Joe, brought over enough moist homemade chocolate cake to last us a week. The next day, Bonnie Melhaff, who with her husband Arlo used to own the town newspaper, the *Northwest Blade*, offered me her soup pot so I could make chicken soup, as she had already heard the rumor that I had left mine at my sister's home in Minnesota. The following week, I was invited to a ladies' tea in my honor, hosted by Claudia Hoffman Merthan, who with her late husband had provided the initial funding for the Eureka Pioneer Museum. Shortly thereafter, Cal Neuharth, a retired teacher in Eureka, greeted me as I was walking downtown. He introduced himself and said to say hello to his classmate, my uncle David, though they hadn't seen each other since David graduated from high school sixty-four years earlier. And Clyde Ottenbacher, the smiling butcher in the grocery store, after reading the local newspaper article about our arrival and our family's history, ran out from behind his counter so he could point out to me the all beef hot dogs "with no pork."

Lincoln and I quickly became accustomed to "the Eureka wave." Everyone who lives in Eureka waves to people in oncoming cars as they drive down the streets of town, even if they can't see who is behind the wheel of the approaching car. It's more than a gesture of neighborliness. It's also a gesture of acceptance — no matter who you are, you are welcome.

When an ice storm recently cut off power to Eureka for several days, the local grocery store, Ken's, let people take groceries out of the store with only a handwritten list of IOUs kept at the front register. The manager reported that all these debts (with the exception of one) were promptly paid once the power was put back on. I was obviously pleased, but not that surprised at these and many other kindnesses. It was consistent with the Eureka in the stories my dad had told.

Another difference between Eureka and the more citified places we'd lived is the tumbleweeds. I'd only seen these naturally entwined grass balls rolling and dancing in the wind in old Hollywood westerns. On windy days, as we drove through and out of Eureka, we saw them fly across the road or pressed against the nearest wire cattle fence, like little league baseball players waiting for their turn at bat. I was told that these prairie grass conglomerates blowing through town are embraced. In many homes, the autumn tumbleweeds are spray-painted bright colors and used as decorations. It didn't matter where they came from, their beauty is recognized.

And the stars at night in Eureka, far from the city lights, were never-ending. When I looked up, in the total quiet, I thought of God's promise to Abraham in the book of Genesis, "I will make your descendants as numerous as the stars in the sky." I called Lincoln outside our first night in Eureka, though we were tired from the move. "Lincoln, you have to come out here!" I said.

"What's wrong?" he asked.

"Just come out, you won't believe it!" I urged. He came out and I told him to look up. He saw the many layers of stars we had never seen before, that went beyond what we used to think of as the heavens. "We never even knew the stars we weren't seeing," I said.

****

Rabbi Ezra Fraser, director of the United States Chidon in New York City, tapped the microphone to make sure it was working. "The three finalists in the fifteen and under public school division—please come up to the stage—are: Lincoln Bernhard . . ." The man who had moved his child's backpack looked at me quizzically as Lincoln said, "Excuse me," and walked past him to the aisle and up to the front of the auditorium. After three more rounds of video questions, the winner was announced for the public school, junior high division United States champion, "Lincoln Bernhard!" After pictures and a snack with his dad and half-brother living in Massachusetts, we returned home to Eureka. Then the work really began.

There were now twenty-nine books to study, most of which Lincoln had never read or studied before. They included Genesis, Exodus, Leviticus, Numbers, Deuteronomy, Joshua, Judges, Samuel 1, Samuel 2, Kings 1, Kings 2, Isaiah, Jeremiah, Ezekiel, Hosea, Amos, Jonah, Micah, Zephaniah, Haggai, Zeckahiah, Malachi, Psalms, Proverbs, Job, Ruth, Ezra, Nehemiah, and Chronicles 2. It was a monumental task for anyone, but even more so for a student who had always attended public schools. Lincoln did not shy away from the challenge. In between public school homework, playing on basketball and baseball teams, taking percussion lessons and playing in the school band, Lincoln studied.

Prior to leaving for Israel, Lincoln learned that he was the only United States representative with a public school education who had studied the twenty-nine texts and was traveling to the international contest. Lincoln arrived in Israel and began the whirlwind of activities there before further testing: meeting contestants from as far away as Romania and the Czech Republic, praying at the Kotel (Western Wall of the Second Temple), visiting Maimonides's grave, and feeling the range of human emotions, being in Israel for Yom Hazikaron (Memorial Day) and Yom Haatzsmaut (Independence Day).

***

Lincoln just missed being a finalist in the televised broadcast of the Chidon Hatanach on Israeli TV. However, he had another interesting encounter while in Israel. The seventy-five champions from over thirty different countries were invited to Prime Minister Netanyahu's residence, where he gave them a speech and praised them as Children of the Book. He asked each of the champions to introduce themselves and to tell him where they were from and how old they were. When it was Lincoln's turn, Lincoln said in Hebrew, "*Shemi Shlomo. Ani Me Artzot Habreet. Ani ben hamesh esrai* [I am Shlomo. I am from the United States. I am fifteen years old]."

Mr. Netanyahu posed for a group picture with the Bible students, and then was preparing to leave the room. Lincoln called out, "*Mar Netanyahu* [Mr. Netanyahu]!" The Prime Minister turned to face Lincoln, who then at 6'4" was the tallest person in the room.

"Are you really fifteen years old?" Mr. Netanyahu asked, remembering Lincoln's introduction of himself from among the seventy-five introductions. Lincoln said that he was. The Prime Minister shook hands with Lincoln and said, "What can I do for you?" Lincoln responded, "Mar Netanyahu, would you please tell us what your favorite Bible story is in the Tanach?" The Prime Minister thought for a moment and then responded, "Joseph and his brothers." Then he paused, and realizing how much taller Lincoln was than he, added jokingly, "I also like the story of David and Goliath!" At that point, Chairman of The Jewish Agency and human rights advocate Natan Sharansky, who spent nine years in Soviet prisons after being denied the right to immigrate to Israel, placed his hands on Lincoln's shoulders and tried jumping up to his height, resulting in chuckles from the group.

Lincoln Bernhard of Eureka, South Dakota, had shaken hands and spoken with an important Jewish leader, just as his great-grandfather Yosef Bendersky of Zebricov had done over a hundred years earlier in Odessa, Russia. I was traveling with the group as an English speaking volunteer chaperone and was standing in the back of the room with the Chidon contestants' Israeli army group leaders. "Shlomo is talking to Bibi!" one of them said to me. "He called out to him to ask a question!"

I was a little embarrassed at the brazen way in which Shlomo (Lincoln) had called out to this Jewish leader. On the other hand, I was proud that my son had the chutzpah to ask a question and shake the man's hand. Lincoln was one of three — in the group of seventy-five — who attended public school and had never attended a Jewish day school, where the ancient texts were studied daily. In addition, Hebrew was not spoken in our home. Lincoln's participation as a Bible Champion representing the United States was a testament to hard work, determination, and a strong faith. Lincoln refused to accept that a participant in the International Bible Contest could not come from a public school, or a small town, or be the great-great grandson of Jewish farmers in a remote area of North Dakota. To those surprised at his accomplishment in going from not placing in the National Bible Contest to first place in three years' time, I repeated his gramps's words to the University of Minnesota Law School Dean Fraser: "Nothing in those tests measures determination."

* * *

Two days later, among the rocky hills and sharp grasses, Lincoln hiked up and down along a wadi in the Judean desert on the path that King David, King Saul, and Jeremiah the prophet walked two

Lincoln Bernhard with Minnesota Twins baseball cap, United States National Bible Champion, talking with Israel's Prime Minister Benjamin Netanyahu, 2014. *Photo by Amihai Bannett, The Jewish Agency.*

thousand years before. It was a long way from Kiva Bendersky in Zebricov dreaming of freedom to Lincoln Bernhard in the Judean desert in Israel, hiking with fellow Bible champions from all over the world. Lincoln's feet trekked on the dusty earth that Jewish kings had walked on, and he felt the strong sun on him that they had also known.

When Lincoln was participating in the International Bible Contest in Israel, there was limited free time in the busy schedule. The one item he wanted to purchase in Israel was a *mezuzah*.[224] He found one that he liked in an open market in Jerusalem. The mezuzah is a way to remind Jews to infuse our daily doings with holiness and good deeds, as well as for us to remember that God is with us when we are in our homes and when we go out of them.

The Sh'ma Yisrael (Hear O Israel) is the oldest daily prayer in Judaism. It contains the following words, taken from the book of Deuteronomy, which refer to the concept of the mezuzah:

> You shall love the Lord your God with all your heart, with all your soul, and with all your might. And these words which I command you today shall be in your heart. You shall teach them diligently to your children, and you shall speak of them when you sit in your house and when you walk on the road, when you lie down and when you rise up. And you shall write them upon the doorposts of your house and upon your gates.

Lincoln's father, living in Massachusetts at the time, visited Lincoln in Eureka the summer after the Bible contest. I suggested that he work together with Lincoln to attach the mezuzah Lincoln had purchased to the doorpost of Lincoln's home, and he did.

* * *

The year after the International Bible Contest, Lincoln was in tenth grade. There were auditions to determine which band students

[224]A Mezuzah is a case containing Torah verses on parchment, traditionally placed on the doorposts of Jewish homes.

would be given which parts for their instruments. It was announced that Lincoln was the first chair percussionist for his high school band. This meant that Lincoln was selected to play the coveted snare drum. The band students were also told that they would be marching in the largest parade in South Dakota sometime later in the fall. Gypsy Days is a festival that is held in Aberdeen, South Dakota, with over two hundred marching bands participating and competing against each other.

As luck would have it, Lincoln soon realized that the day of the Gypsy Day Parade was Yom Kippur, the Day of Atonement, the holiest day of the year for Jewish people. As mentioned earlier, Jews do not eat or drink from sundown on the previous night until sundown on Yom Kippur, people pray in the synagogue with fellow Jews, and no work is to be done on this day.

In 1934, Hank Greenberg, the well-known Detroit Tigers Jewish baseball player, made headlines when he refused to play baseball on Yom Kippur. Years later, in 1965, Sandy Koufax became an inspiration for young Jews everywhere, when he refused to pitch Game 1 in the World Series for the Dodgers for the same reason. Though accurate, these stories have become legend-like in every Jewish community, stories told to young children as soon as they are able to understand. Messrs. Greenberg and Koufax stand as symbols of faith and of making decisions to preserve one's Jewish faith.

Lincoln and I had been planning to attend Yom Kippur services in Aberdeen on Yom Kippur in 2014, prior to knowing there was a conflict with the parade. I wanted to know what decision sixteen-year-old Lincoln would make and asked him what he was planning on doing. I mentioned that it probably would be possible for him to both play in the parade and attend a portion of the services, as both events were to take place in Aberdeen.

"I will not play," said Lincoln, without hesitation.

"What?" I asked, wanting to make sure I had heard him correctly.

"I'm going to Yom Kippur services, like Greenberg and Koufax did," replied Lincoln. When I expressed to Lincoln how proud I was of him for his decision, Lincoln stated, "Mom, it's no big deal. Do you really think I'd miss services?" As Lincoln and I walked into B'nai Israel synagogue in Aberdeen, we could hear the wind and brass instruments warming up for the Gypsy Parade.

Once we were in the little synagogue, the noises outside were no longer heard.

EPILOGUE

Part I

When we moved to Eureka in 2013, Lincoln and I were about forty minutes from the Ashley Jewish Cemetery, where members of the Ashley Jewish homesteading community were buried between 1913 and 1932. When we visited to pay our respects to my great-grandfather Kiva Bender, Lincoln began asking me questions about the cemetery and the lives of the Jewish people who farmed nearby. I didn't have as much information for him as I would have liked. I decided that I wanted to learn more and to share the information with others regarding this little known community. On that day, I privately set as my goal to try to have this remote property listed on the National Register of Historic Places.

In 1916, when Grandpa Joe and Grandma Mary Bender moved to neighboring McPherson County, South Dakota, from McIntosh County, North Dakota, to open a general store, they were less than an hour away from the Ashley Jewish Cemetery. By the 1930s, after almost all of the Jewish homesteaders in Ashley had left their farms, Joe was arranging for the cemetery's upkeep with the assistance of local Ashley caretakers.

When Joe and Mary moved from Eureka to Minneapolis after David began attending the University of Minnesota in 1949, all through the 1960s Joe would return at least annually to check on the condition of the cemetery and to arrange for necessary upkeep and repairs. Johnny Salzer, a McIntosh County Commissioner living in

Ashley, alone and later with his son, Mark, were paid annually to keep the cemetery property maintained. The officers of the Ashley Cemetery Committee at the time consisted of Joe Bender (son of Kiva Bender, buried at the cemetery), Pauline Greenberg (daughter of Israel and Sarah Auerbach, buried at the cemetery), and Ben Grossman (son of Isadore Grossman, buried at the cemetery). They also headed up the campaigns to raise funds from the descendants of those buried in order to provide for the property's perpetual care.[225]

By the 1970s, my dad began making arrangements for the maintenance of the cemetery. He, initially with his dad, Joe, and later on his own, drove at least annually to check the property and talk with the caretaker. In 1971, the Cemetery Association was incorporated as a nonprofit North Dakota corporation. To formalize the duties being performed by descendants, in 1979 Kenneth Bender, grandson of Kiva and Rebecka Bender, was unanimously elected president of the Cemetery Association, and Lionel Greenberg, grandson of Israel and Sarah Auerbach, was unanimously elected secretary-treasurer. Also in that year, Pauline Greenberg gifted the cemetery property she held to the Ashley Jewish Cemetery Corporation.[226]

According to the Ashley Jewish Cemetery Association Meeting Minutes, in 1991 one member of the cemetery board wanted the county to take over ownership of the cemetery site as had been done with the Regan/Wing Jewish Cemetery, one of the three remaining North Dakota Jewish homestead cemeteries. He worried that future generations would not find the time to care for the cemetery and that it might fall into disrepair, disrespecting the memories of those buried there. A vote regarding the future of the Ashley Jewish Cemetery took place at a meeting in the party room of a St. Louis Park, Minnesota, condominium. The votes were counted. The Ashley home-

---

[225]Joseph Bender Interview by Al Thal (1974); Pauline Greenberg Correspondence 1951–1952; and Kenneth Bender letter to Lionel Greenberg, January 19, 1986, Jewish Historical Project of North Dakota records; Ted Quanrud, "Keeping faith with the past—Descendants of pioneers preserve Jewish cemetery," *Bismarck Tribune* (December 6, 1987); Bender, *From the Prairies to the Beaches*.

[226]Ibid.; Ashley Jewish Corporation Meeting Minutes, June 6, 1979, Jewish Historical Project of North Dakota records; Deeds from McIntosh County, North Dakota.

steader descendants who felt a moral obligation to continue caring for the cemetery as their parents had done before them outnumbered the one who wanted the security of knowing the county was caring for the property. This vote was one of extreme faith — faith that the Jewish traditions held dear by the children and grandchildren of the homesteaders would be continued with the future generations of descendants, though they may not even have been born yet.[227]

In the mid-1990s, after most of the generations of children and grandchildren of the original Ashley homesteaders had aged or passed away, homesteader Isadore Grossman's great-grandson Bob Kaufman took over the reins as president of the AJCC. In 1999, Stuart Kaufman of Seattle accepted these duties from his brother and made arrangements for the continuing care and maintenance of the cemetery, including fundraising and arranging for the filing of annual reports with the state. He continues in this role today. Rabbi Jon-Jay Tilsen of New Haven also serves on the cemetery board and is in charge of the cemetery website. Rabbi Tilsen and Stuart Kaufman are both great-grandsons of Ashley homesteaders (Louis Reuben and Isadore Grossman) and have something else in common besides their work to preserve the resting place of their ancestors: their grandmothers each married Jewish traveling salesmen while living in North Dakota.

In the spring of 2014, Lincoln and I met with Stuart, visiting from Seattle, and together noted the stones that were in most need of repair. Though the caretakers had done their best to repair some of the stones as they became unstable, time was having an obvious effect on some of the monuments and ledgers. Through Preservation North Dakota, I was given the name of Mark "Tim" Timbrook, a professor at Minot State University, who had been trained in cemetery restoration, applying the same techniques and materials used at Arlington National Cemetery. Generously, he and his wife, Eunice, agreed to repair five of the stones and to help us to clean the stones as volunteers.

[227]Ashley Jewish Cemetery Corporation Meeting Minutes, September 25, 1991, Jewish Historical Project of North Dakota records.

In August of 2014, Tim, Eunice, an eighty-four-year-old Quaker named Raymond Schneider-Kuhn, who heard of the restoration project from our Aberdeen synagogue, Lincoln, and I all arrived ready to work. As luck would have it, the temperature was in the 90s, with 99 percent humidity on the prairie that day. I had arranged through the cemetery caretaker, Claude Meidinger, to have one tote of 275 gallons of water available and to purchase a one-hundred-foot hose. The Timbrooks did the work requiring the most expertise and the rest of us scrubbed. Once the work was done, the Timbrooks and Mr. Schneider-Kuhn had the same responses to our expressions of gratitude: "It was our pleasure. It was an honor." I shared with them that Jewish people believe that a good deed done for those who cannot repay it is the highest form of charity.

***

Eunice Timbrook assists Lincoln Bernhard, cleaning his great-great grandfather Kiva Bender's stone, August 2014. *Photo by Rebecca Bender, author files.*

With the initial restoration work completed, I focused on my research plan. I told the helpful man who cut the grass at our home in Eureka what I was planning on doing and that I hoped to get historical recognition for the little cemetery in Ashley. He responded, "Don't bother. There are hundreds of little cemeteries all over the Dakotas, and I've never heard of anyone getting them on the Register." I also spoke to my cousin Sandra in Council Bluffs, Iowa, who told me that their congregation had paid a historian to prepare the historic nomination for their old synagogue building, years earlier. She was aware of the meticulous, detailed analysis required in order to submit a nomination. She advised me that though she believed I could do anything I set my mind to do, this process would be unlike anything I had been involved in before. Others I knew wondered why I was spending so much effort on this long-shot.

Undaunted, I began. If the Benders could move large boulders of rock to clear their land, I convinced myself that I was up for the challenge and thought of the oft-quoted phrase from the Jewish scholar Hillel found in *Pirke Avot (Ethics of our Fathers)*, "if not now, when?"

I started with online research regarding homesteading in the Dakotas. Then I reviewed reports of the Jewish Agricultural Society, *Ashley Tribune* clippings on microfiche and from Ashley historian Leona Neu, books and articles by Father William C. Sherman and others, homestead patent records, marriage records, census records, and files gathered by Frances Wold (Regan, North Dakota Town Clerk, reporter, and columnist). I also read homesteader family histories painstakingly compiled in the 1970s by the late Toba Geller of Fargo, who was planning a book on the Jews of North Dakota that she unfortunately was never able to complete. Lincoln and I spent hours listening to interviews of Jewish homesteaders by Alfred Thal, including my grandpa Joe Bender's, at the Historical Society in Bismarck. I waded through boxes of documents and pictures in the archives at the University of Minnesota Upper Midwest Jewish Historical Society Archives. I reread my dad's book, *From the Prairies to the Beaches*, and memories written down my grandfather Joe Bender.

When examining land records at the McIntosh County Courthouse in Ashley, the Court Clerk and Recorder, Carol Fey, whom I had just met, came over and said to me, "Excuse me. May I ask you . . . Do you have Jewish blood?" I was at first taken aback by the question, but her helpfulness to me in my research caused me to know that this inquiry came from a good place.

"Yes," I said. "My grandparents and great-grandparents were homesteaders in Ashley."

"I want to take you to see something during my lunch break that might be of interest to you, if you would like," she said.

"Sure, thank you," I responded.

When the court clerk was ready, we left the courthouse and walked about two blocks into a well-manicured residential neighborhood. "This is my home," said Carol. "It used to be the Jewish synagogue. Would you like to come inside?" I was so surprised and took her up on her generous offer. The home had been remodeled extensively prior to Carol and her husband Lyle's purchase of the property. "Other than the foundation and walls, the only original part of the old church and synagogue is the sculptured tin ceiling," she said. I stood quietly in the building, and tried to picture the Ashley Jewish community meeting and greeting each other and then beginning the serious business of praying in this spot. Carol left me alone for a moment. I closed my eyes and tried to hear the sounds of Shacharit (morning prayers) in the silence, under the tin ceiling.

***

The two main portions of any Nomination to the National Parks Service are the "Description of the Property" and the "Statement of Significance." As I began working on the Description of the Property portion first, I realized that my mother, my son, my dad and my sister had inadvertently prepared me well for this task. Every year, from the time I can remember, my mother, Frima Blume (Yiddish for pious flower), used to plant flowers at family members' graves in Minnesota before Memorial Day. As she wanted to make certain that the area was totally cleared of all weeds and roots prior to placing the spike plant close to the monument, and then building the garden forward with plantings of geraniums, petunias, coleus, and

Ashley Baptist Church, then Ashley Synagogue, and now a private home. The structure remains on the site where it was moved in 1924.
Photo by Rebecca Bender, author files.

ageratum, this was a lengthy process. With time on my hands before I was called upon to repeatedly fill the watering can, I would wander. I would examine the symbols on the stones, the content of the Hebrew writing on the stones, the shape and material of the stones, and I would report back to my mom on what I had seen and then was off again to make new discoveries. Cemeteries, to me, were not only sacred places. They were fascinating.

When Lincoln was studying for the Bible contest, I was studying with him. Though I did not absorb as much information as he, in asking him thousands of questions and reading together I learned a great deal more about Judaism and its roots than I had previously known. Who would have expected that when he was studying the Book of Job, I would later notice the quote from the same Book on Lincoln's great-great grandfather's grave monument in Ashley? Kiva Bender's monument refers to him in Hebrew as *taam v'yashar*, a pious and upright man.

After starting out as a violin performance major at college and then switching to major in psychology, I was uncertain what career path to follow. I followed my father and sister in attending the University of Minnesota Law School. As I admired both of them tremendously, it seemed the logical thing to do; to follow in their footsteps. Had I not been exposed to the laws, rules, and regulations when appearing in court and filing legal briefs, I wouldn't have been able to complete the task of drafting the National Register Nomination as a non-historian. I can hear my dad saying to me, "Rebecca, even if you don't practice law for your whole life, what you learn in law school will help you understand the world better for the rest of your life." In hindsight, I believe that I was supposed to use these experiences and tools to meet the challenge of bringing the Jewish homesteaders' stories to light on the National Register of Historic Places.

There were a number of Jewish homesteader cemeteries scattered across North Dakota from the late nineteenth and early twentieth century, including cemeteries in Ashley, Glen Ullin, Dickinson, Fallon, Edmore, Mandan, Wilton, Wing, Devil's Lake, and Regan. All but three of these cemeteries had been entirely or almost entirely lost by the time I began my research, with prairie grasses and earth covering the last remnants of these homesteaders' history. It was heartbreaking to discover the description of some of the other cemeteries in various journals. For example, the Jewish cemetery from the first Jewish homesteading settlement in North Dakota—Painted Woods Colony, 1882—"may have existed in a field or a ravine"; the Mandan cemetery "has no markers"; the Fallon, Edmore, and Dickinson cemeteries can "no longer be located."[228] In addition to the Ashley

[228]International Association of Jewish Genealogical Societies, "International Jewish Cemetery Project," www.iajgsjewishcemeteryproject.org. I took solace from the fact that these other cemeteries literally disappeared into the earth. In contrast, I learned that after the remaining 19,582 Jews living in Odessa had been murdered by the Nazis and Romanians by January 1942 (by shooting, starvation, disease, and burning), and many of the apartments where the Jews had lived had been reassigned with their belongings to the 7500 "ethnic Germans" living in Odessa, the marble tombstones in the Jewish cemetery were removed and shipped to Romania. In 1943, 831 cubic meters of marble (around 500,000 pounds) from the Odessa Jewish cemetery were located in a stone-cutting plant in Bucharest. The gravestone of Shimen Frug, known as the first Jewish Russian national poet, who passed away in 1916, and whose funeral procession was attended by over 100,000 people in Odessa, was found among the marble slabs there. Martin Gilbert. *The Holocaust: A History of the Jews of Europe during the Second World War* (New York: Henry Holt and Company, 1985), p. 289.

Jewish Homesteaders Cemetery, located in what has been called North Dakota's German-Russian Triangle, the two other homesteader cemeteries that remain visible and accessible in North Dakota are the Regan/Wing Jewish Cemetery near Bismarck and the Sons of Jacob Cemetery, of the Garske Colony about fifteen miles from Devil's Lake.[229]

So I began drafting the Description of the Property. Then, after the research, analysis, and writing of that section was completed, I changed my focus to attempting to understand the many requirements for preparing the "Statement of Significance" and the rest of the nomination. The form from the United States Department of the Interior contained detailed explanations of each required category. It was much more complicated than the requirements I had encountered when preparing federal circuit court appellate briefs on interpretations of securities laws. In addition to the specifications required generally, there are even stricter requirements for cemeteries and for religious properties. My first time reading through the requirements took me over three hours. Nevertheless, I was proud when I submitted the Nomination to the North Dakota Historical Preservation Board. I was looking forward to Lorna Meidinger, the North Dakota Architectural Historian and National Register Coordinator, advising me of when the State Historic Preservation Board would vote on whether to recommend the property to the National Parks Service.

Instead of an email advising me of the timetable for the board's recommendation, I received back the marked-up nomination from Lorna, with over 130 comments, questions, and suggestions. For one day I was crestfallen. I felt I had put everything I had into the research and writing. I had stayed up all night some nights, getting the language as perfect as I could. I had taken pictures of the property

[229]Garske Village (Colony) was formed in 1883, and was the second North Dakota Jewish agricultural settlement in North Dakota. The Wing and Regan Jewish farming colonies were formed around 1901. Gordon Iseminger, "McIntosh County German-Russians: The First Fifty Years": Bernard Postal and Lionel Koppman, *A Jewish Tourists Guide to the US* (Philadephia: Jewish Publication Society, 1954).

and the stones, indicating the point of view. Lincoln had helped me place the pictures on the required disks. I had thought I was done, but I had a choice to make — whether to begin again. After a night's rest, I thought of how important it was that persons happening by the cemetery would know about the people who were buried there. I began the process of doing more research and answering each and every comment and question that had been posed to me. I returned to Bismarck and Minneapolis for more research. I read more articles and family histories, and I rewrote the text. Lincoln assisted me in embedding key documents and pictures in the nomination, and slowly, the document began to come alive.

* * *

Strangely, when I was working on the nomination into the night until morning, I was frequently visited by an owl hooting outside the window. Maybe the owl came to the only light still on in Eureka, or maybe it was sent to keep me company. Either way I looked forward to my late night immersion, surrounded by papers, pictures, history, and the hooting owl. I felt that some force much bigger than myself was guiding me. I came to realize that the comments by Lorna Meidinger had caused me to dig deeper and discover more than I otherwise would have.

Once I had completed researching and writing the Description of the Property portion of the Nomination, I began working again on the Statement of Significance, i.e., why the property is worthy of historic recognition. Thirty-nine percent of the land that now makes up North Dakota was homesteaded, making it the second highest percentage of any state that allowed homesteading. The total number of acres transferred from the public domain in North Dakota to private landowners, beginning in 1870, was 17,417,466.[230] Between 1879 and 1886, the first population boom into the area now known as North Dakota occurred, with over one hundred thousand immi-

---

[230]Clay Jenkinson, "Federal Money Boosts North Dakota Living," *Bismarck Tribune*, August 16, 2015.

grants entering the Northern Territory. The second boom took place between 1898 and 1915, when 250,000 more people moved into the region.[231] In 1885 there were 390 people in McIntosh County, where Ashley is located. By 1910 there were 7,251.[232] The Jewish population of about four hundred people was approximately 5.5 percent of McIntosh County's population in 1910.

North Dakota Jewish history was unlike that in any other states, as most of the first Jewish settlers "came to till the soil."[233] About 1200 Jewish farmers and their families lived in North Dakota on around 250 farms, in at least fifty settlements spread out over twenty-seven North Dakota counties between the 1880s and 1920s. The Jewish agriculturists owned about 86,000 acres in North Dakota in 1910.[234] The Ashley Jewish Homesteaders Cemetery was the cemetery for the largest Jewish agricultural settlement ever in North or South Dakota, and it is the largest Jewish homesteader cemetery in North or South Dakota.[235]

Of the three remaining visible North Dakota Jewish prairie cemeteries, the location of the McIntosh County Jewish homesteaders'

---

[231]State Historical Society of North Dakota: "American Settlement," history.nd.gov/ndhistory/settlement; www.ndstudies.org/getting_and_living_on_a_homestead#sthash.ncuMHrkC.dpuf

[232]Iseminger, "McIntosh County German-Russians"; United States Census Bureau, 13th Census North Dakota (1910); The Dakota Territorial Census of 1885, Collections of the State Historical Society of North Dakota, IV (Fargo, ND: Knight Printing Co., 1913), pp. 361–72.

[233]Postal and Koppman, *A Jewish Tourist's Guide to the US*.

[234]Ibid.; Schultz, "Proving Up and Moving Up," 2010, citing William C. Sherman and Playford v. Thorson, *Plains Folk: North Dakota's Ethnic History* (Fargo: North Dakota Institute for Regional Studies, 1988); Jewish Agricultural Society, Annual Report (New York: JAS 1909), containing summary of first ten years of organization; JAS Annual Report (1910); Oliver B. Pollak, "Jews," *Encyclopedia of the Great Plains* (University of Nebraska Omaha).

[235]J. Sanford Rikoon, *Jewish Farm Settlements in America's Heartland* (Bloomington: Indiana University Press, 1995), p. 132, n. 55; and Jewish Agricultural and Industrial Aid Society, *Annual Report* (New York: JAS 1908), p. 25; William C. Sherman, *Prairie Mosaic: An Ethnic Atlas of Rural North Dakota*, (Fargo: North Dakota Institute for Regional Studies 1983), p. 53; ashleyjewishcemetery.com (Ashley Jewish Cemetery website); Frances M. Wold August 8, 1976, report on Wing/Regan Jewish Cemetery at North Dakota Historical Society; findagrave.com (Regan Jewish Cemetery); sojnorthdakota.org (Garske/Sons of Jacob Cemetery website).

land (and cemetery), not close to any "bigger" towns, caused these farmers to be more isolated from fellow Jews and Jewish institutions than those Jews living in the Garske Colony or the Regan/Wing settlements. The closest "big" city to Ashley was Aberdeen, South Dakota, about eighty miles away.[236] Another distinction between the three cemeteries is that the Ashley Jewish Cemetery is the only one of these that has been continually maintained by descendants (and those hired by the descendants) without the properties having been turned over to the counties or neighbor volunteers for caretaking.

In the early 1900s, there were more Jewish farmers in North Dakota than in any other states except New Jersey, Connecticut, and New York. Some Jewish agricultural settlements were not listed in articles or books describing the time period, as they either consisted of small groups of Jewish farmers, making the "colony" designation strained, or the farming operations were short lived, or the settlements were located far away from larger population centers and did not seek help from the available Jewish organizations.[237]

I was surprised to discover that prior to 1882, Jewish immigration to the United States was negligible. It was no coincidence that the May Laws passed in Russia around this same time, which restricted Jews in so many ways, was the impetus for the start of "the great migration."[238] I also learned about the four main reasons why Russian Jewish immigrants came to the United States: conditions in Russia, the Am Olam movement, favorable United States homestead and immigration laws, and the support of Jewish charitable organizations.

A corollary reason for Jews turning to farming, sometimes contained within a discussion of the Am Olam movement and some-

---

[236]The remoteness of the Ashley homesteaders' land affected their timely access to supplies, markets for their goods, communication, and ability to gather together a minyan. These factors made their retaining their Jewish identity all the more compelling.

[237]Jewish Agricultural Society Annual Report (1910); Schulte, "Proving Up and Moving Up," (2010); Sherman and Thorson, *Plains Folk: North Dakota's Ethnic History*.

[238]Jewish Agricultural and Industrial Society Annual Reports (1903, 1909).

times analyzed separately, is the biblical basis for the Jewish "consciousness for the land." Gabriel Davidson, in *Our Jewish Farmers: The Story of the Jewish Agricultural Society*, refers to the then one hundred thousand Jews making their living on farms in the United States, the biblical journey of the Jews from slavery in search of fertile lands and green pastures, and the "pastoral note" that runs through the songs, proverbs, and prophecies of the Old and New Testaments.[239] Davidson also cites to the advice given by renowned author Leo Tolstoy to a rabbi visiting Russia (Rabbi Joseph Krauskopf, then the leader of the oldest reform synagogue in Philadelphia) to "spread the good name of your people throughout the land . . . by leading Jews out of the city and into the field as producers of bread." Rabbi Krauskopf promptly became one of the founders of the National Farm School in Doylestown, Pennsylvania, in 1894, which had many Jewish students studying agricultural science on its campus.[240]

Whether or not there was a biblical basis for the North Dakota Jewish farmers, there is no doubt that without the help of other Jews, very few of the farming Dakota Jews would have gotten their start on the land. In addition to local synagogue and charitable organizations to assist Jewish immigrants, the two main nationwide charities that assisted the North Dakota Jewish homesteaders were the Hebrew Immigrant Aid Society and the Jewish Agricultural and Industrial Aid Society (later the Jewish Agricultural Society, "JAS"), incorporated in 1900 as part of the Baron Maurice de Hirsch Fund. De Hirsch was a German Jewish philanthropist who had made his money in railroads, banking, and imports/exports. After his only child passed away, he gave large sums of money to assist European Jews to escape the harsh conditions in their homelands. He even considered

---

[239]Gabriel Davidson, *Our Jewish Farmers: The Story of the Jewish Agricultural Society* (New York: L. B. Fischer, 1943).

[240]The School is now known as Delaware Valley University. Lawrence Bush, "The National Farm School" (September 23, 2015, Jewish Currents), jewishcurrents.org/tag/tolstoy/.

settling half a million persecuted Russian emigrants on fertile land in Argentina, until officials in Buenos Aires nixed the plan.[241]

The first objective of the JAS was "the encouragement and direction of agriculture among Jews in America and the removal of those working in crowded metropolitan sections to agricultural and industrial districts."[242] Though there was a strong humanitarian basis for this agrarian resettlement effort, especially after the Russian pogroms began, there was also a fear by American Jewish leaders, most of whom were from Germany, that there would be a wave of American anti-Semitism against these "Yiddish-speaking, impoverished immigrants flooding the urban slums."[243]

These charities were able to assist Jewish immigrants, as it was not until 1924 that immigration laws changed with the passage of the Johnson-Reed Act signed by President Coolidge. This Act limited the annual number of immigrants from any country to two percent of the number of people from that country living in the United States in 1890. Its main purpose was to restrict the numbers coming from Eastern Europe, Southern Europe, Africa, and India, though it was sold to Congress as a means to "preserve the ideal of American homogeneity."[244]

The three main reasons why Russian Jewish Immigrants came to North Dakota—specifically "The Great Northwest"—to homestead in the early 1900s were that land was still available, homesteading was the only way they could own land, and fellow Jews had already been living in North Dakota. Though the Dakota Territory was opened to white settlers as public domain in 1864, the land that would later become the State of North Dakota was not homesteaded

[241]Peter Adams, *Politics, Faith and the Making of American Judaism* (University of Michigan Press, 2014).

[242]JAS Annual Report (1909); W. Gunther Plaut, "Jewish Colonies at Painted Woods and Devils Lake," *North Dakota History* 32, no.1 (Bismarck: North Dakota State Historical Society January 1965); Schwartz, "Early Jewish Agricultural Colonies in North Dakota"; JAS Annual Reports (1965).

[243]Uri D. Herscher, *Jewish Agricultural Utopias in America, 1880-1910* (Wayne State University Press, 1981).

[244]US State Department, Office of the Historian, history.state.gov, *The Historian*; North American Immigration, northamericanimmigration.org.

that quickly due to the ongoing Civil War, reports of conflicts with Indians, blizzards, droughts, prairie fires, grasshoppers, the economic Panic of 1873, which caused a decline in wheat prices, the Great Sioux War of 1876, and a lack of efficient transportation to many parts of the Territory.[245] So once the Jewish immigrants arrived, there was still land to homestead.

Also, as the Russian Jewish immigrants lacked funds to buy farmland outright, homesteading was their only real option to farm their own land. Most didn't arrive with much due to leaving their home countries in haste in order to survive. In addition, Jewish charitable organizations generally preferred to finance selected Jewish farmers with money for equipment or seed, rather than paying for the purchase of land.

The final reason why the Russian Jews found their way to McIntosh County was that many had heard that Jewish people had lived and were living in North Dakota, or close by. The earliest reported Jewish settler in the Dakota Territory was Dan Eisenberg, who operated a trading post on the Missouri River, south of Bismarck, beginning in 1869. His first store was opposite Fort Lincoln on what was called "the Point," but was then washed away by the river. When he moved into town, he became one of the founding fathers in Bismarck.[246]

It was in my second round of research that I learned more about Zebricov, Zebrikov, Zebrykowe, Tsebrykov, Cebriks, Cebricowo, Hoffnungstal, and the Valley of Hope. All of these names refer to the same little town near Odessa, Russia. It is the town where the Michelovich winemaking business was located, where Kiva Bender walked for further Jewish education and met his future bride, Rebecka, and where my grandfather Yosef Bender was born.

---

[245]The Soo Line Railroad did not have a stop in Ashley until 1901, though ox-cart and stagecoach routes existed between North Dakota settlements. Gordon Iseminger, "The McIntosh County German-Russians" (1984); Postal and Koppman. *A Jewish Tourists Guide to the US* (1954)

[246]*Bismarck Weekly Tribune* (March 3, 1911), Schwartz, "Early Jewish Agricultural Colonies" (1965)

Learning the name Hoffnungstal as another name for Zebricov opened up another source of information. I came across reference to a magazine online, entitled *Heritage Review*, published by the Germans from Russia Heritage Society, based in Bismarck, and in one of the volumes was an article entitled, "Massacre of Jews at Hoffnungstal/Odessa 1941." It took me a few days to actually make the call to order the periodical. I felt I should know what happened, as a researcher, but I really didn't want to know the details, as a Jew descended from citizens of the town.

The article told of a fifteen-year-old Hoffnungstal resident's eyewitness account of some of the horror that took place in September 1941. Paul Reeb, very active in the preservation of data regarding North Dakota's Germans from Russia, was the interviewer who submitted the article to the publication. He set the stage, explaining that the German armies had rapidly advanced after their attack of the Soviet Union in June of 1941 and controlled the entire Black Sea region west of the Dnieper River when this incident occurred.

> Andreas Keller and four other boys were witnesses to the executions, which took place on a foggy Sunday morning. The victims were transported to a ravine at the end of the village by 2 and 3 ton army trucks. There they were told to undress and kneel at the edge of the wash-out. Each man, woman, and child was shot in the back with a Luger pistol. The bodies were only partially covered with dirt when the soldiers took a short break to smoke and tell filthy stories. When they noticed there was some movement under the dirt, they shoveled more into the ravine and trampled it down. When curious onlookers showed up, the mother of Andreas Keller one of them, the S.S. soldiers turned them away. Besides this massacre, there were 2 others, bringing the total to more than 100 persons who were killed.

The interviewer then states, "It never entered the mind of young Keller that what he witnessed was a horrendous evil deed. In fact, the incident was considered just retribution for the loss of his father and grandfather to deportation by the Communists. According to

Andreas, "Somehow we had the feeling that the Jews were the underlying cause for all the bad things that happened to us."[247]

I thought about the power of propaganda by a ruling government. Even once the czars were no longer in power, their falsehoods about the Jews lived on and were built upon by the Communists and then the Nazis.

Though this information about my grandpa Joe's hometown was not relevant for the Nomination, and was not, therefore, included, it was relevant and important for me to know. As an American daughter of Zebricov, I felt the increased importance of telling the stories of those who escaped this shtetl to lead free lives in America and the legacy they have left. I also vowed to place this little village's name in my book about faith. In so doing, the Axis nations were not successful in trying to erase its name and its residents' existence.

Shortly after this time, I was returning with Lincoln from Mobridge, a city on the Missouri River about forty-five miles from Eureka. We had passed the Lutheran Cemetery about eight miles west of town many times since Lincoln and I moved to South Dakota. I had even stopped once a year or so before to examine the gravestones there, looking for the names of some of my late dad's classmates. Maybe it was the turquoise sky, close to sunset that caused me to look up at the ornate scrolling metal designs at the entrance to the cemetery. But this day, I noticed something I had never noticed before. Above the words "Lutheran Cemetery," there it was: Hoffnungstal.

"Lincoln," I said, "do you realize that the families buried here came from Zebricov, like your great-grandpa Joe? Before I researched for the book, I went past this cemetery at least fifty times and never looked up high enough to notice that!"

***

[247]Interview of Andreas Keller by Paul Reeb, *Heritage Review* (Germans from Russia Heritage Society): Vol. 14, no. 3 (1984): 71.

It was also in my second round of research that I read the touching family history written by Rachel Minenberg Baker about her family's experiences in Ashley. It caused me to realize that deep religious faith by these homesteaders was something else that many of them shared. Nathan Minenberg had come to Ashley via a different route from most. He heard a spokesman of the Jewish Agricultural Society speaking on a street corner on Dumont Avenue in Brooklyn, New York, and arrived with his family in March 1907 to a dark town with deep snow untouched by footprints. Rachel and her family stayed at a way station for immigrants until spring, so crowded that they slept by the door, and were oftentimes covered by snow that drifted in when they woke in the morning. Rachel's father was an artist, and even though he rarely had much financially, he painted murals on the insides of some of Ashley's churches for free or next to no payment. Nathan placed ads in the Ashley Tribune, offering to teach students how to draw and paint.[248] Rachel recalled at Passover time, when most of the settlers had by then moved into their shacks on homestead claims, she and her parents were alone, still at the way-station. She looked down from the top of a tall box where she slept, while her father and mother celebrated Passover and her father sang Hallel, praising God and thanking Him for His blessings.[249]

I also read of the Kreitzman family, who married in Russia and moved to North Dakota in 1907, and I realized how luck sometimes entered into a homesteader's success or failure. In 1908, Mrs. Kreitzman had boy triplets, the first surviving male triplets born in North Dakota. As a reward for their birth, the United States Government gave William Kreitzman a free homestead. The family grew vegetables and raised poultry for themselves, hanging both from the rafters of their house in the winter to preserve until spring. They had no need to prove up anything, as with the typical homesteaders. The Kreitzmans eventually sold their land and set up a successful hide

[248]Rachel Minenberg Baker, "Minenberg Family History," Jewish Historical Project of North Dakota records, Nathan and Theresa Berman Upper Midwest Jewish Archives, University of Minnesota Libraries.
[249]Ibid.

and fur business.[250] Mrs. Parkansky, buried at the Ashley cemetery, was the grandmother of the triplets.

I learned that the prevalence of the attitude regarding what occupations Jews could and could not do was by no means confined to Russia, where the Benderskys had lived. In *Inventing the Jew: Antisemitic Sterotypes in Romanian and Other Central-East European Cultures*, Andrei Oisteanu explores the gap between the "imaginary Jew" and the "real Jew":

> Sayings commonly have a way of being endorsed by historical fact, in this case the fact that Jews were prohibited by law to own land: "Jews are for all times prohibited from buying estates" (Callimachi Code of Law, Jassy 1816); the acquiring of landed property, vineyards, and Gypsies is rightful only for individuals of the Christian rite" (The Caragea Code of Law, Bucharest 1818), "In keeping with the old custom, the Jewish nation shall be banned from holding estates in ownership" (Organiz Regulation, Jassy 1832).[251]

Mr. Oisteanu then refers to common sayings among Romanians that were meant to denigrate the Jew without reference to the historical reasons behind their occupation choices, e.g., Jews "cannot scratch the soil . . . they are not allowed to work" (Romanian novelist Felix Aderca in 1922) and "Itzic" (referring to a generic Jew) "does not plow, does not own a patch of barren land, and does not own two lanky oxen" (Romanian writer Zaharia Stancu, 1938).

This background, when the Jewish homesteading immigrants to the Ashley area were from both Russia and Romania, helped me to understand my great-grandfather Kiva Bender's often repeated quote, "We wanted to prove to the world that the Jew could be a farmer." I discovered that his quote was actually based directly on

---

[250]William Kreitzman, "Kreitzman Family History," Jewish Historical Project of North Dakota records, Nathan and Theresa Berman Upper Midwest Jewish Archives, University of Minnesota Libraries.

[251]Andrei Oisteanu, Trans. from the Romanian by Mirela Adascalitei, *Inventing the Jew: Antisemitic Sterotypes in Romanian and Other Central-East European Cultures* (Lincoln: University of Nebraska Press, 2009), p. 198.

one of the Am Olam movement's expressed goals, as well.[252] The last part of Kiva's quote, "and we did," was not able to be stated by participants in the Am Olam colonies in the United States before the early 1900s. Father William Sherman's research showed that Painted Woods (the first Jewish colony in North Dakota in 1881) was a failure; that the second one, Garske, was a mixed blessing, as some families suffered while other prospered moderately; and that the Jews who came to the colonies after the turn of the century (including those who farmed in Ashley-Wishek) generally did well.[253]

Perhaps most revealing in my follow up research was what I found when I returned to my grandpa Joe's many handwritten papers. I had, by this time, gotten better at reading his script, and I was determined to try to read every word. I had always previously focused on the pages he had written to educate his children and grandchildren about his life. Now I looked carefully at the tiny print that was fading on several other pages. Here, my grandpa Joe, by then living in Minneapolis, who after leaving Russia had no further opportunity for education, had written for no one in particular his views on anti-Semitism. He said, in part:

> How nice and wise and intelligent it would be if the Hebrews could convince the Gentiles to agree that if Ginsberg, Cohen or Epstein are in the wrong, let us only blame them (rather than all Jewish people). No nation has had as much hardship, misery, destruction and bloodshed against them as the Jews and we do not blame all the peoples who are part of the same nations that have treated us badly.

I emailed news of this find to my uncle David Bender, who told me that Joe had been a member of the Golden Valley Country Club when he and Mary moved to Minneapolis in 1949. After playing a round of golf shortly after joining and thoroughly enjoying the beauty of the course, Joe was in the locker room and witnessed anti-Semitic remarks being made by some of the members. He promptly

[252]Goering, "Am Olam."

[253]Sherman, *Prairie Mosaic.*

walked into the office and resigned his membership. The course's beauty did not outweigh the ugliness he heard. My uncle said, "Dad had a fine sense of fairness that was a part of him."

This discussion brought back another old memory involving my grandpa Joe. In the late 1960s, we were eating at the Di Napoli, an Italian restaurant in downtown Minneapolis on Hennepin Avenue, having our usual fare of meatless spaghetti with a slice of cheese pizza (so as not to mix meat and milk), when my grandpa said quietly to my parents, when mentioning a fellow's name, "He's an M-O-T." I asked my parents later, "why did Grandpa spell mot?"

My dad explained, "It's not mot, it's M-O-T. It stands for 'member of the tribe.' It means that someone is Jewish."

"Why didn't he just say he was Jewish?" I asked.

"That's a good question," said my mom. "Sometimes in public places, Jewish people don't want to identify other people as Jewish, because religion is a private thing." I remember thinking, do people whisper that someone is Catholic or Buddhist? Looking back now, I realize that this not-so-secret acronym at that time was, at least in part, a vestige of the anti-Semitism that Jews had faced, which caused them to feel they had to speak in code about their religion in a public place or to identify who they were.

My additional research also involved looking at a wonderful online resource, called "Digital Horizons" that links many of North Dakota's archives together from the late 1800s to the present. There I found many positive references to Jewish people from other cities in North Dakota that were in line with the feelings expressed towards Jews in Ashley. I also found a few that were not positive. I couldn't determine any pattern from this research, other than the fact that only a small percentage of North Dakotans seemed to hold some negative views regarding Jewish people (and other minorities) and that fewer still felt free to express these opinions in print. From my limited research, it seemed that generally, those who expressed negative views had not lived and/or worked with any or many Jewish people. As such, I unscientifically (and optimistically) chalked these comments up to ignorance. The research also showed that Jewish people were in all parts of North Dakota, even in locations I had not previously heard of, and that as of 1934, there were six known synagogues in the state.[254]

In the *Wishek Golden Jubilee Book*, 1898–1948 in McIntosh County, the Jubilee Committee stated:

> About 24 years ago, Wishek [also in McIntosh County] had about a dozen Jewish families among its residents. A Jewish synagogue was built. It was dedicated by Rabbi Hess of Ashley and served as a temple of worship for a number of years. Later with the exodus of our Jewish families to other places of residence, the synagogue was discontinued, the building sold and moved away. However, while these Jewish people lived among us they contributed their part to the city's development.

In a book entitled, *The Churches of St. John* (McIntosh County), *St. Andrew* (Zeeland) *and St. David* (Ashley) *in North Dakota (1979)*, the history of Zeeland, North Dakota, is provided, with recognition of the religious diversity of its original leaders:

> In September of 1902, the railway was brought in from the then-terminal, Eureka, S. Dakota. Zeeland was organized into a village in 1905. Its first townboard consisted of Frank Kraft (Cath.), Adolph Boschee (Prot.), and Adolph Feinstein (Jew).

In the Valley City, North Dakota *Times Record* (July 11, 1907), the following story was printed:

> The Jews who are being driven out of Europe because that spot on the globe is several centuries behind the United States in civil and religious liberty, are coming to the United States in droves. Big colonies have sailed and will settle in North Dakota.

In *Sheridan County Heritage '76: A Bicentennial Project*, the author states:

[254]At the same time, there were 600 Norwegian Lutheran churches, 350 Catholic churches, and 225 Methodist episcopal churches. *A History of Wells County North Dakota and its Pioneers* (1934)

> The melting pot of America worked well in McClusky. Representatives from Russia, Germany, Sweden, Norway, Denmark, Syria, Ireland, England, Scotland, France and even Jewish people made up the county population.

In *Nelson County History*, Volume 2, Mrs. Lawrence Hopkins, talking of the Grass Lake Township, states:

> In 1912 there were 77 families recorded in the township, today there are 20. But many of these early names are still familiar to us: the Sachs, Handlemans, Marcovitz, Baronys, Poplingers, and Billows. Most of these early-day settlers have passed away, many entirely forgotten, except as their names are listed in early records. But they built schools and roads, conducted the township business, lived their rugged lives as they saw fit, and in so doing left their mark upon a growing community.

In the Odessa, North Dakota, newspaper (September 1915), under the headline "Many Jews Attend Gathering at Odessa From Many Towns," the following article appeared:

> Friday evening and all day Saturday was "Yom Kippur" or the Big Fast Day in the Jewish religion and was fittingly observed over until Sunday morning at Odessa by the Jewish class of people over this section of the state including the towns of Mott, Elgin, New Leipzig, Hebron, St. Joseph, Richardton, Glen Ullin, Flasher and various other towns in this western territory. Following the end of the fast and ceremonies a large feast was prepared for about sixty people . . . During Sunday afternoon and evening games, singing and various other amusements were carried out and at seven–o'clock the engagement of Max Gandel of Odessa, to Miss Rachel Hartstein of Elgin was announced, who will be married in the very near future. Considerable money was collected throughout the gathering, part of which will be used in fixing the Jewish cemetery at Glen Ullin, while the remainder will be sent to Europe and will be given to the many war widows and orphans.[255]

[255]The Glen Ullin cemetery is no longer able to be located. www.iajgsjewish cemeteryproject.org.

In *Stutsman County in the World War*, Jamestown, North Dakota, reference is made to the Jewish Relief Fund Drive which took place on October 23 and 24, 1918, to give assistance to Jewish sufferers in the European war zone and the willing participation of non-Jews in the charity drive:

> Jamestown's quota was $2500. Jamestown citizens subscribed $2565 to the cause. Morris Beck and Louie Fine, prominent Jamestown merchants, were in charge of the campaign in this city, Harry Wolf, another well-known local citizen, officiating as secretary. These men, assisted by Rev. Father Geraghty, Pierce Blewett and R.R. Wolfer, were responsible for the success of the campaign and the oversubscription of $65. Patriotic Jamestown, as usual, responded to the call for help. The entire amount was turned over to the state treasurer Alex Stern, Fargo. The committee, thru this medium, desires to give expression of its appreciation to the people of Jamestown and Stutsman county for their hearty support and willingness to give comfort and financial assistance to the Jewish sufferers.[256]

In LaMoure County's Bicentennial Celebration book, July 1976, Grand Rapids, ND, the following excerpt referenced the Jews:

> A visit from a peddler to a farm home was a welcome event. They were usually Jews who traveled in a horse drawn spring wagon from place to place, displaying their wares to the families and made many sales. They offered blankets, pillowcases, sweaters, chains of beads, etc. to these people who seldom had an opportunity to go shopping. The children were fascinated, "If you will buy this lovely all wool blanket, I will give you this for nothing, this for nothing, and this for nothing." Who could resist such salesmanship?

Our Fifty Years, Regent, North Dakota: 1911–1961, tells the story of a Swedish man who resided there, Henry Rosander:

---

[256]According to the city/county milestone books, Walsh County, North Dakota also gave a portion of its United War Campaign Fund to Jewish Relief, as did Elgin, North Dakota, and over 75 other towns in North Dakota. William C. Sherman notes, NDSU Institute for Regional Studies and University Archives.

> He had homesteaded near Ray, North Dakota on rocky soil, sold it and bought railroad land northeast of Regent in St. Croix Township, North Dakota. Henry served on the school, township, farmers union and congregational church boards. The oddest experience Henry recalled was the time he received an invitation to join the Klu Klux Klan. Out of sheer curiosity he agreed to attend and was driven, blindfolded, to a remote schoolhouse in the company of several other candidates. There, by candlelight, in a roomful of sheeted neophytes, he listened to a hate-filled address against Jews and Catholics. Years later, telling of this, he remarked dryly, "The KKK movement in North Dakota did not interest many people around Regent."[257]

Some North Dakota town histories merely reference that Jewish people were a part of their town's heritage, in the nature of factual news reports. For example, in *History of Hatton, ND (1884–1959): 75th Anniversary Celebration*, the milestone book refers to the fact that the Golden Lake post office by Beaver Creek Township was established by a Jew, Isaac Golden, hence the name. The *Bowdon Diamond Anniversary, 1899–1974*, references that the hardware store is now in the building in which a Jew named Harry Weisfield started a store. In the book entitled *Wilton Diamond Jubilee (1899–1974)*, the following note is included: "Mrs. Polonsky, who ran a store in Wilton for many years and who raised her family here," came from the Regan-Wing (Jewish) settlement. There is also mention of the fact that in the 1880s, the township of Montefiore was an organized school district when the Jewish colonists lived north of the present city, and Miss Fanny Nudelman was its first teacher.[258] The *Wilton News* entry from January 21, 1910, acknowledges a reception at the home of Mr. and Mrs. Philip Kamins the previous Saturday (referred to as "the

[257]The KKK did gain quite a foothold in Grand Forks in the 1920s, however, according to the city's milestone book. In *They Came to Stay, Grand Forks, North Dakota Centennial 1874–1974*, the authors stated, "While the KKK in Fargo marched around in a show–off manner, their colleagues in Grand Forks proceeded to build a Klan that eventually filled the city commission, the school board and the police department . . . they controlled the city politically."

[258]The town was named after British Jewish philanthropist Moses Montefiore.

Jewish Sunday"), at which time the engagement of Louis Kamins was announced and the traditional "breaking of the plate" took place.[259] In *Golden Jubilee, 1911–1961, Robinson, ND*, it is noted that the general store there is owned by a Jewish man. In *Bottineau County Diamond Jubilee Book (1884–1959)*, the authors report that a Jewish settlement of at least five families was begun in Starbuck township along the river. Finally, in *History of Regan and the Regan Community, 1912–1962, Golden Anniversary Celebration*, the book includes the following reprint from the Regan, North Dakota, newspaper in 1913: "Rabbi Julius Hess left for Ashley, North Dakota Monday for a visit. He will be back to preach the Jewish Easter services at the Harris Weinberg home April 22."[260]

In contrast to the above, were the fewer subtle or directly negative references regarding Jews and others. In *Our Pioneers: the Wing Area, 1892–1976*, the Wing Bicentennial Committee references the project started by the Homemakers Club in 1958 to write the history of the Canfield Township. It begins with a list of the Jewish homesteaders in 1900–1905 and the sections they homesteaded. "These were shipped out from Chicago sweatshops by a Jewish Association in New York City. These people were furnished credit for all they needed for 5 years at 3% interest." Next are listed the Norwegians and their sections of land. The concluding portion of the project from 1958 states, "The following may be classified as Americans . . ." indicating that neither the Jewish homesteaders nor the Norwegians, even in 1958, were "classified" as Americans.

However, as evidence of the fact that this feeling was probably an isolated one in Wing, are the numerous articles from the *Wing Statesman*, the local newspaper, reporting factually on the Jewish community in their midst, from announcing Celia Edelberg—a

[259]The breaking of the plate at some Jewish engagements to marry signifies the finality of the agreement that the couple is making and the end of the childhood home, while remembering that even in joyous times, Jewish people remember the sadness of the destruction of the Temple.

[260]As Jewish people do not celebrate the Easter holiday, but Passover occurs around the same time, it is believed that Rabbi Hess was planning to spend Passover at the Weinbergs in Regan.

Jewish young lady—enlisting as a Red Cross nurse for World War I, to urging non-Jewish people to assist with giving charity to the "war sufferers in Palestine," stating "the Jewish people have been foremost in contributing to all other societies, such as the YMCA and Knights of Columbus, and it is no more than just that all persons contribute liberally to the Jewish Relief Fund . . . If Mr. Turnoy does not call on you then be sure to see him with your donation."

In contrast, in a 1918 article from the newspaper in Bentley, the city's popular Masquerade Ball is described:

> No social event in the history of Bentley was so largely attended or more thoroughly enjoyed. The variety of characters was a special feature . . . with mostly original and homemade costumes. Costumed characters included The Big Sioux chief and squaw who could be seen peering into the window, tramps, cowboys, cowgirls, negros, Jews, Irishmen, Germans, Red Riding Hood, Uncle Sam, flower girls, Queen of Hearts, clowns, fat men, sailors, farmers, prize fighters, wise guys, jail birds, politicians, preachers and many others. All made their entrance in a manner calculated to mimic the actions of the different characters in real life. As they danced to "Home Sweet Home", everyone felt that the "best party ever" was over, one long to be remembered for its atmosphere of culture, refinement, artistic beauty and good fellowship.

In *History of Fordvile and surrounding area, 1973*, the following reprint of a story from 1907 appears:

> A third general store was opened in 1907 by Engebret Rotnem, coming from Petersburg, and Joe Gillis, who formerly had a peddlers' route here. This partnership was dissolved a year later when it was found relations between a Jew and a Norwegian proved incompatible, and Mr. Rotnem because the sole owner.

The Agassiz, the 1910 yearbook for the college in Bismarck, North Dakota, when listing the graduates, states: Melvin Baernstein (Bud), Fargo, ND, Pharmaceutical Chemistry: "Two sharks in one skin; a Jew and a druggist."

In my follow up research, I also learned of an infamous former Jewish resident of Ashley, whose baby brother is buried in the infant section of the Ashley Jewish Homesteaders' Cemetery. Donald Berman, one of the sons of David Berman (a rabbinical student and violinist in Russia) and Clara Berman (from a wealthy family in Odessa, Russia), changed his name to David Berman. After young David and his siblings struggled as homesteaders (including seeing their sod house burn when their exhausted father forgot to close the hearth at night after adding hay and cow chips to the fire), they moved to Sioux City, Iowa.

There the young "Davie" started supporting the family by selling newspapers. He later was involved in bootlegging and gambling and became a major crime boss in Las Vegas in the 1940s and a partner with Bugsy Siegel in the Flamingo Hotel. His daughter, Susan Berman, sadly since murdered, wrote a book about being the daughter of a gangster, though she never was aware of her father's livelihood until after his passing. She told of the family's struggles on the farm in Ashley and going to visit her uncle's grave at the Ashley Jewish Cemetery, where a worn down marker "was all that was left of the Bermans in Ashley." She was a guest for dinner in Ashley at the home of lawyer Max and Viola Wishek, who welcomed her graciously as a fellow pioneer descendant.[261] Max's father, John Wishek, had arranged for the land where the Jewish synagogue in Ashley sat until the Jewish homesteaders moved away. Susan's grandfather, David Berman (Senior), was one of the witnesses for Sarah and Noah Schlasinger's wedding in Ashley, North Dakota, as well as acting as the secretary for a time for the Sulzberger Farmers Association in Ashley.[262]

---

[261]Berman, Easy Street (1981).

[262]In Robert Rockaway's *But He Was Good to His Mother: The Lives and Crimes of Jewish Gangsters* (Jerusalem: Gefen Publishing, 2000), the author quotes from Ms. Berman's book, reporting on David Berman's reaction to learning that the Silver Shirts had invaded Minneapolis and were preaching hatred and violence against the Jews in the 1930s. David Berman organized some of his mob acquaintances, equipped them with brass knuckles, stormed one of the Silver Shirts meetings at a local Elks club and fought the hatemongers. Ms. Berman also referred in her book to her father starting the first synagogue in Las Vegas in someone's home.

By the late 1920s, few Jewish homesteaders were left farming in McIntosh County. Though one in five farmers left North Dakota farms in this time period, I wondered if there was more behind the reasons for the Jewish farmers leaving than their being part of a statewide trend.[263]

In the case of some homesteaders, such as the Dorfmans, the reason for selling was necessity, and not related to religion. Isadore Dorfman had no idea where he was going after getting in touch with the Jewish Immigration Aid Society. They arranged for his train transport from New York City to Eureka, South Dakota. He walked the thirty-five miles to Ashley in the ruts of the freight ox carts to begin farming. While on the farm, his wife Freda died in childbirth, and Isadore was not able to care for the farm and four children alone. After he sold his land for ten dollars per acre, he took the proceeds and set up a butcher shop in nearby Wishek.[264]

Some homesteaders came to believe that the climate of the area was too risky to continue providing for their families and moved off the farm to set up businesses that they perceived to provide greater security. Rose Rapaport Schwartz, born in 1907 and daughter of homesteaders Pearl and Sam Rapaport, told of her father and his brother leaving factory jobs they hated in Pittsburgh to come farm on their own land near Uncle Kiva Bender. After having to take a ship from Russia to Italy and then to Argentina before being allowed in the United States, they were thrilled with the opportunity.

Though Rose's father was a moderately successful farmer, he eventually "took on an agency for selling patent medicines for 'Shores.'" With his little wagon, he traveled to the farmers, selling extracts and medicines for humans and animals. His most popular item was his lemon extracts, and he had a flourishing business, only limited by the number of visits to customers he could physically

[263]D. Jerome Tweton, http://www.ndstudies.org/articles/overview_the_1920s.

[264]Maurice Dorfman, "Dorfman Family History," Jewish Historical Project of North Dakota records; Joseph Bender Recollections

make. Years later, Rose learned that the lemon extracts contained "a great deal of alcohol."[265]

Another cause for homesteaders leaving the farm was catastrophic events like prairie fires, tornados, and blizzards, or the predictable lonesomeness, owing to the distance between homesteads and settlements. The Spanish Flu and the Great Depression also took their toll, while some homesteaders were offered opportunities in bigger cities or towns. Again, these were reasons not related to a particular religion.

The distinctly Jewish reasons for some farmers leaving the area were that they wanted their children to have easier access to a Jewish education or access to future Jewish marital prospects. Finally, a good number of Jewish homesteaders lost their farms to an unscrupulous money lender living among them, who they felt they could trust because he was Jewish. Bottom line, with the money they had saved and the money received from selling their land, many of the McIntosh County homesteaders, like the Benders, had enough money to maintain their independence as small business owners. Fifteen towns within forty miles of the Ashley-Wishek settlement had Jewish-owned stores at one time or another during the first three decades of the twentieth century.[266]

***

I submitted my revised one-hundred-plus page Nomination for listing the Ashley Jewish Homesteaders Property on the National Register for a second time. This time, a date was set for the North Dakota Historical Preservation Board to vote to recommend or not recommend the property. I knew this was a positive sign, but still was a little anxious. A mourning dove's cooing woke me the morning of the vote and Lincoln and I took off for the two-hour journey, west on Highway 10 and north on Highway 83. We were driving the paved version of the approximate route taken by my grandfa-

---

[265]Rose Schwartz, "Rapaport Family History," Jewish Historical Project of North Dakota records.

[266]Sherman and Thorson, *Plains Folk*, p.394.

ther Joseph Bender to claim his homestead. The fog was thick on our drive to Bismarck. I didn't even know when we passed Strasburg, as the prominent billboard with the accordion announcing Lawrence Welk's birthplace was entirely hidden. Once we arrived at the History Center, Lincoln and I listened to several other presentations to the Historical Preservation Board. Then it was announced that next on the agenda was the Ashley Jewish Homesteaders Cemetery. I picked up my notes, walked forward, and began.

I advised the board that not only had I learned that the Ashley/Wishek community of Jewish homesteading farmers was the largest Jewish agricultural group ever in North Dakota, but that this cemetery was the only physical reminder of this community of farming Jews that remained. I concluded that the Ashley Jewish Homesteaders Cemetery is National Register eligible under Criterion A due to three primary patterns of historical events. First, the AJHC is associated with Russian Jewish immigrants with no farming experience, settling near a rural community on the North Dakota prairie for the purpose of becoming farmers on homesteaded land. Second, it is evidence of the ways in which the Jewish homesteaders maintained their Jewish identify in this remote location, far from major cities, which resulted in more challenges and obstacles to their practicing their religion. Third, the AJHC stands as a symbol of the acceptance the Jewish homesteaders felt to remain true to who they were among their Russian-German neighbors, despite their religious and cultural differences.

I also quoted researcher Alfred Thal, who stated, at the conclusion of his Bicentennial taping sessions of Jewish homesteaders:

> The Jewish settlers as a whole became good citizens. They took their part in politics, held political office, were on the school boards, aldermen in the various cities, mayors in the various towns, villages and cities and were members of the legislature. So they lived not as a Jew of North Dakota, but as a public-spirited citizen of the State of North Dakota.[267]

[267]North Dakota Bicentennial Oral History Project, Al Thal Papers, Historical Society of North Dakota State Archives (Bismarck, ND)

The board members thanked me for my research, stated that it was one of the most detailed nominations they had ever reviewed, and unanimously voted to recommend the property to the United States Department of the Interior to list as a historic site. It was exactly fifty years from the first time my dad, Keva/Kenneth Bender, took my sister and me down the little hill near Ashley to show us where his grandfather Kiva Bender was buried. When Lincoln and I left the meeting and went to our car, I danced the *hora* (a Jewish dance of celebration) and sang "Hava Nagila" (Come, let's be joyous) between the empty, parked cars in the Historical Society parking lot, while Lincoln looked on, amused.

* * *

On November 17, 2015, the Ashley Jewish Homesteaders Cemetery was named by the National Parks Service of the United States Department of the Interior to the National Register of Historic Places as a historically significant property to be preserved. This monumental event prompted me to be reminded of a conversation about tribes that I had about two decades previous. I was staying at the Black Bear Casino Hotel in Cloquet, Minnesota, prior to taking a deposition nearby the following morning. After enjoying the salad bar, I headed back to my room to look over my outline for the following day. Waiting for the elevator, an older gentleman asked, "What tribe are you?"

"Oh, I'm not from a tribe," I responded with a smile.

He said knowingly, "I am a healer. You are from a tribe, even if you do not know which. Look into your history." Twenty years later, I finally did.

The Bender family was not unique among the Jewish homesteaders. Even after they left the prairie, these pioneers continued to appreciate the freedoms and opportunities afforded them in America and passed this feeling onto their children. It was possible to be a good American and still maintain one's religious identity, even on the prairie. This stony ground was able to bear fruit.

Descendants of those buried in the Ashley Jewish Homesteaders Cemetery include World War II decorated heroes: Larry Schlasinger (KIA, US Army Infantry Intelligence, Normandy), Kenneth Bender (US Army Infantry, D-Day + 1 invasion, 2nd Division), Kenneth Schlasinger (US Air Force, bombardier European theater and Africa), and Lionel Greenberg (US Army Air Corps, Germany, POW). Other living descendants of the Ashley Jewish community are evidence of the many choices that a free society provides, and include a Rabbi, a Pulitzer Prize winner, an American Bible Contest Champion, a New York Times Bestseller author, a medaling World Synchronized Skater, a National Book Award Finalist, a Canadian Screen Award winner, a playwright and founder/artistic director of a theater company, a life and business coach, a marriage and family counseling therapist, a trusts and estates lawyer, a maker of stained glass windows, four psychiatrists, a school superintendent, an ear, nose, and throat doctor, a baseball broadcaster, an airshow pilot and aircraft component distributor, a comedy writer, photographers, a telecommunications entrepreneur, investment bankers, a choreographer, a dentist, composers, civil rights activists, a member of the United States Foreign Service, an oboist, business owners, tennis and racquetball champions, a landscaper, and other acclaimed doctors, lawyers, judges, authors, journalists, accountants, psychologists, realtors, teachers, homebuilders, social workers, advertising and marketing executives, actors, musicians, and volunteers for a variety of charitable causes.

In the late summer of 2016, I received an email from Carol Fey, the court clerk who lives in the old Ashley synagogue, inquiring on behalf of the Ashley Arts Council as to whether I would be interested in speaking at a celebration they were planning. She told me the name of the event was to be "Jewish Heritage Celebration Day." I told her that I would be honored. I also contacted Bea and Hershel Premack, the long-time lay leaders of the Aberdeen, South Dakota, congregation, and they agreed to participate. I was moved by the fact that more than thirty years after long-time Ashley dentist Dr. Leo Cohen, the last Jewish resident in Ashley, had passed away, the citizens of Ashley were interested in honoring the memories of the Jewish families that used to live among them and their ancestors.[268] When I told my son about the event, he volunteered to speak, as well, discussing his experience studying from rural South Dakota to become the United States National Bible Champion and traveling to Israel for the International Bible Contest.

An unseasonably warm, sunny day in the mid-60s dawned on November 6. My brother-in-law Barry Kelner had driven over 350 miles from Minnesota to attend. I had made three buttermilk *kugels* (noodle puddings) for the guests to taste. The Ashley Arts Council, without one Jewish member, had graciously made potato latkes—potato pancakes traditionally eaten on Chanukah—and *mohn* (poppyseed) cookies, customarily baked for Jewish simchas.

The audience members seemed so appreciative of our coming to talk to them. I was appreciative of the fact that they wanted to learn more. One lady, who was not Jewish, walked over and told me that her aunt was named after Sarah Auerbach, my great-grandma Becky's sister. Her aunt's parents worked in Auerbach's General Store many years ago in Ashley, and so admired Sarah. After our speeches to the audience of about fifty people at the McIntosh County Courthouse, the sun was beginning to set.

I had wanted to visit the Jewish Homesteaders Cemetery to recite the Mourners' Kaddish with my son and brother-in-law after the program at the Courthouse, in order to connect more directly with the people who we were honoring that day. Once we three arrived at the gravesites, in the dim light, we saw the Premacks and their visiting daughter Judy get out of their car, as well as two members of our Aberdeen congregation, and two Jewish reporters from Bismarck,

---

[268]The beloved Dr. Cohen passed away in 1983, after serving the dental needs of Ashley's citizens for 50 years, other than when he was in the army during World War II. He served as a dental officer in the United States Army from 1942 to 1946, serving in France and in Okinawa until the War ended. Ashley Diamond Jubilee Book (1963) He was homesteader and later cattle buyer Noah Dorfman's stepson, and the nephew of Freda Dorfman, buried in the Ashley Jewish Homesteaders Cemetery. Dr. Cohen is buried in the St. Helena's Catholic Cemetery in Ellendale with his wife and son, as his wife was Catholic. A Jewish star adorns his foot marker.

North Dakota, who had all attended the event at the Courthouse. "Exactly ten!" said Lincoln.

"Isn't that wonderful!" said my brother-in-law, Barry. Our minyan had magically arrived. Before we started the prayer, I commented that we were saying the prayer for all of the Jewish homesteaders, and as the sun slipped below the horizon, we began, *"Yitgadal, v'yitkaddish, sh'mei rabbah* (May God's great name be exalted and sanctified)."

I would venture to guess that we all felt honored making up the minyan at that moment, much the same way that Joseph Bender felt to be part of his first minyan on the North Dakota prairie after just arriving from Russia. I know that I will never forget that experience.

Rebecca Bender presenting her speech at Jewish Heritage Day in Ashley, as did Lincoln Bernhard and Bea and Hershel Premack. *Photo by Thomas D. Isern.*

It was dark and getting windy, so we all said good-bye to each other and made our way back to our cars, before the echo of our prayer had fully disappeared.

Table being set up at McIntosh County Courthouse on Ashley Jewish Heritage Day, with pans of kugel, challah, latkes, and mohn cookies. *Photo by Thomas D. Isern.*

Kiva Bender monument. *Photo by Rebecca Bender, author files.*

Part II

After the Ashley Jewish Homesteaders Cemetery was listed on the National Register, I started thinking: what would be a respectful way to have intentional and unintentional visitors to the cemetery learn more about this unique group of North Dakota settlers? Perhaps there should be a memorial. Also, should we try to get homesteader descendants and others together for a rededication of the site? I talked with Cemetery Association President Stuart Kaufman about the seeds of my plan and he encouraged me to send a proposal.

Initially, I pondered what form the memorial should take. Should we commission a sculpture on site, or have a small roofed enclosure with information about the Jewish homesteaders at the place where the little house for mourners used to sit, or maybe a wall with a small stained glass window and information in waves of text. Then, on my way to a basketball practice for my son, we fortuitously stopped at Laura Ingalls Wilder's childhood home in DeSmet, South Dakota. Laura Ingalls Wilder books were among my favorites growing up, and I read each of them numerous times. She told stories about her pioneer family in the *Little House on the Prairie* series of books and graciously invited the reader into her life. Though I had seen some of the historic Ingalls sites in Minnesota and Wisconsin years ago. I hadn't previously been aware of this South Dakota homestead site of the Ingalls family from the early 1880s memorialized in Laura's *Little Town on the Prairie* book.

When we parked, I walked over to a huge boulder holding a plaque that told the basics of the Ingalls story. As I proceeded back to the car through the tall prairie grasses and under the cottonwoods planted by "Pa," I realized, "That's it." A boulder could figuratively signify the obstacles and challenges faced by the Jewish homesteaders, both in Russia and once they arrived, and could connect literally to the stones and rocks they moved from their homestead parcels.

I began searching on the internet for a company that sold boulders. In order to get several bids, I described my vision of the project in numerous voicemail messages to rock companies that were never returned. One company, Dakota Classique Rock in Pierre, South Dakota, was very helpful from the beginning and saw this as the glorious undertaking that I did. Managing Director Nancy Gordon was patient through our many discussions regarding size and color of rocks, and I downsized my original vision of the project due to cost. She sent me pictures of possible boulders until we found the right one. Nancy had the good idea of splitting one rock in half, rather than using two separate rocks for the two plaques of text, and we agreed to keep the backs of the boulders unfinished, while polishing the insides and affixing the plaques with hidden studs.

I located a printing wholesaler, Gemini Signs, that worked with retailer DC Signs in Montevideo, Minnesota, providing long lasting outdoor aluminum installations for a reasonable price. Mitch Collins helped me to select the appropriate print and plaque style and color. After I presented my thoughts for the language on the plaques to the other two board members, Stuart Kaufman and Rabbi Jon-Jay Tilsen, there was a collaborative effort to reach the final product. But the cost was still prohibitive, as we on the Cemetery Board wanted to be good stewards for the future caretaking of the cemetery, by leaving sufficient funds in the treasury for continuing maintenance and necessary repairs.

Enter Mr. Jerry Klinger, President of The Jewish American Society for Historic Preservation. Jerry, the son of two Holocaust survivors, had already been making his charitable mark around the United States by helping to arrange for and pay for historical signs documenting the role of Jews in various aspects of American history in twenty-eight states. "If you can raise half the cost, I'll pay the rest," he said. We did, through an Everribbon funding site and through direct donations by descendants and others, and he kept his promise.[269]

Then I became the logistics team of one. Arranging to send the plaques to the boulder company in Pierre for installation was quite easy. Getting the two 2000-pound half-boulders to Ashley—not as easy. Not sure where to turn, I enlisted the help of one of the organizers of the Ashley Jewish Heritage Day, Carol Fey. She told me that McIntosh County would lend its backhoe for unloading the boulders at the cemetery. She also gave me the name of Neil Schneider, a gentleman who lives in Ashley and who drives cattle back and forth to Pierre and other places.

***

When Lincoln and I arrived at the cemetery in April 2017 to await the delivery of the boulders on the flat bed, we saw that a County crew had generously poured some gravel to even the slope from the road down to the cemetery, so it would be easier for the backhoe to descend. Then we saw in the sunny distance the truck cab and flatbed holding the two boulders coming to their new home. Not only did Neil Schneider do a professional moving job, he, McIntosh County Road Superintendent Dennis Glas, and County employee Bruce Smith took such care in guiding the boulders to be gently lowered. All five of us gave an audible sigh of relief once the huge boulders were on solid ground.

I reported to the Cemetery Board that the boulders were in place. Then, after more discussions, we board members decided on the schedule for the rededication of the cemetery to honor these pioneers as well as to celebrate the recognition of their lives by the United States Department of the Interior. I wanted those in attendance to hear the powerful words of the homesteaders, the same way I had

[269]Jerry, with his experience in historic preservation, also gave me good advice regarding the production of the plaques.

been moved by them. I researched more online to find additional descendants. Invitations were then sent via email, and I was interviewed for articles in various news publications. I also sent information about the upcoming event to North Dakota Governor Doug Burgum. He issued a proclamation recognizing the contributions of the Jewish homesteaders and businesspeople, and he proclaimed May 21, 2017, "North Dakota Jewish Homesteaders' Day." But we wondered, would people come to this place far from the beaten path, and how many?

Boulders with plaques, lifted and ready to leave Pierre, South Dakota; transporter Neil Schneider and Scott Mutschler of Dakota Classique Rock on flatbed; April 2016. *Photo by Nancy Gordon.*

I decided to be optimistic and began cooking for the reception. Having spent my formative years around a mother and grandmother who thought a fate worse than death would be inviting people to eat and not having enough food, my task was clear. The night before the event, in torrential rain, I delivered to the Hayloft (a ninety-nine-year-old barn), eight pans of buttermilk lukshen kugel; multiple bowls of salmon salad with pimiento, black olives, and celery; bagel chips; roasted red pepper humus; grapes; fresh challahs; and cinnamon and chocolate babka brought from Minneapo-

Boulders are taken off the flat bed as Lincoln observes, April 2017, Ashley, ND. *Author's files.*

lis by my sister and brother-in-law. With the help of the wonderful Shlepps, who own The Hayloft and run a dinner theater in the barn, we adorned the tables with fresh lilacs and prairie flowers in old milk jugs and patinaed ceramic vases, American flags, and kosher chocolate truffles.

✲✲✲

On May 21, 2017, a chilly windy spring day, the rain clouds lifted and we were left with some stratus and non-threatening cumulus. I parked our car and—carrying programs with Lincoln—walked down the little hill to the Ashley Jewish cemetery. For a few moments, we stood and faced the wind, saying nothing but feeling the history of the place. Historic integrity, a term from the National Registry, is merely a phrase when it is written on paper, but every time I go to this cemetery, in the persistent strong breeze, it is a tangible feeling of isolation and triumph at the same time. Lincoln and I set up the music stands for my sister Nancy and I to play a duet, and the wind promptly blew both stands down.

Then we waited. Our thoughts were interrupted not by horses hooves, as my grandpa Joe had heard when waiting for his neighbors at Matthias Kapp's farm over a hundred years earlier, but by car engines. And car after car pulled up and parked on the shoulder of 48th Street Southeast for the rededication of the Ashley Jewish Homesteaders Cemetery. They kept coming, more than forty cars in all. People I knew and people I had never met. People from North Dakota, California, Washington, Florida, Minnesota, Maryland, and South Dakota. The McIntosh County Sheriff sat in his squad car on top of the hill approaching the cemetery with his flashers on to ensure that persons used to traveling on this little road would use extra caution with the large number of people getting out of their cars.

On that day, over one hundred people witnessed or participated as two granite boulders with explanatory plaques were unveiled, accompanied by "voices from the prairie," recollections of the pioneers' words and contemporaneous accounts from the *Ashley Tribune* and the Jewish Agricultural Society's Annual Reports.

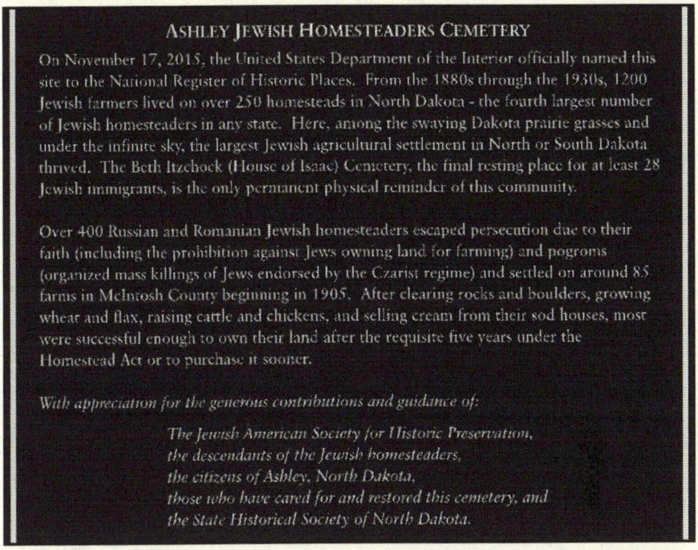

Ashley Jewish Homesteaders Cemetery Historic Plaque 1, May 2017.
Author files.

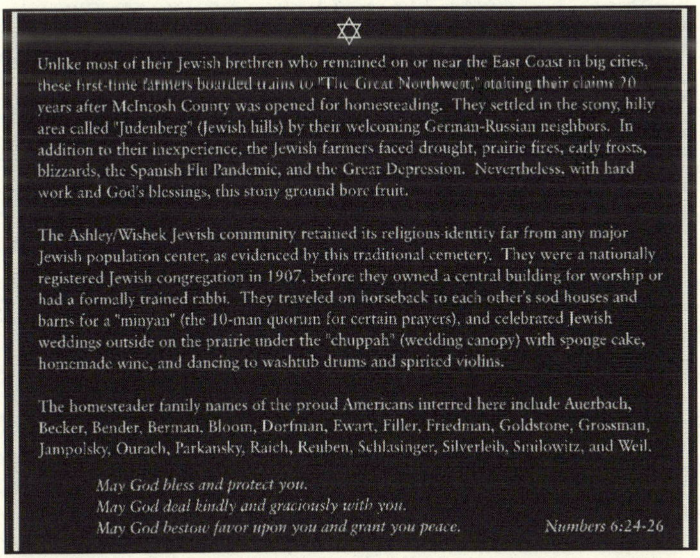

Ashley Jewish Homesteaders Cemetery Historic Plaque 2, May 2017.
Author files.

The following homesteader descendants participated with speaking parts in the program:

Ronnie Hartman, Ann Kay, Nancy Bender-Kelner, and Rebecca E. Bender:

Great-granddaughters of homesteaders Kiva Bendersky and Rebecka Michelovich Bendersky (grandchildren of homesteaders Joseph and Mary Bender and Sarah Bendersky Schlasinger and Noah Schlasinger). Nancy recited recollections of young Ashley Jewish homesteader Rachel Minnenberg

Marshall Kelner, Malcolm Kelner, and Lincoln Bernhard:

Great-great-grandsons of homesteaders Kiva and Rebecca Bendersky (great-grandchildren of homesteaders Joseph and Mary Bender)

Mary Cohen:

Daughter of Dr. Leo Cohen, Ashley's long-time dentist, (granddaughter of homesteaders Noah and Rose Dorfman and great-niece of homesteaders Isadore and Freda Dorfman).

Erwin Grossman:

Grandson of homesteaders Isadore and Ann Berkowski Grossman (great nephew of homesteader Louis Grossman, nephew of homesteader Joe Grossman)

Stuart Kaufman:

Great-grandson of homesteaders Isadore and Ann Grossman (great-great nephew of Louis Grossman, great nephew of Joe Grossman)

Robert Tilsen:

Grandson of homesteaders Yehuda Leib (Louis) Reuben and Mirel Chaplik Reuben (nephew of homesteader Benjamin Reuben)

Rabbi Jon-Jay Tilsen and Jim Tilsen:
Great grandsons of homesteaders Yehuda Leib and Mirel Chaplik Reuben (great-nephew of Benjamin Reuben)

Tova Benson-Tilsen:
Great-great granddaughter of Yehuda Leib and Mirel Chaplik Reuben, and great great-niece of Benjamin Reuben; Tovah recited recollections from descendants of the homesteader Raich family.

Sara Lee Sloven:
Granddaughter of homesteaders Israel and Sarah Auerbach (daughter of Pauline Auerbach Greenberg and Ben Greenberg)

Herschel Premack:
Grandson of homesteader Samuel Smilowitz (nephew of Isador Smilowitz)

Also participating in the ceremony were Jerry Klinger (President of the Jewish American Society of Historic Preservation), Rabbi Yonah Grossman (Co-Director of Chabad Jewish Center of North Dakota), Claudia Berg (Director, North Dakota State Historical Society), Thomas D. Isern (University Distinguished Professor of History, North Dakota State University), Carol Fey (McIntosh County Clerk of Court and Recorder), and Barry Kelner (husband and father of descendants, and editor of plaque language). Dale Bluestein, a volunteer videographer, drove 350 miles one way from Minneapolis to document the historic event, and Carolyn Grueskin, a reporter from Bismarck came to do the same.

When my sister and I began to play "Sim Shalom" (Hebrew prayer meaning "Spread Peace"), she on flute and I on violin, the wind was blowing so strongly into the foot of her flute that no sound would come out. Then Barbara Pressler Altman, a member of the Aberdeen synagogue, who also happens to be a violinist and violist, called out, "Turn your backs to the wind!" We followed the suggestion, began again, and soon our music floated over the prairie.

Nancy (at left) and Rebecca, playing music (held by Malcolm Kelner and Marshall Kelner) on the prairie. *Photo by Suzzanne Kelley.*

An especially moving part of the day was when John Salzer, caretaker for many years at the cemetery and just out of the hospital, appeared with the assistance of his second generation, Mark, to accept a plaque of appreciation. Stuart Kaufman referred to Mr. Salzer's commitment and dedication over the years, honoring our ancestors as if they were his family, too.

The rededication was made all the more special as descendants of the homesteaders, those whose ancestors had known Jewish people, and those who had never met a Jew honored the memories of

Jerry Klinger (far left), founder, Jewish American Society for Historic Preservation, with the three Cemetery Association Board members (continuing from left), Rebecca Bender, Stuart Kaufman, Rabbi Jon-Jay Tilsen, May 2017. *Photo by Nancy Bender-Kelner.*

these pioneers, together. Then it was on to the Hayloft for the reception a few miles down the road with the instructions, "turn right at the covered wagon." When the group arrived after the rededication from the cemetery, we washed our hands from an old blue ceramic pitcher (transitioning from a place of death to a place of life), as chickens clucked and ran around close by. Then we walked up the wooden steps into the barn to eat and share stories.

And just like had taken place on the land nearby almost one hundred years before, a minyan was called together by the two rabbis

Most of the Ashley Cemetery Rededication attendees pose for a picture at the cemetery before heading off to "The Hayloft" for a reception to honor all of North Dakota's homesteaders, sponsored by the descendants of Kiva and Rebecka Bender, May 2017. *Photo by Dale Bluestein/Carolyn Grueskin.*

present, Rabbi Grossman of Fargo, North Dakota, and Rabbi Tilsen of New Haven, Connecticut. It is believed to be the only time that two Rabbis have been officiating together in McIntosh County since around 1918–1922, when the tenures of homesteader Rabbis Hess and Ostrowsky overlapped. A *mincha* (afternoon) religious service was held in one corner of the old barn under the thick beam rafters with the same Hebrew words spoken that have been recited by Jews for generations.

When the reception was declared a success by the attendees and the leftover kugel and babkas were given away, I exited the barn with the large American flag painted on its side and thought of John Cougar Mellencamp's lyrics, "Ain't that America."

* * *

Reception inside The Hayloft near Ashley, North Dakota, May 2017.
Photo by Nancy Bender-Kelner, Marshall Kelner in foreground.

After the rededication, a thought popped into my head that I felt a need to pursue: Was it possible that we held our reception on land that was once homesteaded by a Jewish immigrant farmer? County Recorder Carol Fey checked the McIntosh County land records at my request and found that in 1908, part of the Shlepps' land was originally homesteaded by a gentleman named Strul Itzic. I checked the list I had of Ashley area Jewish homesteaders who had received loans from the Jewish Agricultural Society and saw not Strul Itzic, but Itzic and Strul Brown. This makes sense as the biblical name of Isaac is oftentimes spelled in English as "Itzic," especially so when the Jewish person named was from Romania. So unbeknownst to us at the time, our reception honoring the Jewish homesteaders was partly on land homesteaded by a Jewish man. The old saying from Romania, "Itzic doesn't plow," was literally disproved in McIntosh County, North Dakota.

Shortly before the rededication of the Ashley cemetery in May 2017, Arlo and Bonnie Mehlhaff, the curators of the Eureka Pioneer Museum, showed me a book I had never seen: *Central Dakota Germans*, by Shirley Fischer-Arends, who grew up in Ashley.

Dr. Arends studies, among many other subjects, the historical bases that led to the German-Russians and the Jews being comfortable living and working next to each other in McIntosh County, North Dakota, and in McPherson County, South Dakota. When the Russian and Romanian Jewish immigrants arrived in McIntosh County in the early 1900s, the population was already more than three-quarters Black Sea German Protestants, mostly Lutheran. The special privileges that had induced the Germans to leave Germany and move to Russia were gradually taken away by the Czars, beginning in 1834. So, though the Jews in Russia were never given special privileges, they knew what it was like to be living in a country, minding their own business, and having the laws and rules regarding them shift and change.

Another connection between the Jews and the German-Russians was that they worked together in Russia, and thereby developed a level of trust. The German-Russians raised wheat, corn, and rye; the Jewish grain merchants bought the grain at the farms; and the Moldavian peasants hauled the crop by wagons to the train depot.

In addition, both groups knew what it was like to move to another country seeking religious freedom. Though the German-Russians were not targeted in pogroms as the Jews had been in Russia, they, too, had to sometimes hide their religious affiliation. Arends tells a story handed down over generations of a Lutheran family living in Germany in the early nineteenth century. When Napoleon took power, he decreed that all of the small duchys (territories rules by a duke or duchess) on the west side of the Rheine River would be Catholic. The Lutheran family hid their Bible inside dough baked into a loaf of bread when soldiers belonging to Napoleon's vassals were searching the house, in order to hide their religious identity. Shortly thereafter, many of these Protestant and most Lutheran Germans moved to the Black Sea region of Russia, hoping for a better life.

Last, the Russian Jews and the German-Russians had lived in the climate in Odessa and then had a distinctly different experience in North Dakota. Some of the German-Russians interviewed by Arends recalled fruit growing in abundance in Odessa, and that there were "as many grapes from the vines lying on the ground, as there were rocks lying on the land in North Dakota." In describing the area around Ashley, one German immigrant interviewed by Arends stated so powerfully, yet so succinctly, "the wind was always in the grass."[270]

As if Arends' detailed research would not have been fascinating enough, I came upon this remark:

> One pioneer in my own family, my grandfather Jacob Fischer, arrived too late to homestead and had no collateral for a bank loan. He and his wife, who had four children, worked for other farmers. One day he drove to Eureka, South Dakota, to see Joseph Bender, a Jewish merchant, to ask him for a loan to buy a farm of his

[270]Shirley Fischer Arends. *The Central Dakota Germans.*

> own. Joe Bender gave him the money with only a verbal agreement that it be repaid as he could.[271]

With this family connection, I wanted to ask Dr. Arends more questions. In exchanging emails, I was lucky to learn more personal stories about her family and the Jewish community in Ashley. I discovered that her father, Cristoph Fischer, enjoyed working for Ashley Jewish cattle and horse trader Noah Dorfman for years, and through this association, learned to speak Yiddish in addition to English and the German dialect of the region. Fischer had also told Arends that he was forever indebted to Mrs. Auerbach (the wife of Israel and Sarah Auerbach's son, Nate, who owned a general store in Ashley). When Fischer was a boy, he suffered from terrible boils in his neck. Mrs. Auerbach told him to quit eating pork, and that the affliction would leave him, and it did.[272]

Arends also fondly recalls going to Max Kelber's general store at least once a day, on errands from her grandmother, who suffered with severe arthritis. Kelber's Jewish general store sold everything and was a Watkins Products distributor, selling the infamous Watkins Pain Relieving Liniment, made in Minnesota from camphor of evergreen trees and capsicum of red peppers. Shirley's reward, with permission from her grandmother, was picking up some *halva* (a dense sweet bar made with sesame paste and honey that originated in the Middle East and is a common dessert among Jewish people) as a treat for herself.

In our last email exchange, in addition to Arends indicating that the warm feelings between these two groups of prairie pioneers was evident, she wrote, "I should also thank you for your grandfather loaning money to my grandfather. Now, that is a story."

---

[271]Ibid: Jacob bought a small farm in Greenway, SD, with a sod hut for a home. He repaid the money, sold the farm, and bought a larger place in McPherson County. This was just one of the many stories the pioneers told about the assistance they had received from the Jewish merchants.

[272]Perhaps unbeknownst to Mr. Fischer, Nate Auerbach's wife was the daughter of the former Rabbi in Ashley, Rabbi Hess. One wonders whether her suggestion to stop eating pork was medically or religiously based.

"No need to thank me regarding the loan," I responded. "I'm sure Joe Bender knew a trustworthy fellow when he met him."

When I thanked Arlo and Bonnie for telling me about Arends's book, Arlo then shared another story about my grandparents in their Eureka general store. He said he was just a little boy at the time, but he has heard this story from a number of people over the years, so he strongly believes that it is true. There was something unique about Benders' General Store that he thought I should know. When someone would come into the store to purchase something, there were two sets of prices.

The story is told of a man who came in to purchase a pair of warm boots. "How much are they?" the customer asked my grandma Mary, who was waiting on him. She called back to her husband Joe, working in the back of the store. "How much are the boots, Joe?" Joe responded, "Who is it, Mary?" Mary told him, and then Joe called back the price. In other words, time and again, if the customer was someone who was struggling or down on his/her luck, the usual price of the goods was lowered.

* * *

I feel proud of my small part to ensure that the history of these strong Jewish pioneers will not fade away. The translation of my Hebrew name, Rivka, is to connect or tie together. In hindsight, my desire to connect with the past and bring the stories forward seems bashert—Yiddish for "meant to be." And to those who said they had never heard of anyone getting a remote prairie cemetery on the National Register of Historic Places, I quote my grandpa Joe, "Well now you have."

One lesson that I learned from Lincoln when he was studying ancient texts in preparation for the Bible contest was how long lasting the effects of words can be. In the 1970s, my cousin was working for the family of the president of a college, where her husband was working towards his doctorate degree in education. The president and his wife appreciated my cousin's hard work and grew to like her as a person. Soon they started asking her to babysit their two sweet teenage daughters.

One night, they wanted my cousin to stay over at their home to watch their girls, as the parents were going out of town. My cousin fixed the girls' dinner and they played a board game. Then my cousin told them it was time to go to sleep, so the girls went in to their bedroom. My cousin was reading, sitting on the couch in the living room. The girls kept getting up and walking into the living room. Finally, my cousin asked what they were doing. The older daughter said, "We know that when Jewish people fall asleep at night, their horns come out, so we wanted to see." My cousin was so surprised to be having this conversation in the home of an educated university president. She, obviously, told the girls that their information was inaccurate.

Fast forward forty years. My son was studying with Rabbi Meier Smith on Skype for the International Bible Contest. They were studying the passage in Exodus about Moses receiving the Ten Commandments on Mount Sinai and how his face was glowing when he came down the mountain (Exodus 34: 29–30). Rabbi Smith explained to Lincoln that this passage has been misinterpreted for over a thousand years by non-Jews because of a double incorrect translation. Instead of interpreting the words to mean that Moses' face was glowing with light after having an encounter with God, the wording was misinterpreted to mean that Moses had horns when he came down the mountain. When the Bible was translated from Hebrew into Greek (called the Septuagint), the phrase was first changed to read that Moses' face was "glorified."

St. Jerome in the fifth century, translated the Bible from the Greek into Latin in the Vulgate, the official Bible of the medieval Church, as "*quod cornuta esset facies sua* [because his face was horned]." This inaccurate translation of an inaccurate translation led to years of a foolish falsehood about Jews, which served as a basis for distinguishing Jews negatively from other people. Even Michelangelo's sculpture of Moses, dating to 1515 and housed in the Church of

San Pietro in Vincoli in Rome, shows Moses with horns, holding the two tablets containing the Ten Commandments.

Several years ago, Lincoln attended a basketball tournament at Augustana College in Sioux Falls, a Christian school of higher education in South Dakota. While walking on campus, we were surprised to see a replica of Michelangelo's Moses, complete with horns. I found out that the sculpture was donated to the city of Sioux Falls by an inventor and entrepreneur who hired a famous sculptor, Felix de Weldon, to go to Italy to work with the Italian government to make a bronze cast of both Michelangelo's *Moses* and *David* in the 1960s.[273] The Vulgate's inaccurate translation regarding Moses' "horns" and many of the other mistranslations, had been corrected in the King James Bible in 1611.

Michelangelo's Moses sculpture replica in Sioux Falls still remains on Augustana's campus, the victim of an inaccurate translation corrected about 350 years before this replica was constructed. Learning of this history caused me to realize that falsehoods about a group of people are like a pebble in a pond, with waves spreading almost endlessly.

* * *

Over the years I have learned that Judaism is much more than my religion. It is also a guide as to how to live my life, as it was to my ancestors. My religious background mixes so closely with my family's history that it is impossible to separate the two, like two flowers coming from the same deep-rooted stem.

I have had great examples to follow from five generations of my family, as well as from rabbis and teachers. I also learned from them to recognize and appreciate the special qualities of persons who do not happen to be Jewish, and that all good deeds are on the same level no matter what the person's faith.

---

[273]Felix de Weldon is better known for his sculpture of the Iwo Jima Memorial in Arlington County, VA.

In addition to trying to help others when we are able, Lincoln and I have been the recipients of numerous good deeds during challenging times. None of them were given with any desire for recognition or as a quid pro quo, which is why they meant so much. I believe that all good acts float out into the world and have a positive effect, though we may not personally see that effect immediately, if at all. As we do a mitzvah because we know it's right, and not for applause or recognition, perhaps we are not meant to know all the good that comes from our acts. We should simply trust that good will lead to more good. Tikun Olam (repair of our world) is a core value of Judaism, and I believe we can repair our world with even the smallest of kindnesses — a comforting word or a willingness to listen. This belief in the power of good is one of many gifts from my family and my religion.

I can still hear Rabbi Milgrom's words, while I sat in my Vikings cheerleader uniform at the Minneapolis Talmud Torah: "We Jews were not chosen by God because we are somehow better. We were and are chosen for responsibility. We are chosen to be examples to others of the moral and right way to act. We are chosen to follow God's laws regarding how to treat each other. We are chosen to stand up for the person who has no one to stand up for him or her."

I also distinctly recall one High Holiday sermon of Rabbi Arnold Goodman at the Adath Jeshurun Synagogue related to this subject, in which he stated it so concisely: "Always act as if you are the only Jewish person who someone will ever meet." After September 11, Rabbi Barry Cytron, former rabbi at the Adath and then Chair in Jewish Studies at St. John's University and the University of St. Thomas, quoted from the Book of Job in a press interview, referring to the efforts all humanity should continue to strive to make, especially during times of trouble. Our goal, he stated, is to still "be eyes to the blind, feet to the lame, and to wear righteousness as a robe." Rabbi Harold Kravitz, who has served as a rabbi at the Adath since 1987 and is Past Chair of Mazon, a Jewish Response to Hunger, gave the opening prayer on June 9, 2015, at the United States Senate. He prayed, in part, that "the Senators be guided to do what the book of Deuteronomy describes as that which is right and good in the sight of the Eternal One." Rabbi Kravitz also stated, "We pray for all Americans, especially those who lack sufficient food to feed themselves and their families. May the One who provides sustenance for all (Hazan et hakol), bless this United States Senate with the wisdom and compassion to act on its responsibilities to those who are vulnerable and in need."

In the various chapters of my life, I have attempted to apply the Jewish lessons learned in and out of school. When I mentioned to my brother-in-law's brother, Larry, that someone we both knew had recently become Haredi Orthodox (the most strict interpretation of observant Orthodox Judaism), he said to me, "Rebecca, just because you wear a black mask and ride a white horse doesn't make you the Lone Ranger." This was his way of stressing the importance of living a Jewish life day-to-day in one's dealing with others, in addition to following Jewish rituals and attending religious services.

When two students in a school system where I was employed were struggling with making the right choices, I sent them letters of encouragement at the juvenile detention facility where they had been sent. I wanted them to know that many people, including me, believed in them and their potential. I had confidence in the fact that in sending these positive thoughts to the boys, their chances of success would increase. I recognize that the legacy I've received — of believing in the power of good — includes an ample dose of hope and optimism, as well. When the boys thanked me and told me they hung the letters in their room once they returned home, I realized even more how important this simple act was in their lives at a time of diminished hope.

When I was working at a Hutterite Colony in North Dakota as a teacher's aide several years ago, I was reading with a bright fifth-grade student about holidays around the world.[274] With his German accent, he was reading about "Chanukah, the festival of lights." He

[274]The Hutterite people, Anabaptists who believe in peaceful, communal living and speak Hutterite German as their first language, came to the United States for religious freedom.

commented to me, "I've never heard about *that* one." I told him a little about the origins of this holiday and told him that this is a holiday that I celebrate, because I'm Jewish. With wide-eyed amazement and a smile, he said, "Really? I've never met a Hebrew before!" I volunteered to help the students prepare for the Christmas musical for their parents in English, their second language, and oversaw the older children hiding plastic eggs with candy for the younger students at Easter, because these holidays are important to the children. By doing so, I never changed my beliefs, but showed them that I respected theirs. I fell in love with the students at the Colony, just as I do with all students I am privileged to work with.

I felt the students' love for me, as well—perhaps no more so than when the bird flu was sweeping the Dakotas. As the disease was being spread by infected birds, there were rumors at the Hutterite Colony that they may have to kill all their chickens, rather than risk the consequences. I was getting ready to leave the Colony for home one late afternoon, and the same fifth-grader appeared near my car wearing a large overcoat. I put the window down, and asked him how he was doing. "Not well," he replied, with tears in his eyes.

"What's wrong? " I asked.

"They may be killing the chickens soon and I have been caring for a favorite black chicken, Mrs. Bender," he explained. "Would you be able to bring Black Chicken to Eureka, and care for him, until the bird flu scare is over?" he asked. At that moment, he opened the large overcoat and there was his chicken, a shiny black-feathered bird with a red beak. The chicken sat calmly in the nook of the boy's arm.

I said to him, "I am so honored that you would want me to take your prize chicken. I would do my best to care for him with my son, but I would need to ask the heads of the Colony if this would be OK so we don't spread the bird flu or harm your favorite chicken." His mood improved with this response, and with a smile, he told me to have a good evening. As I pulled out on the dusty road, I saw this young boy, in his big overcoat, heading back to his home with his chicken following behind. Thankfully, the birds at the Colony did not have to be killed. That moment is still a very special one for me;

though this fifth-grader knew our religions were different, he knew he could trust me with being kind to his beloved feathered pet.

There was another day at the Hutterite Colony, when one of the third graders was falling asleep sitting at his desk. During a break, I walked over and asked him if he was feeling OK. "Yes," he said, "I just stayed up too late last night." I explained how important it is for children to get enough sleep at night. He acknowledged that he knew this to be true. "But it was such a good book, Mrs. Bender, I couldn't put it away," he said.

"What was the name of the book?" I asked.

"I brought it with me to read during recess," he said. He opened up his backpack, and showed me the book, *Joseph and His Brothers*. I stared for a moment at the book, realizing that the book that this boy could not put down at the Hutterite Colony in rural North Dakota, just happened to be the Bible story that Israel Prime Minister Netenyahu told Lincoln in Jerusalem was his favorite. I felt so fortunate to be allowed to witness the connection between these two events—between groups of people who on their surface may seem so different. How could I not feel that this was more than mere coincidence, and a beshert moment? "*Joseph and His Brothers* is a wonderful book with good lessons about forgiveness," I said, "but the nice things about good books is that they are still there in the morning for you to read and reread. They don't disappear."

⁂

When I was taking Lincoln to AAU basketball team practices in South Dakota during the summer of 2016, the practices were held in different locations. I would typically wait during the practice and catch up on phone calls or pay some bills. When we stopped at one gym, I dropped Lincoln off to park the car. By the time I came in, he was approaching me at the door, saying, "You wouldn't believe the mascot for this school." I asked him what it was. "It's the Cossacks," he said, "and they have a huge Cossack on a horse with a long sword on their gym wall."

"You're joking, right Lincoln?" I asked. I walked in and was surprised and saddened to see the menacing Cossack that Lincoln had described. Lincoln, knowing that his great-grandfather's brother was killed by a Russian Cossack and that the Cossacks instilled fear into the Russian people as the evil enforcers of the czars' policies, couldn't imagine how a school would have this mascot. I explained to him that some people just don't know history and therefore wouldn't understand how offensive this could be. I told Lincoln that I bet this community was not inhabited by Russians and Poles who immigrated to America, whose family members had been killed by Cossacks, and that I would assume it was not chosen as an intentionally hurtful act.

After checking, I found this to be the case. Though the town has the name of a Russian river, it was originally named by the railroad, solely to attract Russian immigrants to the area. They never came, and instead the area was populated by mostly Norwegians and Germans, whose descendants probably didn't have knowledge of the violent history of the Russian Cossacks at the time the school was picking mascots. Lincoln and I talked about the responsibility we each have to study and remember world history.

Lincoln continues to remember his family history and his late grandparents. Every Memorial Day for the last eight years, he has played the snare drum for the color guard at Temple of Aaron Cemetery in St. Paul, Minnesota, where his grandparents Frima and Kenneth Bender are buried. He also places a stone on top of the monument honoring them. Many Jews place stones on top of gravestones to show honor to the deceased, and to show that the person who is buried at that site has not been forgotten. As evidence of the different approaches to traditions and customs among Jewish people, I recall my baba Minnie's comment regarding this practice of placing stones. She said, "Becca, when I die and you visit the cemetery, please don't put a stone on my monument."

"Why?" I asked her, perplexed.

"I don't want the other people who are buried there to feel bad if they don't have a stone on theirs," she replied. And who could argue with that concern for others, even after her death.

⁂

As I've gotten older, I appreciate the Jewish traditions even more — dropping matzoh balls into hot, bubbling water on Passover, like my female ancestors did, adding my voice to sing Psalm 3:17–18, "Etz Chaim He" (Tree of Life) with fellow congregants at the synagogue, the smell of onions and soup chicken on my hands that reminds me of the smell of my mother's fingers when she was preparing a *yontif* (Jewish holiday) meal, the way the ten days of repentance between Rosh Hashanah and Yom Kippur give me a time-out to reflect on the past and look ahead, as leaves change color and fall from the trees, the sizzle of potato latkes as I flip them in hot oil for Chanukah dinner and make my kitchen windows steamy.[275]

Among the favorite memories of my lifetime are those when I was called upon to participate in a Jewish family milestone. One occurred on my dad's side of the family in New York City about twenty years ago. I was asked by my younger cousin Karen and her husband Robert to represent the older generation of the Bender family in handing their son Jonah to Karen as part of his naming ceremony. Another occurred on my mom's side of the family in Omaha, Nebraska, in 2017, when I was asked to be one of the two witnesses on the wedding contract for my first cousin Sandra's daughter Shayna and her husband, Ben. Prior to signing my name in English on the delicate hand-cut Ketuba, I was asked to write it in Hebrew. As is done for Conservative Jewish religious contracts, one does not just sign a name. Rather one writes his or her name and the names of one's parents. I wrote, "Rivka, bat Akiva v Timeema," Rebecca, daughter of Kenneth and Frima.

Besides feeling extremely honored to have been asked to fulfill these roles during special simchas, these were times when I recognized my generational responsibility. I was standing in the shoes of family from generations past, whom I had never met, following the

---

[275]Translation from Hebrew, " She (the Jewish belief system) is a tree of life to those who hold fast to it, and all who uphold it are happy. Her ways are ways of pleasantness and all her paths are peace."

same traditions they had, while recognizing that someday the baby, bride, and groom would do the same mitzvahs for generations they had yet to meet. I felt both times like I was a direct link, standing between the past and the future for one beautiful present moment. And both times I was overwhelmed with powerful emotions.

***

There are rare times in life, when you just know you are where you are supposed to be. Jewish people refer to this feeling as bashert, in Yiddish, meant to be. I had one of those days when I was getting ready to send my finalized manuscript to North Dakota State University's editor, Dr. Suzzanne Kelley, for a final edit, design work, and preparation for publication. Lincoln and I were visiting my sister, Nancy, and brother-in-law, Barry, at their home, when Nancy said to me, "Do you think you want to look through any of the bins of old pictures we organized after we sold Mom and Dad's house, to make sure there isn't something you might want for your book?" I told Nancy that I thought I had looked through all those bins prior to working on the Nomination for the National Historic Register, but as long as I was there, and there was a thunderstorm causing me to not feel like driving the several hundred miles home, I would look through the Joseph and Mary Bender bin once more. As I was going through the pictures, there was a folded-up letter that was stuck between a few pictures. I opened the letter and read:

> Mrs. Sam Geller
> 417 Oakland Avenue South
> Fargo, North Dakota 58102
>
> October 1, 1975
>
> Dear Mr. Bender –
>
> Thank you very much for your quick response to my inquiry about my parents. I thought you might be pleased to know that we have your complete history on the oral tape you did for Mr. Alfred Thal of Bismarck last

> year. We sent a member of our research committee to Bismarck recently, and he taped all the material that Al had contributed to the State Historical Society. Among them was your tape. One of our volunteer typists has just finished transcribing your tape on the typewriter.
>
> What a marvelous story you told — I wish we had more like it. I assure you it will have a prominent place in our book and will be of great interest to all who read it. I'm sorry that we have not met — perhaps we shall one day. Your story indicates that you must be a very fine man, and that you take pride in the years you spent in the Dakotas. We shall be proud to have your story on the pages of our book. Many many thanks.
>
> Sincerely,
> Toba Geller

I found it so special that this lady, whom I had admired for taking her time to urge North Dakota Jewish families to write down their histories, was communicating directly with my grandpa Joe, whom I admired for the history he had lived. Though I was not given the opportunity to meet Toba Geller, I had already felt close to her during the time I was involved with my research. Now I felt her warm spirit, in the over forty-year-old letter my grandfather received about three years prior to his death. Toba passed away two months before Grandpa Joe did. Maybe they did eventually meet and have been part of the supportive force I have felt assisting me to eventually get some of these "marvelous" stories told.

As I was rechecking facts in this book, I realized that I didn't know when my grandpa Joe had served as mayor of Eureka. I went to Eureka City Hall and Nicole, the City Clerk, helpfully went in the walk-in-vault and brought out the heavy minute books from 1925–1949, covered in burgundy-colored leather. I got to work.

In the April 15, 1925, minutes, I saw mention of my grandfather. He was among a group of citizens selected for a committee to handle the case of August Martell against the City for damage to his land by the city's lake. Clearly, Eureka's mayor and aldermen were not ones to hold a grudge. In the very next month's minutes, the same August

Martell applied for and received a license to operate a pool and billiard hall. Also, according to the City Council minutes, in June 1925, Ordinance 88 passed. A motion was made and seconded to have signs painted and erected north, south, east, and west of town, stating, "Welcome to the City of Eureka—please drive within reason." I smiled at this good old-fashioned common sense approach to a problem. The July 1, 1927, minutes referred to Joe Bender again, this time applying to rent City Hall for the purpose of a moving picture house. The charge was twenty-five dollars a month plus a license fee.

I learned that elections were held in May in Eureka in the 1920s, and after turning page after page, I finally saw that on May 4, 1928, Joseph Bender was elected 2nd Ward Alderman, with seventy-five votes. The following year, on May 6, 1929, Mayor Schamber and two aldermen resigned. On motion on May 7, 1929, Joseph Bender was elected by the councilmembers as President and Acting Mayor with a salary of $150, payable quarterly. During Mayor Bender's term, May 7, 1929–May 7, 1930, the typical types of issues facing rural small towns were discussed at Council meetings, everything from an effective sewer system, to paying the City's bills, approval of rates for Northern Light and Power Company, tax levies, installing street lights, appropriating money to maintain and operate a Municipal Bathing Pool, to pay the "Leader of the City Band," and to hire a night watchman for the City (which was referred to the Police Committee, with the direction to "hire a good man" at a salary of less than $50 a month). Mayor Bender also introduced an ordinance that was later passed "prohibiting the opening or removal of covers of any manhole or catch-basin in the City of Eureka and providing a penalty for violation thereof."

But something atypical occurred in April 1930, which never occurred in the history of Eureka before or since. It caused me to give a double-take and then feel tears well up in my eyes. Every set of city council minutes (regular and special) was signed by the City Auditor and the Mayor. I had been taking note of how impeccable Joseph Bender's cursive signature was next to the typed "Mayor" signature line for the year he served, despite having had no schooling in the United States. In April, Joe Bender had chosen not to run in the election to continue as mayor, though he planned to continue representing his ward as Alderman. On April 4, 1930, as Joseph Bender bid adieu to his time as mayor, and before Doc Gerdes took over as Mayor in May 1930, Joe Bender did not sign "Joseph Bender" next to the title "Mayor" in the minutes. He signed his name in Hebrew. Not an English transliteration of his Hebrew name, but his name in Hebrew letters — from right to left, as Hebrew is written and read.

I sat in the room where the Eureka City Council now meets, feeling the power of this quiet act by my grandfather in 1930, eighty-seven years earlier. I felt it was Joe Bender's way of letting anyone who reviewed the minutes in later years to know that a Jew had been mayor of Eureka — his way of stating who he was and how important his religion was to him, while praising the country that allowed him to serve and the city that chose him to do so. In Russia, his brothers had been killed just for being Jewish. In the United States, the remaining Bendersky male had served as mayor of his town, without regard to his religion.

***

During the time I was concluding the writing of this book, I realized that I was humming a tune, subconsciously. Lincoln said to me, as I was preparing dinner one evening, "What are you always humming lately?" Then I realized that it was a song that my dad sang, with full baritone Broadway projection, on family car trips when Nancy and I were little. It's from the musical *Camelot*, written by Alan Jay Lerner and Frederick Lowe, and is called, "If Ever I Would Leave You." It goes through all the seasons of the year and the reasons why it would be difficult to leave during those times. I can hear my dad singing it as he drove our Buick across America, filling in certain words he didn't know with his own new lyrics, and sometimes with "dum, dyum, bum, bum." But the words to the last stanza he knew: "Oh, no! not in springtime! Summer, winter or fall! No never could I leave you, at all![276] Though I appreciate that Bender family members have written to me, saying how proud my dad would be that I have preserved the Bender family's history by getting the Ashley Jewish Cemetery on the National Register, I haven't told them, until now, that he has been here with me the whole time.

***

When the newspaper editor asked if I was "*still* Jewish," I responded, "Yes." I now understand that this simple word did not come just from me. As every note played on a musical instrument has harmonic tones that are produced simultaneously when the fundamental tone is played, my voice does, also. My voice speaking had the overtones of Russian orphan Kiva Bender saying, "I want to learn more about my religion," and my farming grandpa Joseph Bender saying, "We did for you what you would have done for us," and my great-grandma Becky saying, "You are born a Jew, you will die a Jew," and my dad, Kenneth Bender, saying, "I will not change my dog tags," and my son, Lincoln, saying, "of course, I will miss the parade to go to Yom Kippur services. Did you really think I would consider anything else?" These are the powerful chords of faith.

In the 1954 book *A Jewish Tourist's Guide to the U.S.*, the Ashley Jewish Cemetery is listed among sites for Jewish tourists to visit. It is referred to as "an abandoned cemetery." The authors got it wrong. Despite its remoteness, it never was. It never will be.

I have faith.

Still.

[276]"If Ever I Would Leave You (from *Camelot*), Music by Frederick Loewe, Lyrics by Alan Jay Lerner, Copyright © 1960 (Renewed) by Alan Jay Lerner and Frederick Loewe Publication and Allied Rights Assigned to Chappell & Co., Inc., All Rights Reserved, Used by Permission of Alfred Music.

ACKNOWLEDGEMENTS

FOR MY SON, Lincoln Bernhard, whose inquiries about our family prompted me to investigate further, and whose determination, creativity, accomplishments, and sense of humor I look up to; for my mom, Frima Gordon Bender (z"l [*zichrona livracha* in Hebrew for may his/her memory be for a blessing]), and my dad, Kenneth Bender (z"l), who are with me every day as in life, encouraging and celebrating; for my grandparents Mary Rievman Bender (z"l) and Joseph Bender (z"l), Minnie Goldberg Gordon (z"l), and Samuel Gordon (z"l), who left a tangible legacy of generosity and hope; for my sister, Nancy Bender-Kelner, my brother-in-law, Barry Kelner, and my uncle David Bender, who were my trusted, patient, and wise first draft book editors and who are members of my lifetime advisory team; for my nephews Marshall Kelner, Malcolm Kelner, and Jackson Kelner, and my niece, Sage Kelner, for being the unique, talented, and caring individuals they each are; for my supportive and innovative aunts, Josephine Berg Simes, Meri Bender, Frances Bernbaum, (z"l), Sara Lee Plachte (z"l), and Bernice Ellison (z"l); for my "Sweet Sixteen" first cousins, all for one, and one for all: Sandra Kurland, David Berg, Jim Berg, Sherna Posner, Melvyn Bernbaum, Lorna Bernbaum, Natalie Plachte White, Michelle Plachte-Zuieback, Steven Plachte (z"l), Jim Ellison, Jean Milofsky, David Ellison, Kathy Ellison, Karen Bender, Suzanne Bender, and Aimee Bender (and spouses, children, and children's children).

FOR MY FRIEND Renita James, whose genuine interest in learning about my family's traditions and sharing her own, helped me realize the great similarities in people of faith; for Suzzanne Kelley (Editor in Chief of NDSU Press) and the publishing book team and anonymous reviewers, Lorna Meidinger (ND Architectural Historian), Claudia Berg (Director, State Historical Society of ND), and Steve Hunegs (Executive Director JCRC, whose belief in the importance of my work spurred me to greater heights); for my friends Minnie Pietz, Stephanie Hannah, Laura Herfurth, Sonja Davy, Barbara Sanders, and Lisa Ausman, whose dedication to children and goodness I admire.

FOR ALL THE STUDENTS I've had the honor to teach in Minnesota, South Dakota, Wisconsin, Arizona, and Hutterite Colonies; for Johnny and Mark Salzer, Carol Fey, Claude Meidinger, Leona Neu, Neil Schneider, Dennis Glas, Delores Schneider, Shirley Fischer Arends, Bruce Smith, Scott and Ermalene Schlepp, honorary citizen Thomas D. Isern, and the other special people, past and present, of McIntosh County, North Dakota; for Toni Schaeffer, Bonnie and Arlo Mehlhoff, Claudia Merthun, Elsie and Lester Heilman, Edmund and Hulda Opp, Jannel and Paul Bentz, Joan and Jim Anderson, Ron and Wendy Brockel and family, John and Renee Schwingler, Gary Krein, Bob Weber, Cal Neuharth, Clyde and Bobbie Ottenbacher, Wanda Jundt, Les Merkel, Debie Bernhardt, the Kary brothers, Sally Davis, Barbara and Bob Billotto, Don and Susan Fischer, Gerald Beutler, Julie Hoff, Randy Hermanson, Kay Krein, Darlene Kary, Susan Imberi, Bruce Alexander, Dwain Schwan, Kelsey and Nick Weismantel, Tonya and Sid Maier, Stan and Rose Marie Stabler, Estella and Bill Merkel, Charley Glaesman, Antonio Alandy, Ronda Lapp, Susan Ostrowski, Daren Fischer, Blake Aman, Mark and Elisa Opp, Cindy Dosch, Lana Hilgemann, Kelly Odenbach, Dale and Alison Batie, Lloyd Miller, Nina Kunz, Nicole Frerk, Paulette Bauer, Sully Knoepfle, Cindy and Jim Schumacher, Ray Rohrbach, Linda Bergman, Gary and Merilee Ackerman, Ric Weisbeck, Bruce and Wendy Fauth, Scott Lien, Michael Dosch, Dan Vander Wal, Susan Wolf, Jackie Rau, Craig and Janeen Connell, Nancy Kindelspire, Dana Leibel, Pat and Melissa Lapka, Gwen Wolf, Doreen Emery, Pam Dunn, Curt Walz, Alvin Kallas, Vickie Lapka, Monica Hilgemann, Tricia Erickson, Julie Nikolas, Charlie H., Holly H., Jean Bertsch, Margie, Oreen, Tim, Dennis, Kathy Opp, Scooter, Ivy, Karri, Bonnie, Natalie, and the other special people, past and present, of McPherson County, South Dakota.

FOR ALL THE RESEARCHERS and information gatherers who came before me, especially Toba Geller(z"l), Father William Sherman and Alfred Thal(z"l); for my teachers and Lincoln's teachers, and Rabbis A. Goodman, B. Cytron, A. Ettedgui, M. Smith, H. Kravitz, G. Davy (z"l), R. Younger (z"l), L. Milgrom (z"l), Y. Grossman, M. Alperowitz, D. Ettedgui, Cantors M. Amsel (z"l), S. Buckner, lay leaders Herschel and Bea Premack, David and Suzon Gordon, Jim Sherman, and David Liss, and linguists Pamela Russ and Uri Koppel; for my Kelner "siblings" Diane, Larry and Marcie, Ron and Rita, children and grandchildren.

FOR THE DESCENDANTS of the Ashley Jewish Homesteaders, those who participated in the May 21, 2017 event, and especially, Stuart Kaufman and Rabbi Jon-Jay Tilsen for their dedication; for Jerry Klinger, Mark "Tim" and Eunice "ET" Timbrook, Raymond Schneider-Kuhn, Dale Bluestein, Lance Nixon, Carolyn Grueskin, Kelda Pharris, and Lauren Donovan, who showed compassion for preserving the memories of people they never knew; for Joel Bernbaum, Abby Guiver, Steven Bernstein, Virginia Catt, Linda Dweh, and Vicky Korlewala Doe, who honor people everyday with their selfless acts of kindness.

FOR THOSE WHO SMILED with me, including Justin J., Anthony J., Hy S. (z"l), Marvin and Gloria (z"l) W., Shelley F. and Virgil P., Grete and John K., Rachel B., Ronnie H., Ann K. Mary Co., Ervin G. Robert T. Saralee S., Joy G., Rae B. (z"l), Judy S., Ian D., Logan D., Trista D. Kevin M., Matt J., Vladimir P., Tyler R., Connie S., Bernice and Mike F., Shirley T., Toni Sw., Kevin M., Lisa S., Vicky D., Amy M., Lee S., Lisa C., Jessica and J.R. S., Cindy K., Cindy C., Cindy W., Cindy J., Ashley B., Cathy P., Ruth A., Sarah E., Tami S., Ann P., Marie H., Evan M., Harold N. (z"l), Candi B., Jon B. (z"l), Jim O., David G., Jeff L., Lee Ann H., Sigrid S. (z"l), Mary S. and Marshall C., David M., Laurie R., Gillian A., Ed L., Loretta D., Linda B., Karron H., Suzanne G., Brian L., Lisa R., Joy S., Sally M., Flo and Ted F., Jane F., Julie K. (z"l), Nancy K., Debbie S., Joni F., Rae K., Susan R., Rae Lynn S., Susan and Jonathan G., Pauline R., Elizabeth B., Mark B. (z"l), Roberta B., Eileen B., Alvin B. (z"l), Nancy C., Mary C., Jay R., Rori E. (z"l), Hunter H., Sarah B. (z"l), Lori, Jean M., Alex H., Rich and Mitzi G., Elaine L., Gail B., Rodney J., Judy R., Lizz T., Ellen T., Debbi J., Susan A., Pesach G., Barb L., Debbie F. Jennifer D., Debbie J., Lori M., Mary B., Joan F., Karen C., Kristi T., Marcia B., Steve M., Eric T., Elmer T., Ellyn W., John O., David I., Damon D., Marsh E.,

Pat and Laurie D., Tiffany, Terry F., Delores, Pam E., Mark R., David R., Bradford D., Anne K., Joanne R., Sharon G., Sandra D., Dick E., Ethel C., Lorie A., Kathy M., Matt M., Tom B., Eric D., Gare E., Bruce H., Mindy B., Rachel L., Carol B., Margaret and Irvin R., Mike and Ruth M., Walt and Dodie S., Joy B., Helen H., Johanna B., Gail P., Joyce and Doug K., Carol D., Carol G., Stan and Barbara A., Jerry T., Jessica S., Matthew and Liz P., Cecilia S. Robyn A., Jayme S., Nicole, Eric A., Rich and Rachel E., Dan and Carol C., Dan N., Jon N., Bob A., Cindy and Olaf M., Melissa R., Laurel G., Ned W., Jeff H., Bob G., Damon W., Tracy A., Nelly R., Pams, Mr. H., Nicki, Youa X., Wendy B., Erica K., Merrilee J., Janice M., Stuart T. Mike H., Stuart H. Bob J., Robin D., Paul Hi, Judy S., Peter Hi, Jim and Andrea D., Bob and Laura S. Allen K., Judy B., Gerry P., Randy K., Robert S., Mark M., Ruvane K., Mendel K., Shayna K., Roberta A., Tiffany G., Danielle B., Britanni B. Ellie B., Judah B., Ari P., Rami P., Amira P., Madalina K., Ari B., Ilana B., Sam K., Josh K., Beverly P. (z"l), Marlene S., Marian and Oscar R., George N., Becky, Buzz, Wesley J., Sarah G., Maureen R., Lisa and Jon D., Marshall M., and Sammy S.

AND WITH APPRECIATION to all the Bendersky/Rievman and Gordon/Goldberg ancestors, descendants and spouses who have lit the path for me to follow and have sweetened my life with their love, laughter, and stories.

APPENDIX

Largo
Still
Lyrics and Music by Rebecca E. Bender
c. 2016, used by permission of composer
Violin
Piano
Verses 1 & 2
In the quiet of the night when no
When it's close to the dawn do you think of
one is awake when you think of your life and how
those before how they led you to here, how they
choice transcends fate do you ever wonder how you
breathe in your pores? In their black and white pictures, when you
came to be you? In the still of the night,
see your own eyes what else still continues
what do you still hold true?
through your lows and your highs?
1

Refrain A

What we keep and we throw, who we hug and re- lease does what's
left in your heart bring you heart-ache or peace?
Does your link still hold strong in the chain they be- gan? In the
still of your soul do their i- deals still stand?

Verses 3 & 4

If they met you today and had 2 minutes to talk
Then at that divine moment when the lake be comes clear
Would they say "job well done" or conti- nue to walk
and you see your re- flection and beliefs you hold dear ...
If you'd run after them then, then why not now
Then your path will be even, your load will feel light
to put still in your life, find your an- swers some how.
all be- cause you're still you and your still feels so right.

Refrain B
What we keep and we throw,
who we hug and release
Does what's
Rallentando
Fermata
left in your heart
Does what's left in your heart
bring you
heartache
or peace?
Diminuendo
Violin

BIBLIOGRAPHY

Books

Adams, Peter. *Politics, Faith, and the Making of American Judaism*. Ann Arbor: University of Michigan Press, 2014.

American Jewish Committee. *American Jewish Year Book, Volume 9*. Philadelphia: Jewish Publication Society of America, 1907.

Anavy, Regina M., ed. *Larry's Letters: The Personal Correspondence of Larry Schlasinger*, 2nd ed. San Francisco: Hummingbird Imprints, 2005.

Arends, Shirley Fischer. *The Central Dakota Germans: Their History, Language, and Culture*. Washington DC: Georgetown University Press, 1989.

Ashley Golden Jubilee Historical Book Committee. *Ashley Golden Jubilee Book*. 1938.

Ashton, Dianne. *Hanukkah in America*. New York: New York University Press, 2013.

Bartelt, Pearl W. "American Jewish Agricultural Colonies." In *American Communal Utopias*, edited by Donald E. Pitzer. Chapel Hill: University of North Carolina Press, 1997.

Bender, Joseph. *From the Prairies to the Beaches: An American Soldier's Story*. Minneapolis: 2005.

__________. *This is Your Life, Joseph Bender*. Minneapolis: 1970.

Berman, Susan. *Easy Street: The True Story of a Gangster's Daughter*. New York: Bantam Books, 1981.

__________. *Easy Street: The True Story of a Mob Family*. New York: Dial Press, 1981.

Brandes, Joseph. *Immigrants to Freedom: Jews as Yankee Farmers! 1880s to 1960s*. Philadelphia: University of Pennsylvania Press, 1971.

Eureka Golden Jubilee Committee. *Eureka, South Dakota: 1887-1937 Golden Jubilee Book*. 1937.

Flannery, Edward. *The Anguish of the Jews: Twenty-Three Centuries of Anti-Semitism*. New York: Macmillan Company, 1965.

Herzl, Theodor. *Der Judenstaat*. Trans. Sylvie D'Avigdor and Jacob De Haas. Public domain, 1896.

Hill, Leonidas, E. "The Nazi Attack on 'un-German' Literature, 1933–45." In *The Holocaust and the Book: Destruction and Preservation*, ed. Jonathan Rose. Amherst: University of Massachusetts Press, 2001.

Goering, Violet and Orlando Goering. *Jewish Farmers in South Dakota: The Am Olam*. South Dakota Historical Society, 1983.

Judge, Edward H. *Easter in Kishinev: Anatomy of a Pogrom*. New York: New York University Press, 1992.

Kinghorn, Jonathan. *The Atlantic Transport Line, 1881–1931*. Jefferson: McFarland, 2012.

Klier, John D. and Shlomo Lambroza, eds. *Pogroms: Anti-Jewish Violence in Modern Russian History*. Cambridge: Cambridge University Press, 1992.

Laqueur, Walter. *History of Zionism: From the French Revolution to the Establishment of the State of Israel*. Knopf Doubleday Publishing Group, 2009.

Long, John H., ed. "Dakota Territory, South Dakota and North Dakota: Individual County Chronologies." In *Dakota Territory Atlas of Historical County Boundaries*. The Newberry Library, 2006.

Mangione, Jerry. *The Dream and the Deal: The Federal Writers Project, 1935–1943*. New York: Syracuse University Press, 1996.

Mendes-Flohr, Paul and Yehuda Reinharz, eds. *The Jew in the Modern World*. Oxford: Oxford University Press, 1995.

National Conference of Jewish Charities. *Jewish Charities: Bulletin of the National Conference of Jewish Charities*. 4th ed. Baltimore: 1912.

Patterson, Carl. *I Remember B Company, 38th Infantry Regiment, 2nd Infantry Division.* Leawood: Leathers Publishing, 2000.

Pendergast, Tom and Sara Pendergast. *St. James Encyclopedia of Popular Culture.* Detroit: St. James Press, 2000.

Robinson, James Harvey and Charles Beard, eds. *Readings in Modern European History.* Vol. 2. Boston: 1908.

Sherman, William C., and Playford V. Thorson, Jr., eds. *Plains Folk: North Dakota's Ethnic History.* Fargo: Institute for Regional Studies, North Dakota State University, 1986.

Sherman, Williams. *Prairie Mosaic: An Ethnic Atlas of Rural North Dakota,* 2nd ed. Fargo: North Dakota State University Press, 2017.

Spickard, Paul. *Almost Aliens: Immigration, Race and Colonialism in American History and Identity.* New York: Routledge, 2007.

Sreenivasan, Jyotsna. "Jewish Agricultural Communities, 1881–1941." In *Utopias in American History.* Santa Barbara: ABC-CLIO, 2008.

Sutton, Robert P. "Nineteenth Century Jewish Farm Communities." In *Communal Utopias and the American Experience: Religious Communities 1732–2000.* Westport: Praeger, 2003.

Journals, Periodicals, Conference Presentations

Abrams, Jeanne. "Jews in the Wild West." *Jewish Action,* May 26, 2011. http://jewishaction.com/.

"Al Jolson Remembered." *Paramount News,* Dec. 6, 1950.

Common Council for American Unity. *Common Ground,* Autumn 1946.

"Four Great U.S. Wheat Belts Yield a Rich Harvest." *Life Magazine,* Aug. 1937.

Devine, Edward T. "War Relief Work." *The Annals of the American Academy of Political and Social Science,* 79, no. 1 (1918): 1–8.

Donovan, Lauren. "Between a Rock and a Hard Place." *Bismarck Tribune,* May 6, 2017.

Iseminger, Gordon L. "The McIntosh County German-Russians: The First Fifty Years." *North Dakota: Journal of the Northern Plains* 51, no. 3 (1984).

Jewish Agricultural Society. (1909). *Jewish Agricultural Society Annual Report.* New York: Jewish Agricultural Society.

"Jewish Massacre Denounced." *New York Times* (New York, NY), Apr. 28, 1903.

Lucas, Albert. "American Jewish Relief in the World War." *The Annals of the American Academy of Political and Social Science,* 79, no. 1 (1918): 221–28.

Menes, Abraham. "The Am Oylom Movement." *YIVO Annual of Jewish Social Science* 4, (1949): 9.

The Reform Advocate: America's Jewish Journal 9. (1913).

Saeks, Alan. "When Law Firms Wouldn't Hire Jewish Lawyers." *American Jewish World,* July 31, 2015.

Schulte, Janet E. "Proving Up and Moving Up—Jewish Homesteading Activity in North Dakota 1900–1920." *Great Plains Quarterly* 10, no. 4 (2010): 228–44.

Schwartz, Lois Fields. "Early Jewish Agricultural Colonies in North Dakota." In *North Dakota History,* Vol. 32, 217–32. Bismarck: State Historical Society of North Dakota, 1965.

Sherman, William. "Jewish Homestead Communities in North Dakota, 1900–1920." Bemidji: 17th Annual Northern Great Plains History Conference, 1982.

Vossler, Ron. "The Lost Jews of McIntosh." *North Dakota REC/RTC,* July 1986.

Weber, Laura E. "Gentiles Preferred, Minneapolis Jews and Employment." *Minnesota History* 52, no. 5 (1991): 166–82. http://www.collections.mnhs.org/.

Whitfield, Stephen J. "Where They Burn Books . . ." *Modern Judaism* 22, no. 3 (2002): 213–33.

Wishek, Nina. "Along the Trails of Yesterday: A Story of McIntosh County." *Ashley Tribune,* 1941.

Websites

Aspenleiter, Gayla. "German-Russian Village List." Last modified February 2012. http://www.blackseagr.org/pdfs/village_list.pdf.

The Editors of Encyclopedia Britannica. "October Manifesto." In Encyclopedia Britannica. http://www.britannica.com/.

Eilfort, Yeruchem. "Why Do Mourners Recite Kaddish?" http://www.chabad.org/.

Gliksberg, Shimon Yakov. "Jewish Odessa, Chapters from My Memoirs." http://kehilalinks.jewishgen.org/.

Gottheil, Richard and Wilhelm Bacher. "Aramaic Language Among the Jews." In *1906 Jewish Encyclopedia*. http://www.jewishencyclopedia.com/.

Heylen, Philip. "The Red Star Line." Speech, Sarasota, August 6, 2011. Erratic Impact. http://erraticimpact.com/~feminism/html/pdf/fuentes_en_sarasota_speech.pdf.

Klier, John. "Pogroms." In *The YIVO Encyclopedia of Jews in Eastern Europe*. YIVO Institute for Jewish Research, 2010. http://www.yivoencyclopedia.org/.

"Leopold Stein's Maoz Tzur 'Schirm und Schutz.'" *Stein Families from Upper and Lower Franconia*. Last modified March 18, 2018. http://leopoldstein.net/.

Mayrent, Sherry. "Why Listen to Scratchy Old 78s?" Last modified September 23, 2016. http://klezmeracademy.com/.

"Modern Jewish History: Pogroms." *Jewish Virtual Library*. https://www.jewishvirtuallibrary.org/.

"Odessa Mama - אדעסא מאמא." *Yiddish Songs and Lyrics* (blog). May 16, 2007 (3:52 p.m.). http://yiddishlyrics.blogspot.com/.

Prell, Riv-Ellen and Sarah Atwood. *A Campus Divided: Progressives, Anti-Communists, Racism, and Anti-Semitism at the University of Minnesota, 1930-1942*. http://acampusdivided.umn.edu/.

"The Red Star Line: Changing America's Face and Place in the World." *National Archives at Philadelphia* online. Last modified August 15, 2016. https://www.archives.gov/.

Rosenthal, Herman and Max Rosenthal. "Kishinef." In *1906 Jewish Encyclopedia*. New York, 1906. http://www.jewishencyclopedia.com/.

Rosenthal, Herman and S. Penn. "Odessa." In *1906 Jewish Encyclopedia*. http://www.jewishencyclopedia.com/.

Rosenthal, Max. "Agricultural Colonies in the United States." In *1906 Jewish Encyclopedia*. http://www.jewishencyclopedia.com/.

"Searching for Shelter." *Nebraska Studies*. http://www.nebraskastudies.org/.

Speakman, Joseph M. "Into the Woods: The First Year of the CCC." *Prologue*, Fall 2006. https://www.archives.gov/.

Spiro, Ken. "The Czars and the Jews." https://www.simpletoremember.com/.

"SS Belgic." *White Star Line History Website*. http://whitestarhistory.com/

Stanislawski, Michael. "Kahal." In *The YIVO Encyclopedia of Jews in Eastern Europe*. YIVO Institute for Jewish Research, 2010. http://www.yivoencyclopedia.org/.

Archival Sites

Becker, Goodye. "Al Thal Papers," article. State Historical Society of North Dakota Archives.

Bernshteyn, Avrom-Moyshe. "Am Olam (Eternal People)," sheet music. Vilna, African and Middle Division, Hebraic Section, Yiddish Sheet Music. Library of Congress.

Jewish Historical Project of North Dakota. Nathan and Theresa Berman Upper Midwest Jewish Archives, University of Minnesota Libraries.

Sherman, William C. Notes from interview with Ashley residents Max Wishek and Dr. Leo Cohen. 1980. NDSU Institute for Regional Studies and University Archives.

Thal, Alfred. Taped interviews with Joe Miller and with Joseph Bender. 1974. State Historical Society of North Dakota Archives, Bismarck Heritage Center and Museum.

Thal, Alfred. Interview with Mrs. Jake Marcovitz and Mrs. Julie Lewis Ourach. 1974. State Historical Society of North Dakota Archives, Bismarck Heritage Center and Museum.

Interviews

Bender, David. By author. November 2017.
Friedman, Harry and Kenneth Bender. By author. 1974.
Rievman, Frances and Lenore Haasl. By author. 1990.
Ristow, Irvin and Margaret Ristow. St. Louis Park, MN. By author. 1998.
Stabler, Stan. Eureka, SD. By author. 2015.
USD graduate. Eureka Centennial Celebration, Eureka, SD. By author. 1987.

INDEX

Hebrew and Yiddish words/terms are shown in *italics*.

Abelson (Rabbi), 229–30
Aberdeen, SD
  Gypsy Days Parade, 258
  holiday services, 61, 108, 258–59
  population, 2
  synagogue, 88n118, 251
Aderca, Felix, 279
Adon Olam (Lord of the Universe), 13
African Americans, 89, 118, 200
The Agassiz (college yearbook), 287
Akiva ben Yosef (Rabbi), 13–14, 16
alav hashalom (peace be on him), 15
Alexander I (Czar), 74
Alexander II (Czar), 9–10, 16–17, 74
Alexander III (Czar), 16–17, 32, 74
Alteuland (Herzl), 28
Altman, Barbara Pressler, 307
Am Olam movement, 31–35, 272–73, 280
American Indians, 50, 75, 275
American Jewish War Relief Committee, 92
American *Jewish World*, 189, *191–92*
American Jewish Yearbooks, *xiv*
American Revolution, xii, 123, 216
Anavy, Regina, *xiii*
Anti-Defamation League (ADL), 214
anti-Semitism
  Czarist Russia, life in, 16, 22, 25, 28, 37–39, 74, 242 & n221
  efforts to stop, 214–16 & n213
  exclusion from employment, 116–18
  Grandpa Joe's response to, 46, 94–97, 109–10, 280–81
  Jewish stereotypes, 32, 279–80
  Jews are not Americans, 286
  KKK in ND, 110n145, 285 & n257
  M-O-T code, 281
  Silver Shirts, 117, 288n262
  U.S. immigration and, 274
Arends, Shirley Fischer, xv, 312–15
Ascension Catholic Church, 224
Ashley Arts Council, 293–94
Ashley Baptist Church, 89, *267p*
Ashley Jewish Cemetery Association/Corporation, xv, 262–63
Ashley Jewish Homesteaders Cemetery, *4p*
  author's first visit, 4–7
  burials, 77–78, 93–94 & n128, 262, 279, 288, 293
  Kiva Bender grave, *6p, 7p, 238p, 264p*
  memorial, origin of plans, 299–301
  in National Register of Historic Places, 261, 265, 268–77, 269–71, 290–92, 299, 315, 328
  rededication ceremony, 301–12
  repairs and upkeep, 261–63, 272
  restoration, 263–65
  See also Jewish cemeteries
Ashley Jewish Synagogue, 89–90, *267p*
Ashley Tribune, xiv, 76, 91–94, 265, 278, 304
Auerbach, Israel (Uncle Auerbach), 5, 39, 41–42, 55, 66, 91–93, 262
Auerbach, Nate, 92–93
Auerbach, Nate (Mrs.), 314 & n272
Auerbach, Sarah Rievman, 5, 39, 74, 294
Auerbach's General Store, 294
Augustana College (Sioux Falls), 317

Baba (grandmother), 173n181
Baernstein, Melvin ("Bud"), 287
Baggett, Stokes, 163–*65p*
Baker, Rachel Minenberg, 75, 278
Baron Maurice de Hirsch Fund, 273–74
Barony (homesteader family), 283
bashert (meant to be), 315, 324
Bauer, Alice, 111
Bauer, Dave, 111
Bauer, Marlene, 111
Beck, Morris, 284
Bender (Bendersky), Joseph Moses (Yosef), life in Russia
    birth, childhood, education, 19–20
    enters resistance movement, 34–38
    hearing the Herzl message, 26–31
    leaving for America, 39–42
Bender (Bendersky), Joseph Moses (Yosef), making a home in America
    as source of stories, *xiii*, 10n11, 19n26
    coming to America, 43–49, 95–96
    confronting anti-Jewish attitude, 94–97, 109–10, 280–81
    determination of, 14, 115, 255
    homestead claim, 42, 50–59, 69–70
    learning to read English, 98–99
    maintaining the cemetery, 261–62
    marriage to Mary, 79–86
    marriage to Rae, 188
    operating the General Store, 98–100, 315

photograph, *67p, 80–81p, 100p, 111p, 187p, 219p*
selling the General Store, 167
serving as mayor, 110, *111p*, 325–27
showing kindness, 99, 200, 313–14, 315
working for the railroad, 94–97
Bender (Bendersky), Kiva Mychal, life in Russia, *x*
birth, 5
death of father, 11–15
leaving Russia, 39–42
marriage, 15–16
message of Theodor Herzl, 26–31
Bender (Bendersky), Kiva Mychal, making a life in America
cemetery gravestone, *6p, 7p, 238p*
conducting services, 60–61, 87 & n116
death and burial, 94
founding farming cooperative, 63–64
homestead claim, 42, 69 & n88
registering the Ashley Jewish community, 63
Bender (Bendersky), Lena, *23p*
birth and family, 16 & n19
departure for America, 41–42
enroute to ND, 43–48
featured in magazine article, 66
homestead claim, 49–51, 69 & n88, *73*
horseback racing, 72
marriage, 76–77
selling the homestead, 109
Bender (Bendersky), Rebecka (Grandma Becky), *x*
children, 16 & n19
grandchildren, 103–04, 108
helping in the General Store, *100p*
marriage to Kiva, 15–16
preparing Passover cakes, 109
Bender, Bernice, 103, 113, 161
Bender, Charles Albert ("Chief"), 141 & n164
Bender, David
as source of stories, *xiii*, *xvi*, 280–81
birth, 112
graduation from high school, 167
preparing for bar mitzvah, 251
relationship with Keva, 122, *124p*, 141–42, 161
school presentation, 157–58
university student, 261
Bender, Frances, 97–98, 103–04, 113
Bender, Frima Blume Gordon
children, 171
courtship and marriage, 168–*70p*
education, 232n217
helping others in need, 219–20
high score bowler, 174–75
photograph, *168p, 177p, 182p*
tending the family graves, 266–67
Bender, Karen, 323
Bender, Kenneth (Keva), childhood and education
birth in Minneapolis, 98
Eureka (SD), growing up in, 2, 103–12
facing anti-Semitism, 115–19
high school/college, 113–14
law school, attendance, 114–15
learning to play golf, 111–12
photograph, *102p, 162p*
relationship with grandmother, 107–08
rescued from Lake Eureka, 101–03
studying for *bar mitzvah*, 104–06
Bender, Kenneth (Keva), life in America
adjusting to a post-war life, 161–68
as storyteller and historian, *xiii*, 2
courtship and marriage, 168–*70p*
employed as lawyer, 119, 121–22
helping others in need, 219–20
maintaining the cemetery, 262
photograph, *7p, 177p, 187p, 238p*
Bender, Kenneth (Keva), war service
confronting discrimination, 138–39
enlistment and training, 122–32
honorable discharge, 161–66
invasion of Normandy, 143–48
letters from home, 157–58
photograph, *124p, 129p, 137p, 149p, 159p, 165p*
promotions and awards, 130, 148–49, 158
saving Lt. Baggett, 163–64
serving in Europe, 148–54
wounded, 152–53, 155–56, 220
Bender, Mary Rievman
as source of stories, *xiii*
being a "real farmer's wife," 86–87
children, 94, 97, 98, 103
death and burial, 185–87
marriage to Joseph, 79–86
photograph, *81p*
operating the General Store, 98–100, 167, 315
Bender, Rae Feldman, 188, *219p*
Bender, Rebecca Ellen (Rivka Esther)
birth and childhood, 171–77
growing up Jewish, 219–20

law career, 232–35, 238
marriages and divorce, 239–40
memorial plans/rededication, 299–312
memories of dad, 220–21
memories of Grandpa Joe, 199–200, 229–30
photograph, *7p, 177p, 180p, 187p, 202p, 219p, 233p, 308p, 309p*
preparing for bat mitzvah, 205–10
speaking at Heritage Day, 293–94
St. Louis Park Parkette, 217–18
summers at White Bear Lake, 179–85, 213
testing the Jewish compass, 196–99, 233–35
university student, 223–32, *233p*, 268
Bender, Rose, 94
Bender, Sara Lee, 103, 108, 113
Bender-Kelner, Nancy
bat mitzvah, 206, 208
family car trips, 176–77, 327
first trip to Eureka and Ashley, 1–7
growing up in St. Louis Park, 171–72, 186–89, 201–02, 214
growing up Jewish, 194–95
holiday celebrations, 174–75
marriage, 189–*90p*
memorial ceremony, 304–*08p*
memories of dad, 220–21
photograph, *7p, 177p, 180p, 187p, 190p, 202p, 308p*
summers at White Bear Lake, 179–85
Bender's General Store, 98–*100p*, 136, 141, 251–52, 315
Bendersky, Bessie, 16 & n19
Bendersky, Chaim, 16n19, 35, 37, 40
Bendersky, Channah Nechie, 9, 12
Bendersky, Chaya, 16 & n19
Bendersky, David, 16 & n19
Bendersky, Ephraim, 16n19, 35, 37–*38p*
Bendersky, Samuel, 16 & n19
Bendersky, Sarel, 16 & n19, *23p*, 25, 35, 39. *See also* Schlasinger, Sarah
Bendersky, Schmeri, 9, 10, 12–15, 61
Benson, Elmer, 116
Benson-Tilsen, Tova, 307
Bentley, ND, 287
Berg, Claudia, 307
Berg, David, 179–*80p*, 183–84
Berg, Jim, 179–*80p*
Berg, Josephine, 213
Berg, Robert, 183–84, 213
Berg, Sandra, 179–*80p*, 265, 323
Berger, Zdena, 212
Berman, Clara, 288
Berman, David, Sr., 288 & n262
Berman, Donald (aka "Davie"), 288
Berman, Nathan, *xi*
Berman, Nathan (infant), 94n128
Berman, Susan, *xiii*, 288
Berman, Theresa, *xi*
Berman family, *xii–xiii*
Bernbaum, Frances. *See* Bender, Frances
Bernhard, Lincoln (Shlomo), *267p*
bar mitzvah ceremony, 243–45
determination, 255–56
given Keva's compass, 243
honoring the dead, 322
memorial ceremony, 306
photographs, *238p, 241p, 249p, 256p, 264p, 303p*
playing AAU basketball, 321–22
participation in Bible contest, 247–48, 253–56, 267, 315–16
relocation/move to Eureka, 249–53
speaking at Heritage Day, 294
visit to Ashley cemetery, 237
Bessarabetz (newspaper), 24
Bethelem Yehuda colony, 32
Billow (homesteader family), 283
BILU movement, 31 & n41
Bismarck, ND, *xii*, 51, 61, 69, 77, 88–89, 108, 269, 275, 287
Bismarck *Daily Tribune*, 38–39
Blewett, Pierce, 284
Bloom, Lipman, 5, 60, 93
Bluestein, Dale, 307
B'nai Isaac Synagogue, 88n118, 259
Boschee, Adolph, 282
Bottineau County Diamond Jubilee Book (1884-1959), 286
Bowden Diamond Anniversary Book, 1899-1974, 285
Braddock, ND, 77
bris ceremony, 169 & n177, 228n215
Brown, Itzic and Strul, 312
Brudnoy, Fanny Miller, *xii*, 109, 179
Buddy (dog), 240, *241p*, 250
Buffalo County, ND, 50, 50 & n67
Burgum, Doug, 302

Camelot (musical), 327
Camp McCoy, WI, 127–31
Catherine II (Russian empress), 10, 74
Catholics/Catholic Church, 109–10 & n145, 139, 244, 281, 282n254, 285, 294n268, 313
Census of 1910, 66, 68

Central Dakota Germans (Fischer-Arends), 312
challah (bread), 180
Chanuka (Festival of Lights), 21, 30 & n38, 174 & n182, 189–90, 228, 294, 319–20
Chanukah menorah, 21, 174 & n182
chuppah (canopy), 16, 83, *190p*, 242
The Churches of St. John, St. Andrew, and St. David (Schill), 282
citizenship, 286
Civilian Conservation Corps, 113
Coates (Monsignor), 224
Coffman, Lotus, 118
Cohen, Ben, 323
Cohen, Leo, 293, 294n268, 306
Cohen, Mary, 306
Cohen, Rebecca, 93
Collins, Mitch, 300
Coolidge, Calvin, 274
Cotopaxi, CO, 32
Cremieux colony, 32 & n44
Cytron, Barry (Rabbi), 318
Czarist Russia, life in, 9–42, 74, 242 & n220, 272, 312, 324

The Daily Tribune (Bismarck), 38–39
Dakota Classique Rock, 300–301
Davidowitsch, Fanny, 16 & n19, 45
Davidowitsch, Moische & Rachel, 45
Davidson, Gabriel, 273
Dayton, George Draper, 235
Dayton's Department Store, 117, 195, 235
DC Signs (Montevideo, MN), 300
De Hirsch, Maurice (Baron), 273–74
Deinard, Amos, 167
Der Judenstaat (Herzl), 28–29
DeSmet, SD, 299
Devils Lake, ND, 119, 268
Devin (pseudonym), 224–28
Dickinson, ND, 268
Digital Horizons, 281–85
Dizengoff, Meir, 19n25
Doland, SD, 167
Donaldson's Department Store, 221
Dorfman, Freda, 289, 294n268, 306
Dorfman, Isadore, 289, 306
Dorfman, Noah, 306, 314
Dorfman, Rose, 306
Doylestown, PA, 273

Edelberg, Celia, 286–87
Edmore, ND, 268
Eisenberg, Dan, 275
Elgin, ND, 283, 284n256
Ellis Island, *xiv*, 45–46, 48, 50, 95–96, 169
Ellison, Bernice. *See* Bender, Bernice
emunah (faith), *ix* & n, 328
Erhardt, Dick, 172
Ess Gezunterhait! (eat in good health), 181
Eureka Pioneer Museum, *xiv*, 252, 312
Eureka, SD
  as "Odessa of the North," 47
  as "Wheat Capital of the World," 2
  Bender's General Store, 98–*100p*, 167, 315
  Jewish population, 2
  Joseph and Lena's arrival, 47–48
  Joseph as mayor, *111p*, 325–27
  recalling the family trips to, 2–7, 177, 237–38
  relocation of author to, 249–53
Eureka High School, 112–13, *162p*, 167, 249
Eyn Kelohaynu (There is none like our God), 13

fabissen (sour person), 181
Fallon, ND, 268
Federated Stores, 167–68, 176–77, 224, 236–37
Federation of Jewish Farmers, 63–64
Feinstein, Adolph, 282
Feldman (army Private), 136
Fenick, Wolf and Alta, 84
Fey, Carol, *xiii–xiv*, 265–66, 293, 301, 307, 312
Fiddler on the Roof (movie), 242 & n220
Fine, Louie, 284
Fischer, Cristoph, 314
Fischer, Jacob, 313–14 & n271
Fisher, Luke, 153, 155
Flasher, ND, 283
Fort Benning, GA, 125–26, 143
Fort Blanding, FL, 161
Fort Lincoln, ND, 88, 275
Fort Sam Houston, TX, 126–27
Fort Snelling, MN, 123–25
Fraser (Harvard dean), 114–15, 256
Fraser, Ezra (Rabbi), 253
Frug, Shimen, 268n228

Gackle, ND, 119
Gandel, Max, 283
Garske Village, 269 & n229, 272, 280
gedicht (type of food), 25 & n183
gefilte fish, 180, 181n187
Geller, Toba, *xii*, 265, 324–25
Gemini Signs, 300

Geraghty (Rev. Father), 284
Gerdes, O. H. ("Doc"), 101–03, 107, 250, 327
German-Russian Triangle, 74–75, 268–69
Germans from Russia Heritage Society, 276
Gillis, Joe, 287
Gilman, Frank ("Frankie"), 166
Gilman, Henrietta, 166
giv a keek (take a look), 181
Glas, Dennis, 301
Glen Ullin, ND, 268, 283 & n255
Gliksberg, Shimon Yakov (Rabbi), 21
Goebbels, Joseph, 112
Goldberg, A. B., 169, 205n200
Golden, Isaac, 285
Golden Jubilee, 1911-1961, Robinson, ND, 286
Golden Lake, ND, 285
Goloni (Mr.), 211–12
Goloni (Mrs.), 211
Goodman, Arnold (Rabbi), 203, 210, 217, 318
Goodman, Harold ("Hal"), 215
Gordon, Frima. See Bender, Frima Gordon
Gordon, Harold H. (Rabbi), 169, 204
Gordon, Jacob (Rabbi), 228
Gordon, Jacob (Rev.), 169
Gordon, Minnie Goldberg ("Baba"), 173n181, 179–85, 205n200, 208, 216, 226, 251, 322
  photographs, *182p, 185p, 219p*
Gordon, Nancy, 300
Gordon, Sam ("Zada"), 173 & n181, 175, 179–85, 232
  photographs, *180p, 185p, 219p*
Gorky, Maxim, 22n31
Gottheil, Gustiv, 30n39
Graham (Mrs.), 220
Grand Forks Herald, 58
Grand Rapids, ND, 284
Great Depression, 106–07, 112–13, 119n157, 290
Greenberg, Ben, 307
Greenberg, Hank, 258
Greenberg, Lionel, 262–63, 293
Greenberg, Pauline Auerbach, 262, 307
Greenway, SD, 314n271
Grossman, Ann, 306
Grossman, Ben, 262
Grossman, Erwin, 306
Grossman, Isadore, 262, 263
Grossman, Joe, 306
Grossman, Louis, 306
Grossman, Yonah (Rabbi), 307, 311
Grow, Doug, 236
Grueskin, Carolyn, 307

Haag, Benny, 122
HaAretz (newspaper), 203
Hagadah, 18n24
hakafpt (circling the chuppah), 243
Halakha (religious law), 204n199
Handleman (homesteader family), 283
Hanukiah (menorah), 21, 174 & n182
Hartman, Ronnie Sigal, 94n128, 306
Hartstein, Rachel, 283
Harvard Law School, 114–15
Hebrew Immigration Aid Society, 47, 273
Hebron, ND, 283
Heilman, Lester and Elsie, 250
Heine, Heinrich, 112n147
Herbert, Ann, 224
Heritage Review (magazine), 276
Herzl, Theodor, 22–31, *27p, 83p*, 109, 127, 188
Hess, Abraham Lincoln, 88
Hess, Francesca Feist, 87
Hess, Julius (Rabbi), 87–91, 282, 286 & n260, 311, 314n272
Hillsview, SD, 109
History of Fordville and surrounding area, 1973, 287
History of Hatton, ND (1884-1959): 75th Anniversary Celebration, 285
History of Regan and the Regan Community, 1912-1962, 286
Hitler, Adolph, 112, 140, 242n221
Hoffnungstal. See Zebricov, Russia
Hoffnungstal Lutheran Cemetery, 277
Holocaust survivor, 211–12
Homestead Act, *xiv*, 42, 49, 52, 69
homesteading in ND
  accessing resources, *xi–xiv*
  Bendersky plans/land claim, 39–42, 50–52, 69 & nn88–89
  clearing the land, 52–56
  colony success/failure, 280
  employment off-farm, 56–58
  farmer organizations, 63–66
  finding time for religion, 58–63
  helping neighbors in need, 72–74
  Jew and German-Russian connection, 312–13
  National Register criteria, 291–92
  1909-10 farming conditions, 68–69
  population and acres, 270–73

Schlasinger land claims, 49
selling the land, 97–98, 289–90
socializing/homemaking, 70–72, 75–77
Hoover, J. Edgar, 166
Hopkins, Lawrence (Mrs.), 283
hora (dance of celebration), 292
Humphrey, Hubert, 167
Hutterites/Hutterite Colony, 319–21

immigration
accessing the resources, *xi–xvi*
assimilation, 74–75, 193–94
discrimination, 138–39
Ellis Island processing, 45–46
keeping one's Jewishness, ix–xi, 58–63, 194–99, 291–92
promotion of Russian, 26–33, 272, 322
sponsors, 47–48, 55–58, 273–75
stories of arrival, 278–79
Immigration Act of 1924, 274
Influenza Pandemic of 1918, 77
International Bible Contest, 247, *249p*, 254–57, 294, 316
International Jewish Cemetery Project, *xiv*
In Inventing the Jew: Antisemitic Stereotypes...(Oisteanu), 279
Isern, Thomas D., 307
The Israel Store (Ashley), 91–92, 93

Jamestown, ND, 284
Jampolsky, Isadore ("Izzy"), 62
Jampolsky, Leo, 77–78
Jampolsky, Sol, 60, 77–78
Jastrow, Marcus, 30n39
The Jazz Singer (film), 89, 228
Jewish Agricultural Society, *xiv*, 55, 57–58, 63–67, 79, 216n213, 265, 273–74
Jewish American Society for Historic Preservation, 300–301
Jewish cemeteries
abandoned/lost, 268–69, 328
county ownership, 262–63
Glen Ullin, ND, 283 & n255
Odessa, Russia, 268n228
online resources, *xiv*
restoration projects, *ix*, 263
Temple of Aaron (St. Paul), 322
See also Ashley Jewish Homesteaders Cemetery
Jewish Chautauqua Society, 87, 88
Jewish Dating Service, 238–39
Jewish faith. *See emunah; koech; mezuzah*
The Jewish Farmer, 64–67

Jewish foods
Chanukah, 294
holiday fasting/self-denial, 172–73
pareve, 206n202
Passover, 21, 24, 109, 175–76
Purim holiday, 110
Seder, 18, 175, *187p*
traditional dishes, 110, 181, 186, 189, 206, *296p*, 303, 323
See also kosher/"keeping kosher"
"Jewish Heritage Celebration Day," 293–97
Jewish Publication Society of America, 63
Jewish Relief Campaign, 92, 284 & n256, 287
Jewish School and Family Bible, 88
Jewish Synagogues
1934 count of, 282
Adath Jeshurun, 174, *190p*, 202–05, 208–10, 318
Ashley, ND, 89–90, 266, *267p*
Beth El Synagogue, 230
B'nai Isaac Synagogue, 88n118, 251, 258–59
Brodsky (Broder) Synagogue, *26p*
Sons of Israel Congregation, 88n118
Wishek, ND, 90–91, 282
Jewish Theological Seminary, 210
A Jewish Tourist's Guide to the U.S., 328
Johnson-Reed Act of 1924, 274
Jolson, Al (aka Al Hesselson), 89
Joseph and His Brothers, 255, 321
Judaism, branches/denominations
Ashkenzai Jews, 203 & n195
Conservative, 87, 191n189, 201–05, 208–10, 242–43 & n222, 251, 323
Haredi Orthodox, 243n222
Orthodox, 191n189, 203–04, 210n207, 233, 243n222
Reform, 203–04, 209n205, 210n207, 273
Sephardic Jews, 203 & n195

Kaddish (prayer), 5 & n9, 12, 59–60, 237, 294–95
Kamins, Louis, 286
Kamins, Philip (Mr. and Mrs.), 285–86
Kasden, Lorraine, *xii*
kashrut (dietary laws), 208
Kaufman, Bob, 262–63
Kaufman, Stuart, 263, 299–300, 306, *309p*
Kaufmanis, Karlis, 224–25
Kay, Ann Overby, 94n128, 306
Keeton (Mr., school principal), 199
Kelber, Max, 92, 314
Keller, Andreas, 276–77

Kelley, Suzzanne, 324
Kelner, Barry, 189–90, 232, 294–95, 307
Kelner, Jackson, 329
Kelner, Larry, 319
Kelner, Malcolm, 306
Kelner, Marshall, 239, 306
Kelner, Sage, 237, *238p*
Keriah (symbol of mourning), 197
ketubah (wedding contract), 240, 242
Ketuvim (section of the Tanakh), 16
Killibrew, Harmon, 221
Klinger, Jerry, 300–301 & n269, 307, *309p*
koeach (strength), *ix*, 33–34, 98, 103, 107, 196–99, 201–02, 244–45, 263
Kol Nidre (prayer), 229 & n216
Korean War, 89, 215
kosher/keeping kosher
  eating restrictions, 21, 44 & n62, 62–63, 183–85, 189, 247
  foods for bar/bat mitzvah, 208–09
  foods for Passover, 175–76, 191
  retaining the practice of, 194, 205
  Torah construction, 60–61
  See also Jewish foods
Koufax, Sandy, 258
Kraft, Frank, 282
Krauskopf, Joseph (Rabbi), 273
Kravitz, Harold (Rabbi), 318–19
Kreitzman, William and Mary, 278–79
Kristallnacht (Night of Broken Glass), 122
Krushevan, Pavel, 24
Ku Klux Klan, 110n145, 285 & n257
Kulm, ND, 76
Kurland, Sandra. *See* Berg, Sandra
Kurland, Shayna, 323

Lake Eureka, 237
LaMoure County, 284
Landfield, Ruth, *xii*
Langer, William, 118–19 & n157
Lehr, ND, 76, 119
Lenz (Professor), 110–11
Little House on the Prairie (Wilder), 299
Loeb, Morris, 79 & n108
Logan County, ND, 50n67
Luther, Hans, 117
Lutherans/Lutheran Church, 277, 282n254, 312–13

makhn zikh nisht visnidik (ignore what is happening), 181
Mandan, ND, 268
Manders, Frank, 107
Maoz Tsur (hymn), 30 & n39
Marcovitz (homesteader family), 283
Margolin family, 39, 42, 47
Marshall, George C., 89, 126
Martell, August, 325–26
Mayrent, Sherry, 70n90
Mayrent Institute, 70 & n90
McArtor, William S., 150–51, 154–55, *165p*
McClusky, ND, 283
McIntosh County
  arrival of immigrants, *xi, xv*
  arrival of Rabbis, 87–91, 311
  created from Logan County, 50 & n67
  German-Russian Triangle, 74–75, 269
  homesteaders leaving the farm, 289–90
  Jewish population, 270–73, 282
McIntosh County Heritage Center Museum, *xiv*
McWilliams, Carey, 116
Mehlhaff, Arlo & Bonnie, xiv, 252, 312
Meidinger, Claude, 264
Meidinger, Lorna, 269–70
Meir, Golda, 208, 242n220
Merricourt, ND, 77–78
mezuzah (sign of faith), 257 & n224
Michelangelo (sculptor, painter), 317
Michelovich, Aryeh Yehoshuah, 15
Michelovich, Esther. See Rievman, Esther Michelovich
Michelovich, Faige Tolbe, 15–16
Michelovich, Rivka (Rebecka). *See* Bender (Bendersky), Rebecka
Michelovich, Sarah, 15
Milgrom, Louis (Rabbi), 218
Miller, Deborah, *xii*
Miller, Fanny. *See* Brudnoy, Fanny Miller
Miller, Joseph, 63n83, 76–77, 104, 109
Miller, Lena Bender. *See* Bender (Bendersky), Lena
Minenberg, Nathan, 75–76, 278
Miniutti (Lieutenant), 150, *165p*
Minneapolis, as "Anti-Semitic Capital of America," 116–18
Minneapolis Star Tribune, 236
Minnesota Vikings, 217–18
Minot, ND, 88
minyan (quorum of ten adults), 50–60, 62, 209–10, 272n236, 295, 310–11
Mitchell, SD, 32 & n44
Mobridge, SD, 277
moel (circumciser), 169 & n177, 228 & n215
Montefiore, Moses, 285n258
M-O-T code, 281, 292
Mott, ND, 283
Mutschler, Scott, *302p*

Nachshon (Dr.), 218
Nash (Mr., teacher), 197–98
National Anti-Defamation League, 214
National Bible Contest (Chidron Hatanach), 247–48, 256, 294
National Conference of Jewish Charities, *xiv*, 88
National Farm School, 273
National Jewish Population Survey, 196n192
National Parks Service, 269, 292
National Register of Historic Places, 261, 265, 268–77, 290–92, 299, 315, 328
Native Americans, 50, 75, 275
Nazis/Nazism
  book burnings, 112 & n147
  invasion of Poland, 121
  Jews, suppression of, 121–22, 134–36
  killing Jews/concentration camps, 164, 211–14, 268n228, 276–77
  Nurenberg Laws, 117
  occupation of Norway, 133–34
  The Sound of Music and, 216–17
Nelson County History, Vol. 2, 283
Netanyahu, Benjamin, 254–55, *256p*
Neu, Leona, *xiv*, 265
Neuharth, Al, 250 & n223
Neuharth, Cal, 252
Nevi'im (section of the *Tanakh*, aka "Prophets"), 16
New Leipzig, ND, 283
New Odessa, OR, 32
The New York Times, 25
Nicholas I (Czar), 9–10
Nicholas II (Czar), 24, 28, 32, 37
Nicholson, Edward, 117–18
Nicole (Eureka city clerk), 325
North Dakota Historical Society, *xi–xii*, 119n157
North Dakota Jewish Historical Project, *xii*
"North Dakota Jewish Homesteaders Day," 302
North Dakota State Historic Preservation Board, 269–70, 290
North Dakota State University, *xii*, 324
Northwest Blade, 140–41, 252
Nudelman, Fanny, 285

Odessa
  anti-Jewish pogroms, 16–20, 36–40
  Bendersky origins, 9, 12–16, 275
  Bendersky's departure, 40–42, 51
  Dakotas, comparison to, 47, 313
  Jewish pogroms, 20–36, 96
  marriage of Sarel and Nuchen, 49
  Nazi executions, 164, 268n228, 276–77
  See also Czarist Russia, life in
Odessa, ND, 283
"Odessa Mama" (song), 70–71
"Odessa of the North", 47
Oisteanu, Andrei, 279
Olympic Games, 117–18, 128, 213–14
Oneg Shabbat, 208–09
Ostrowsky (Rabbi), 89, 311
Ottenbacher, Clyde, 252
Our Fifty Years, Regent, North Dakota: 1911-1961, 284–85
Our Jewish Farmers...(Davidson), 273
Our Pioneers: the Wing Area, 1892-1976, 286
Ourach, Gertrude and Getzel, 93
Overby, Ethel Schlasinger, *xii*

Painted Woods (colony), 268, 280
Palestine, 27, 31–32, 92, 287
Panic of 1873, 275, 304, 312
Paradise, Jonathan, 218
Passover (Pesach), 18 & n24, 21, 24, 61, 109, 175–76, *187p*, 189, 191, 278, 286n260
Patterson, Carl, 127
Peshkov, Aleksey Maksimovich, 22n31
Pew Research Center, 196 & n192
Pierre, SD, 300–301
Pirkei Avot (Ethics of the Fathers), 265
Plachte, Sara Lee. *See* Bender, Sara Lee
Pobedonostsev, Konstantin, 17–18
Polonsky (Mrs.), 285
Poplinger (homesteader family), 283
Poulten, Charlie, 128, 148
From the Prairies to the Beaches... (Bender), *xvi*, 103n140, 265
Premack, Bea, 293, *295p*
Premack, Hershel, 293, *295p*, 307
Preservation North Dakota, 263
Purim (holiday), 110

Rabbinical Association, 88
Rabinovich, Solomon Naumovich (aka Sholen Aleichem), 184 & n188
race/racism
  ending discrimination, 167
  Jews/Judaism as, 46n63
  Nazism and, 117
  See also Ku Klux Klan (KKK)
Raich (homesteader family), 307
Rapaport, Pearl and Sam, 70, 73, 76, 289
Ray, ND, 285

Reeb, Paul, 276–77
Regan-Wing colonies, *xii*, 68, 88, 262, 268–69 & n229, 272, 285–86
Regent, ND, 284–85
Religion and Public Life Project, 196 & n192
Reuben, Benjamin, 306–07
Reuben, Louis, 75
Reuben, Mirel Chaplik, 306–07
Reuben, Yehuda Leib, 306–07
Richardton, ND, 283
Rievman, Claire, 177–78
Rievman, Esther Michelovich, 15, 80–81
Rievman, Mary. *See* Bender, Mary Rievman
Rievman, Max, 80–81
Ristow, Irwin, 138–39
Robertson, Walter, *149p*, 156
Robinson, ND, 286
Romania, 268n228
Roosevelt, Franklin D., 112–13, 125, 137, 142
Rosander, Henry, 284–85
Rosh Hashanah (Jewish New Year), 61, 88, 172, 189, 232, 323
Rotnem, Engebret, 287
Russia
  Nazi persecution of Jews, 164, 211
  Orthodox Church, 9, 12, 17–18
  Revolution of 1905, 36–39
  Soviet treatment of Jews, 191, 223, 276–77
  See also Czarist Russia, life in; Odessa

Sachs (homesteader family), 283
Salzer, John and Mark, 261–62, 309
Schaeffer, Arvilda ("Toni"), *xiv*, 252
Scheiner, Sam, 214
Schlasinger, Ethel, *xii*, 119n157
Schlasinger, Kenneth, 293
Schlasinger, Larry, *xiii*, 155, 162–63
Schlasinger, Marcella, 119n157
Schlasinger, Mary, 94n128
Schlasinger, Noah (Nuchen), *23p*, 25, 35–36, 39, 49
Schlasinger, Sarah Bendersky, 49, 54, 57, 64, 155, 288
Schmedeman, Keith, 135
Schneider, Delores, *xiv*
Schneider, Neil, 301, *302p*
Schneider-Kuhn, Raymond, 264
Schwartz, Rose Rapaport, 61–62, 289–90
Schweinalas (little piglets), 229
Seder, 18, 175, *187p*
Shabbat, 104–05, 180, 191, 208–09
Shabbos goy (non-Jew helper), 233
Shahecheyanu (prayer), 43n59
Shankland (Mr.), 140
Sharansky, Natan, 255
Shavuoth (Feast of Weeks), 43 & N60
Shehechyanu lazman hazeh (prayer), 82n111
Sheridan County Heritage '76: A Bicentennial Project, 282–83
Sherman, William (Fr.), *xi*, *xiii*, 92, 265, 280, 287
Shlepps (family), 304, 312
shochet (Jewish butcher), 62, 169 & n177, 228 & n215
Sholen Aleichem (aka Solomon Naumovich Rabinovich), 184 & n188
shtetl (small town)
  life in Russia, 9–18, 242n220
  support, creates feeling of, 42, 191
  telling stories of escape, 277
Siegel, Benjamin ("Bugsy"), 288
Siegel, Robert, 323
Silver, Alice Gordon, 228–29
Silver Shirts (hate group), 117, 288n262
Simchat Torah, 61–62
Sioux Falls, SD, 88n118, 317
Sloven, Sara Lee, 307
Smilowitz, Isador, 307
Smilowitz, Samuel, 307
Smith, Bruce, 301
Smith, Meir (Rabbi), 248–49, 316
Sons of Israel Congregation, 88n118
Sons of Jacob Cemetery, 269
Spanish Flu pandemic of 1918, 77
Spitz, Mark, 213–14
Spitzer, Edwin, *162p*, 163
St. Helena's Cemetery, 294n268
St. Joseph, ND, 283
St. Louis Park, MN, 1–2, 171, 188, 195–97, *202p*, 217–18, 224–25, 244, 249–50
Stancu, Zaharia, 279
Stern, Alex, 284
Still, lyrics and music, *v*, 333–36
stock market crash. *See* Great Depression
Strobel, Harvey, *162p*, 163
Stutsman County in the World War, 284
Sukkot (holiday), 21, 61, 64, 88
Sulzberger, Cyrus, 216n213
Sulzberger Colony, 63–64
The Survey, 79 & n108

Talmud (source of religious law and theology), 16, 204n199
Talmud Torah (Hebrew School), 188, 212, 217–19, 318
Tanakh (Hebrew Bible, aka Mikra), 15

tefillin, putting on/wearing (black leather boxes), 108, 112
Tell Me Another Morning (Berger), 212–13
Temple of Aaron Cemetery, 322
Thal, Alfred, *xii*, 19n26, 265, 291, 324–25
This Is Your Life, Joseph Bender (Bender), *xiii*
tikkun olam (repairing a broken world), 242
Tilsen, Jim, 307
Tilsen, Jon-Jay (Rabbi), 300, 307, *309p*, 311
Tilsen, Robert, 306
Timbrook, Eunice ("ET"), 263–64
Timbrook, Mark ("Tim"), 263–64
Times Record (Valley City), 282
Tolstoy, Leo, 273
Torah (the Five Books of Moses), 16
treyst (comfort), 12
Trud School (Odessa), 19 & n25
Turnoy (Mr.), 287
Twain, Mark, 215–16 & n213

United War Campaign Fund, 284n256
University of Minnesota, *xi–xii*, 113, 117–18
Upper Midwest Jewish Historical Society, *xi*, *xv*, 265
U.S. Bureau of Land Management, *xiv*
U.S. Federal Bureau of Investigation, 166
U.S Immigration Office, *xiv*
U.S. Veterans Administration, 166
USS *Florence Nightingale*, 131–32

Valley City, ND, 282

Wagner, Whihelm Richard, 242n221
Walder (Mrs.), 75
Walsh County, 284n256
Washington, George, 123
Weinberg, Harris, 286 & n260
Weisfield, Harry, 285
Weismann, Si, 214–15
Weitz, Max, 218
Welk, Lawrence, 291
Wilder, Laura Ingalls, 299
Willie (from the Northside), 200
Williston, ND, 88, 119
Wilton, ND, xii, 68, 88, 268, 285
Wilton Diamond Jubilee (1899-1974), 285
Wilton News, 285–86
Wing, ND. See Regan-Wing colonies
Wing Bicentennial Committee, 286
Wing Statesman (newspaper), 286
Wingate, Charles, 235–36
Wishek, John, 89, 288
Wishek, Max and Viola, 288
Wishek, ND, *xii*, 79–80, 87, 90–91, 94–95, 280, 282, 289–91
Wold, Frances, *xii*, 265
Wolf, Harry, 284
Wolfer, R. R., 284
Wong, Thew Yuk, 130–31
Works Progress Administration, 119n157
World War I, 77–78, 92, 169, 216n214, 284, 287
World War II
  attack on Pearl Harbor, 125
  Dr. Cohen service, 294n268
  end of the war, 161
  enlistment of Kenneth Bender, 122
  invasion of Normandy, 141–48, 162–63
  Jews serving in, 214–16 & n214
  Uncle Bob service, 213–14
  veterans buried at Ashley cemetery, 293

Yiddish (language)
  about the family stories in, *xvi*
  children losing the ability, 181
  identified new arrivals, 32n44, 45
  keeping the cultural connection, 173n181, 193–95, 315
  missing the "th" sound, 188
  multi-lingual ability, 74, 97–98
  publications, 64, 66
  source/origins of, 11
The Yiddish Daily News, 25
Yiddish music, 70 & n90, 194
Yom Haatzxmaut (Independence Day), 254
Yom Hazikaron (Memorial Day), 254
Yom Kippur (Day of Atonement), 61, 105, 172–73, 229 & n216, 232, 258, 283, 323

Zada (grandfather), 173n181
Zebricov, Russia (aka Hoffnungstal), 12, 15, 255, 257, 275–77
Zeeland, ND, 282
zichrono(ah) livracha (honorific for the dead), 329
Zion, 13n16
Zionist movement, 27

ABOUT THE AUTHORS

Rebecca Bender, a former securities litigator in Minnesota, now works with children, first as a volunteer Cub Scout den leader and then t-ball coach, and more recently as a special education aide and as a substitute teacher. Some things have never changed for her: enjoyment of history and hearing uplifting stories, taking pride in family and Jewish traditions, gratefulness and appreciation for life in America, where she and her son are free to practice their religion and to work hard to achieve their goals.

Her co-author for portions of *Still* is her late father, Kenneth Bender (1916–2006), who Rebecca says would be the first to tell you that he was an ordinary guy who just worked hard and always tried his best. His story, reflected in this book, belies his modest characterization. During the last two years of his life, he hand-wrote page after page of his vivid memories. Rebecca typed up his notes with the agreed-upon compensation at the end of each of their working sessions: a shared chocolate milkshake.

ABOUT THE PRESS

North Dakota State University Press (NDSU Press) exists to stimulate and coordinate interdisciplinary regional scholarship. These regions include the Red River Valley, the state of North Dakota, the plains of North America (comprising both the Great Plains of the United States and the prairies of Canada), and comparable regions of other continents. We publish peer reviewed regional scholarship shaped by national and international events and comparative studies.

Neither topic nor discipline limits the scope of NDSU Press publications. We consider manuscripts in any field of learning. We define our scope, however, by a regional focus in accord with the press's mission. Generally, works published by NDSU Press address regional life directly, as the subject of study. Such works contribute to scholarly knowledge of region (that is, discovery of new knowledge) or to public consciousness of region (that is, dissemination of information or interpretation of regional experience). Where regions abroad are treated, either for comparison or because of ties to those North American regions of primary concern to the press, the linkages are made plain. For nearly three-quarters of a century, NDSU Press has published substantial trade books, but the line of publications is not limited to that genre. We also publish textbooks (at any level), reference books, anthologies, reprints, papers, proceedings, and monographs. The press also considers works of poetry or fiction, provided they are established regional classics or they promise to assume landmark or reference status for the region. We select biographical or autobiographical works carefully for their prospective contribution to regional knowledge and culture. All publications, in whatever genre, are of such quality and substance as to embellish the imprint of NDSU Press.

Our name changed to North Dakota State University Press in January 2016. Prior to that, and since 1950, we published as the North Dakota Institute for Regional Studies Press. We continue to operate under the umbrella of the North Dakota Institute for Regional Studies, located at North Dakota State University.